JAMES C. JENKINS
with
WILLIAM MATSON LAW
Foreword *by* JOHN BARBOUR

Creator and co-producer of NBC's *Real People*. Director and writer of the 1992 documentary *The JFK Assassination: The Jim Garrison Tapes*, and *American Media & The Second Assassination of John F. Kennedy* in 2017.

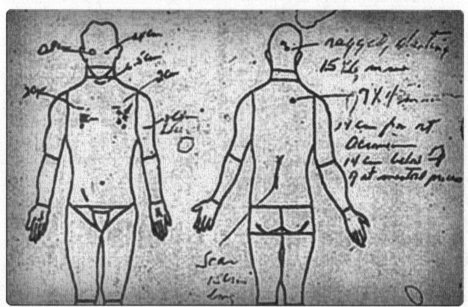

AT THE COLD SHOULDER OF HISTORY

The Chilling Story of a 21-year-old Navy Hospital Corpsman Who Stood at the Shoulder of JFK During the Bethesda Autopsy

Published by:
Trine Day LLC
PO Box 577
Walterville, OR 97489
1-800-556-2012
www.TrineDay.com
trineday@icloud.com

Library of Congress Control Number: 2018956440

Jenkins, James C.
At The Cold Shoulder of History—1st ed.
p. cm.
Epub (ISBN-13) 978-1-63424-212-7
Kindle (ISBN-13) 978-1-63424-213-4
Print (ISBN-13) 978-1-63424-211-0
1. Jenkins, James C. -- 1942- 2. Kennedy, John F. -- (John Fitzgerald) -- 1917-1963 -- Autopsy. 3. Kennedy, John F. -- (John Fitzgerald) -- 1917-1963 -- Assassination. 4. United States -- Politics and government -- History. 5. Conspiracies -- United States -- History. I. Title

FIRST EDITION
10 9 8 7 6 5 4 3 2 1

Printed in the USA
Distribution to the Trade by:
Independent Publishers Group (IPG)
814 North Franklin Street
Chicago, Illinois 60610
312.337.0747
www.ipgbook.com

PUBLISHER'S FOREWORD

That's a valiant flea that dares to eat its breakfast on the lip of a lion.
– William Shakespeare

Success is not final, failure is not fatal:
it is the courage to continue that counts.
–Winston Churchill

Which way did he go, George?
–John Steinbeck

We are not here to curse the darkness, but to light the candle that can
guide us through that darkness to a safe and sane future.
– John F. Kennedy

J ust what will it take? There has been so much water under the bridge. John Fitzgerald Kennedy was our 35th president. We are now up to number 45. Where has the time gone? Where has our country gone? Many of us find it hard to recognize our world today. There was so much hope in our youth. JFK used the slogans "A time for greatness 1960" and "We Can Do Better." He presented a "New Frontier," asked what *we* could do for our country, created the Peace Corps, signed the Partial Nuclear Test Ban Treaty, said "We choose to go to the Moon," gave us a "A Strategy of Peace," and vibrantly lived in Camelot with his beautiful family.

Today's discourse seems so far away, yet so painfully near. Decorum appears to have been left behind, while appeals to our lowest base instincts are standard fare. We are long way from JFK's inauguration words: "...civility is not a sign of weakness, and sincerity is always subject to proof.... Let both sides explore what problems unite us instead of belaboring those problems which divide us." Yes, those words were spoken about US/Russia relations in the Cold War, but I feel that they speak directly to us today.

TrineDay is honored to bring to you James Jenkins personal testimony of what he saw and experienced as he stood by a murdered President. *At*

The Cold Shoulder of History: The Chilling Story of a 21-year-old Hospital Corpsman Who Stood at the Shoulder of JFK During the Bethesda Autopsy is an amazing story that all Americans should read.

Jim Jenkins, with Paul O'Conner, prepared the morgue in anticipation of receiving the body. Jim stood at JFK's right shoulder assisting Dr. Boswell during the autopsy, moving the President's body, removing and examining internal organs, helping infuse the brain and positioning the body for x-rays. He and Paul helped the mortician dress a dead John F. Kennedy, and then were given the job of cleaning up the morgue. Jim was in the morgue from 3:30 in the afternoon until 9:00 the next morning. He was there.

Can you imagine?

Jenkins wasn't called to testify before the Warren Commission. He was interviewed in 1977 for the House Select Committee on Assassinations, but these were to be hidden from the public until 2029. While working for the Assassination Records Review Board Douglas Horne was told directly to *not* interview either Jim Jenkins or Paul O'Conner. The interview was finally released because of the President John F. Kennedy Assassination Records Collection Act of 1992.

In 2015 at a JFK conference in Dallas, speaking about one of the most famous JFK autopsy pictures, I heard Jim say something earth-shaking: "We didn't use that type of head rest in Bethesda." I got in the question line and asked him to confirm what he had said. He did, and also confirmed that the Bethesda Morgue didn't have a phone on the wall where the same picture showed one to be. I was floored and flabbergasted. A picture is worth a thousand words, right? Does this mean that photographic lie is …?

Here we have the personal testimony of what a 21-year saw and participated in November 1963, and the travails that it brought.

I want to thank James Jenkins for his service to our country and his courage to stand and deliver his recollections of this most unfortunate affair. And a huge thanks to William Matson Law for his continued steady hand and thoughtful inquiry. We are so lucky!

Onward to the Utmost of Futures!

Peace,
Kris Millegan
Publisher
TrineDay
Sepember 6, 2018

This book is dedicated to the memories of Paul Kelly O'Connor and Dennis Duane David.

James Jienkins as a young Naval Corpsman.

FOREWORD

In 1963 had the eyewitness information in this book of the non-autopsy, but actual alteration of the head wounds to President Kennedy's corpse been made public, more than a dozen of the major perpetrators might also be corpses, hung or shot for treason for the crime that changed America and the world for the worse ... like no other in history. Also, we may have seen arrested scores more including some of our most revered names in the Media.

But sadly, like the truths of District Attorney Jim Garrison's provable case that: "Elements of our CIA murdered our President," these too were ruthlessly crushed by every facet of Government and Media hungry for war in Asia – and the Fake Wars that plague us to this day. Crushed till this book. Jim Garrison is dead; but fortunately for history his amazing American story is alive in two documentaries. Now, just as fortunately for us, and history, James C. Jenkins, who as a 21-year-old medical technician stood at the shoulder of the President's naked bloody body, finally tells of the horrors he witnessed, perpetrated by Drs. Humes and Boswell. And fortunately for us, the readers, James found the perfect investigative journalist and writer to help him tell his totally riveting, terrifying tale, William Matson Law.

To me, *At The Cold Shoulder Of History* is not a strong enough title for the rage I felt in what James was recalling and reporting about what his superiors were actually doing to the body, and the heartbreak I felt for this young man who suffered in silence, not just in that room, but for years. Imagine what it must have been like for this young southern boy. As a young man wanting to be a doctor ... to help humanity. Wanting to be in the Navy ... to help his country. Then quite by accident ends up at Bethesda Naval Hospital and is called in to assist in what he thought was going to be a *real* medical autopsy of the President. His first shock comes when he sees the body removed from an ordinary casket, not the one the body was placed in at Parkland. A bucket is placed under the autopsy table for the convenience of Dr. Humes. Imagine young James' shock when he sees Dr. Humes pull the blood-soaked towel from off of the president's head and just toss it on the floor, ignoring the bucket. Then also ignoring his medical oaths, treating the body as so much trash to be simply discarded. *The possibility of two brains!!* A gaping frontal neck wound. And a small bullet hole in the right temple, which they try to conceal. Well, you do not have to imagine it. You will see it in this riveting read. It is more than *At The Cold Shoulder Of History*. It is: "A Stab In The Back Of Justice." And for James, "A Stab In the Heart of Truth": The death of his American Dream.

Following the outrage of the public when they finally saw the Zapruder film in 1975 on Geraldo Rivera's TV show with Dick Gregory and Robert Groden, Congress was forced to set up the House Select Committee on Assassinations. When this happened, James felt he could finally unburden himself and tell the truth of what he had been witness to thirteen years earlier. But, this Committee was quickly sabotaged again by the CIA and its Media and Congressional assets. Richard Sprague, the tough Philadelphia lawyer and lead investigator who said he'd solve the case and would investigate both the FBI and CIA, was removed. He was replaced by G. Robert Blakey who turned the entire hearings over to the CIA. And heartbreakingly, James was once again silenced.

Not being able to put down James and William's book, I began to wish I was watching an old Frank Capra movie with a happy American ending. The happy ending will have to be that TrineDay finally published the story. Now, I'm going to tell you briefly why this book, perhaps small in size, is so gigantic in History.

On September 5, 1981 when I was fortunate enough to be interviewing Jim Garrison, I still recall his passion for eventual justice for President Kennedy's deliberately public execution as he called it; he leaned across his desk showing me Dr. McClelland's death certificate signed shortly after 1:30pm: "Death by gunshot wound to the right temple."

"John," Mr. Garrison intoned, "In a murder case, nothing is more important than the autopsy. Which never occurred." Dr. Fink, who is mentioned in this book, under cross examination as a defense witness in the Clay Shaw trial, reaffirmed that under oath. This was never reported by the Media. It is now finally, finally, movingly affirmed in *At The Cold Shoulder Of History*. The final nail in the coffin of American Injustice.

James' and William's long needed story, for me, completes the quartet of the four major works anyone needs to read or see about the murder of President Kennedy. First would have to be Mark Lane's *Rush To Judgement*, which legally shreds the fiction of The Warren Report. Second is Oliver Stone's brilliantly crafted film, *JFK*, which brought to life for America and the World, Jim Garrison's story, resulting in the passage of The President Kennedy Assassination Records Act. Third, Mr. Garrison telling his own story in *The Garrison Tapes*, and more importantly in Part Two: *The American Media & The 2nd Assassination Of President John F. Kennedy.*

Now fourth, and every bit as strong as all the aforementioned, maybe even more so: *At The Cold Shoulder Of History!*

John Barbour
8/22/2018

John Barbour is an actor, comedian, television host, and is the only performer in TV to win Emmys for both entertainment and news shows. Barbour is known as one of the hosts of the NBC reality television series *Real People*, for which he was also a creator and co-producer. He also directed and wrote the 1992 documentary *The JFK Assassination: The Jim Garrison Tapes*. This film covers the investigation of District Attorney Jim Garrison, who, after the 1963 assassination of John F. Kennedy, decided to further investigate the official report given by the Warren Commission. The documentary hypothesizes connections between the assassination and the FBI, the CIA, the Mafia, the Cuban Missile Crisis, the Vietnam War, and other organizations and foreign affairs issues. The film won an award in 1993 at the San Sebastian Film Festival in Spain. He released the film, *American Media & The Second Assassination of John F. Kennedy* in 2017.

ACKNOWLEDGMENTS

I would like to acknowledge and give special thanks to my friend William Law without whose journalistic knowledge and skills this book could have never been written.

First and foremost, I would like to thank my wife, Jackie and William's wife Lori, whose invaluable input and support made this lengthy endeavor possible.

I would also like to thank my sister Sara, an artist, and my niece, Carol, for their help in my attempt to picture the morgue as I remember it and to my nephew Charlie, a professional photographer, who is responsible for the back-cover photograph.

To Phil Singer, who so willingly shared his vast knowledge of the Kennedy assassination and to Rick Russo, who freely shared the New York recordings for transcription in this book.

I would also like to thank Jim Metzler and Bill Lynch, two old friends and fellow classmates at Bethesda in 1963. Thank-you to Dr. Micheal Chesser. They have given me valuable information as to what occurred outside the morgue and helped clarify the events leading up to the autopsy.

I would like to thank Hugh Clark, James Felder and Tim Cheek, members of the Honor Guard whose shared knowledge of the Dallas casket delivery helped me to clarify some of my vague memories which I discuss in this book.

I would also like to thank my publisher at Trineday, Kris Millegan ,for standing behind this project from the beginning. I would also like to thank Pete Mellor from the UK, for providing me with his own personal transcript of the 50th November in Dallas conference. Special thanks to Wim Dankbaar for providing me with film of Thomas E. Robinson. And A big thank-you to John Barbour for his wonderful foreword.

As always, I am sure that I have forgotten someone and for that I apologize, but their input was not considered less valuable. This book has been a collaborative effort of countless people and to all of you I extend my heartfelt thanks.

TABLE OF CONTENTS

James Jenkins and William Matson Law at JFK Conference in 2015.

PROLOGUE

In November 2013, I attended the 50th anniversary conference on the assassination of President John F. Kennedy in Dallas, Texas. I attended this conference more as a favor to a friend than out of any curiosity or interest. My role as an assistant in the Bethesda autopsy has always been more of a burden than any highlight in my life. It has caused an intrusion into my private life by individuals who have sought to use what I saw and heard during the autopsy to support their personal hypophysis. For this reason, I have only participated in a limited number of interviews with a few researchers. I later even regretted this limited exposure, because I felt that my words were often used to support conclusions other than those I intended. This is not to say that the things that were attributed to me by the researchers were totally false, but some parts of the interviews were often left out or taken out of context, to support the researcher's personal theory or conclusion.

At the 50th Dallas Conference, I was asked to take questions concerning what I saw and did in the morgue that night. I expected to answer a few questions from a few researchers and authors but was surprised when we went for more than an hour and were asked to return later. That later session lasted until 1:30 in the morning. I was also surprised at the interest of people from other countries. Many people from Japan, Australia, Germany, the Netherlands and the Scandinavian countries stopped me to ask questions about what I saw and did that night. These people seemed to have a great interest in the assassination and the answers I had to their questions. I came away from the conference feeling somewhat selfish, because I had refused to participate in the truly passionate interest of so many people for many years. I also became acutely aware of the corrupted and sometime outright misinformation that had been attributed to me and Paul O'Connor, the other corpsman assisting the Doctors in the morgue that night.

At this time, I was pretty much unaware of the information that was being attributed to Paul and me. I had received many books written by the few interviewers that I had talked with and had tried to read the parts that pertained to my interviews but became disillusioned with the way my words were used to support conclusions that were never intended by me. Therefore, I decided to limit my discussion with other researchers. This did not stop the phone calls and request for information. I agreed to participate with a few other authors at the urging of Paul. I was disappointed by most of the writings of these researchers with the exception of one, who wrote my words as they were told to him. Over the years he has tried to encourage me to participate more but I have resisted, not wanting to get into the "he said, she said" controversy that has become commonplace among researchers and bloggers.

It has become apparent that if the events of the President's autopsy are to be told as I remember them, then I must do the telling myself. So, with the encouragement of author, researcher and friend William Law, this is my attempt to do so.

CHAPTER ONE

Who would have thought that a small town southern boy would find himself standing at an autopsy table assisting with the postmortem on an assassinated president of the United States of America. Certainly not I. But, please allow me to digress for a moment and tell you a little about that southern boy.

I was born in a little town in North Mississippi called Eupora. My dad was drafted into the Navy during World War II and my mother and I went to live with her parents until my dad returned from the service. When he returned from the Navy in 1944, we moved to South Mississippi, and my dad bought a couple of sawmills and went into the timber business with my mother's father.

We lived in the country, a little village called Auburn. When the timber played out in this southeast area, my dad moved his sawmills to Louisiana close to Lake Charles and purchased timber tracts there. My dad would transport the sawn timber back to Summit Ms., where we were living at the time. My mother had become ill, and my father moved us to Summit, which was a town of 200 or 300 people, to be close to a doctor. Summit is where my interest in the medical profession started. When I was about 9 or 10 years old, I lived down the street from the town physician. The town I was raised in had a population of about 200 people and only one doctor. The doctor's hobby was developing different varieties of camellias. He was always working with his camellias when I rode my bicycle past his house and I would stop and watch him grafting and pruning his camellia bushes. He would talk to me and tell me what he was doing, and I would ask annoying questions, but he never seem to mind. He was a little man, balding, and wore glasses – just what you think a doctor would look like in a little boy's eyes. He wasn't a jovial kind of person, but he always had a quick and ready smile and always had something encouraging to say to me. Everyone went to him for treatment because he was the only doctor in town. Somehow, and I don't remember how all these years later, I got interested in what he did. I was curious as a kid and I started asking the doctor questions like "what do you do as a doctor"? He took the time to talk to me about it, and I was intrigued. That's when I decided that's what I want to do when I grow up. I never told my parents of these visits because I was afraid they would have stopped me from bothering the doctor. He seemed to enjoy the visits talking with me and I think that he was a little surprised at my interest at that age. Though my parents never knew where my interest in medicine came from, they liked the idea of me pursuing a medical career. In those days, kids would usually go to the six or seventh grade, drop out of school and pick up some type of manual labor or mechanical work. Very few of the kids that I knew pursued a professional career. A couple of the kids became lawyers or accountants, but most of the ones from my hometown went into the timber business, worked for the railroad, or went into the family business straight out of high school. There wasn't much opportunity for college. Being in the medical field was something I really wanted, and that was the goal I set for myself.

I lived in Summit until I went into the Navy. I attended school there, until the ninth grade. The school system consolidated, and I was moved to McComb High School where I completed my high school education and received my diploma. My dad was the kind of person who believed in work. If I didn't work I didn't get an allowance. But if I worked, I got an allowance and a salary. It was a great incentive to work. I started out at about 12 or 13 years of age, working at a drive-in malt shop waiting on cars and serving milk shakes, hot dogs and burgers. I would work after school till about 10 o'clock at night a couple of nights a week and weekends. I made about $.35 an hour but it was fun because I got to associate with the "big" kids from school and ride in their cars. I worked doing that through a couple of summers. So, I was well acquainted with working by the time I went to work with my father at the tractor company. One of the men there was an older man in his late 60s. I was pretty much his "go-fer." I did the heavy lifting. My dad had purposely assigned me to him. Dad paid me about $35.00 a week, no allowance. So, for a 15-year-old kid in high school, I had money for gas for my car, which I usually charged to my dad's account at the gas station when I thought I could get away with it, and hanging-out at the drive-in and money to take a date to the midnight movie on Saturday night. Any excess money I put into my car. It was 1957, like most teenagers I loved cars. My car was a thing of beauty in my eyes but not my father's. She was a 1952 Chevrolet Coup. I worked on the engine myself. I had a three-quarter cam and a home-built three carburetor intake manifold. The 1950s was the era of hot rods. And we built our own cars. This particular car was a six-cylinder with a home-built split exhaust manifold. I painted the car – well, I helped paint the car. One of the guys who worked at the Chrysler dealership next to the tractor company, was an excellent painter. He must've seen me working on my car because one day he walked over and asked me "why don't we paint your car?" "I already painted it" I said." Yeah, I see that" he said. He was trying hard not to laugh, without much success.

He told me that if I would buy the paint and bring the car to his house over the weekend that he and his five kids would repaint it for $50.00. He sprayed the car sierra gold. It was really a bronze color more than gold, and he put a candy-flake in the paint which was a common thing that kids did in those days to make it sparkle. If you were 15 to 25 in the 1950s, cars were a big deal, and customizing your own car was even bigger. That was life for me back then – always trying to do something different to my car to make it cool. There were kids at school who had cars that might've been flashier than mine, but I can truly say that there was not another car in town that was faster (at least in my mind).

Chapter Two

After high school, I went to Southwest Mississippi Jr. College which was located in my home town of Summit. After the first year, I realized I wasn't going to be able to go on to a University because I didn't have the financial resources. So, I decided to join the Navy, not because I wanted to go into the Navy in particular, but because that was the only way I would be able to continue with my education. My father had been in the Navy and so that seemed the best way to go. The Navy offered me educational opportunities that I couldn't have gotten in other branches of the military. Besides I always liked being in or around water.

I always thought that I would like to learn to fly so, I went in as a Naval Aviation Cadet, but when I went through the physical, it was discovered that I was red-green colorblind. Being colorblind would have restricted my flight options. I was told the only things I would be able to fly were propeller driven or rotary driven aircraft, and that wasn't exciting enough for a naive southern boy nor was it what I was really interested in. I was told I could pick any other thing that interested me. I wanted to go to medical school, so the opportunity to be a hospital corpsman,was more of an interest for me than any of the other options offered. While I wasn't training to be a doctor it was the closest I could get to my goal at the time without an MD. After boot camp, I went to hospital corps school, which taught me basic diagnosis, treatment of disease, and medical terminology, allowing me to be semi-independent treating patients under the supervision of a physician. Later, I went through a course in field medicine, which taught emergency treatment of battle wounds and other types of trauma. Hospital Corps School lasted about three months. I was single,18 years old living in the barracks and learning. The barracks were open rooms that had double bunks and lockers. It housed anywhere from 100- 250 men. It was a two-story barracks with living quarters on both sides, and in the middle were the heads (bathrooms for you civilians) and showers. The petty officer in charge of the barracks had a small office and living quarters off to the side. After I finished corps school, I was stationed at Cecil Field, a Navy air base in Florida. For my first duty station, I was fortunate to have a commanding officer that took an interest in his people. Captain Nauman stood about 5 foot-nine and was stocky. He had a very gregarious personality. He was the type of person, to use an old adage, whose bark was worse than his bite. He had more the personality of a drill sergeant than a" four striper," navy slang for a Captain. There was a group of us that were pranksters and it was a little bit like being in college with these guys – our antics would often get us into trouble and on one such occasion, we had to go before the Captain and he was giving us a thorough dressing down for what we had done and one of guys spoke up and said, "Captain, hold it down your rattling the blinds! The Captain gave us a stern look and shouted, "Just get the hell outta here!" We got!

For whatever reason, the Captain liked us, and we certainly benefited from it. The Captain had a great deal of trouble at times with his back and he would occasionally have to have it looked at – there was a chance that he would have to have surgery on his spine. The Captain kept putting the surgery off because it might keep him from making Admiral. When he would go to the Bethesda Naval Medical Center for checkups, one of us was required to go with him.

I suppose that he liked me, because when I was first stationed at Cecil Field I worked in sick bay where we had the "sick call." If base personnel were sick you went to "sick call." Usually, the corpsman would examine you first to determine what your particular ailment was. If it wasn't something life-threatening, the corpsman would treat you and tell you to return if there was no improvement. If a person came in for a cold or minor laceration he usually never saw the doctor. We would examine them and according to their complaint, check the throat, look at the ears, check the sinuses, listen to the heart, check the pulse rate, blood pressure or maybe suture a minor laceration. If the corpsman was not able to diagnose the problem or the trauma was severe, the doctor would see the patient.

Allergies would be treated with antihistamines, infections were treated with antibiotics. We used a lot of procaine penicillin in those days, which was administered by injection. The one thing I didn't care for was when I had the duty on the weekends, we had a dependent's clinic at the dispensary and we saw a lot of military dependent children, and doctors would put kids on penicillin for respiratory infections. These kids would get a regimen of shots that would last 3 to 5 days. So, the parents would bring the kids in to get their shots on weekends. I was usually the youngest and lowest rated corpsman on the watch section, and the older corpsmen would always push the distasteful chores off on me. I would always be the guy to deal with the kids and give them their shots. One day, I had this little boy, probably three or four years old. We always gave the shot in the hip and had never had any trouble before, but this kid went ballistic! The kid was screaming and crying, and his dad was trying to hold him down. As his pants were pulled down, I took an alcohol swab and wiped his buttock where I was going to give the injection. Suddenly, all of his "crocodile tears" dried up, he turned his head and looked up at me and said in a small plaintive voice, "be careful." I just put the syringe down and walked away. But those were the good times.

We also had an ENT clinic (ear, nose and throat) next door to sick bay. The Captain's interest in medicine was ENT. I would always clean up after the Captain had finished for the day. One day after I had finished cleaning up I was in the clinic reading some of the medical books. The Captain came in and asked me what I was doing, and I told him I was reading, and he asked me, "Are you interested in ENT medicine?" I told him that I was, but I didn't really know much about it. The Captain didn't say anything, he just turned and walked out of the room. The next day, my boss, a second-class hospital corpsman, in charge of the sick bay, told me that I would be working with the Captain in ENT today. Everybody there was kind of leery and afraid of the Captain because he was – how should I put this- very direct and a "little" gruff. But I knew the Captain reveled in rattling the people around him, and it only made me like him all the more. I wasn't afraid of him, I had a lot of respect for him, but a lot of the enlisted men were afraid and avoided him. I think that's part of the reason he took me under his wing. I know most of the reason I went to Bethesda Naval Medical School to attend the clinical laboratory and blood bank course was because Captain Nauman told me that I had three years left in the Navy and I was going to spend them under him and if I didn't go on to school he would make it "hell on me" and then he walked away laughing. I took this as a "military suggestion" and filled out my application and he had the personnel officer put me in for school. Now, at first, I didn't want to go to Bethesda for training. My goal was to get out of the Navy and go to college. I'd been at Cecil Field for about a year at that point and unsure of my direction, but unbeknownst to me, the Captain had made arrangements to get me into the Bethesda clinical laboratory and blood bank school before our discussion. I enjoyed the Navy, I never had any problems in the military, and the Captain gave me a lot of support – though he would never have admitted it. Your life can sometimes take unimaginable turns, and when Captain Nauman made the decision to put me in for laboratory and blood bank school at Bethesda Maryland, how could he or I have known that his act of kindness, whatever his reasons, would change the course of my life and I would find myself part of some of the darkest hours in the history of this nation? History that, whether I like it or not, follows me to this very day.

Chapter Three

The captain pushed me a lot. If he hadn't I would have not taken promotion as it came, all I wanted was to wait my time out in the military and get back to my primary purpose for going into the military, which was to get the financial resources to continue my college education. He saw that I had taken an interest in the laboratory there in the clinic and that my interests were more along the scientific path than treatment, though I didn't realize it myself at the time. I was interested in testing for diseases. I wanted to work in the laboratory at the Dispensary, but I didn't want to leave the ENT clinic and the opportunity working with the Captain. He took a lot of interesting in teaching me. He pushed my education far beyond what I had learned at Corps school especially during the ear, nose and throat part of my training. I learned how to determine an external otitis from an internal otitis infection of the ear and how to treat them among other things.

So, in pursuing my medical career I wound up in the military at Cecil Field Florida, which not only accounted for my being at Bethesda Naval Hospital but also led to the meeting of my future wife. Several of my friends and I were asked to escort a group of young ladies to a weekend on-base dance at the NCO club. Unescorted civilians were not allowed on base due to the critical nature of the base's mission. I wasn't particularly interested in any girl at the dance, but my friend Larry was very interested in dating one of the girls and she wouldn't go out with him unless it was a double date. So, I agreed to go out with her best friend. You might say I got drafted. I had never thought of getting married but there was something about this girl that I couldn't put into words. I really enjoyed her company and our shared interests, and how she made me feel when we went to the beach, to a movie, or just being together. Meeting her, like being at Bethesda Naval Hospital on the night of November 22, 1963, would change my life forever.

We were married in August after I received orders to Bethesda, and when I left my duty station at Cecil Field, I was a newly married corpsman with what I felt was a bright future ahead of me. My wife and I were headed for an exciting new life in Bethesda, Maryland.

For the first year of our married life my wife and I didn't have much money. It took every penny we had just to live. People laugh at me when I tell them that the first year of our married life together we ate a lot of chicken pot pies, because they only cost $.15 apiece. There was another married couple in our building and we would get together on Friday night and play cards. We didn't have much money, but we managed with sodas and chips; gone were the days gathering with my friends and having drinks and dinner at the NCO club. You could buy a Coke for $.10 and a bag of potato chips was maybe $.15, especially if we bought them at the base exchange. I was lucky because I was able to be home every night except the nights I had duty in the morgue. My wife did not like being alone on the nights I had duty, but she had no choice. Her uncle whose family my wife had lived with during high school, had retired from the military, so my wife knew what she was in for. It was just something that was expected, and life went along for us as it did for thousands of young married couples in the service.

The military gave me a stipend of $125 a month, money that was to aid married families with living expenses, food and things like that, which was a good thing, because I was only making $48-$50 twice a month straight military pay. We found a two room "efficiency" apartment in Gaithersburg, Maryland which cost $125 a month, all utilities paid. My wife soon found a job and we stopped eating Swanson pot pies so often and were able to buy some modest furniture. So, things weren't so bad for us financially now, as we started our life together. I set about completing 18 months of training at the Bethesda Naval Medical School.

Chapter Four

My first year at Bethesda was filled with classes in laboratory sciences, courses in hematology, microbiology, cytology, blood-banking, pathology and serology, which today is considered immunology. In serology we dealt with antigens and antibodies and their reactions in the serum and their ability to detect diseases with properly prepared serums. We didn't really know much about the reactions we were dealing with – we just knew that certain tests worked if we prepared the serum correctly.

A typical day for me went like this: In the morning we would gather for muster, roll would be called and any information needed for the day was given. Then we would be released to go to various classes. We did this for the first 6 to 8 months. Then came the practical portion. We went into the laboratory departments and did patient testing under supervision of the staff. We still had classes, but not every day, all day, like we had in the first months at Bethesda. These new classes where directed toward developing special tests and skills. Even as students, we had regular military duties, and every fortnight we had to man the duty sections. All of us had various duties, some drew patient blood for testing, others were assigned administrative duties. There were eight of us that had duty in the morgue. I did my first autopsy at Bethesda, though I don't remember much about the experience. I found doing autopsies interesting because it was a new learning experience. Little did I know that I was about to be involved in the most infamous and controversial autopsy in modern times.

The following is my memory of that autopsy.

On November 22, 1963 I was stationed in Bethesda, Maryland, at the Naval Medical School, where I was a student at The Navy laboratory and blood banking school. As a student I was responsible for the duty every fourth day. My duty consisted of assisting in performing autopsies with resident pathologists. We usually performed two or three autopsies each duty night.

On the 22nd at about 3PM, I was in serology class when Bill Lynch, a fellow student, returned from break and told us that the President had been shot during his visit to Dallas. The instructor came in shortly afterwards and told us that the President was dead. He said that classes were dismissed, and the duty crew should report to the morgue, to prepare for an autopsy in case the President's body came to us at Bethesda.

Paul O'Connor and I had the duty and Bill Lynch, who had the duty the night before, gave Paul the keys to the morgue. Paul and I went to the morgue and began to prepare it for the possible autopsy.

Later, Paul and I were joined by a first-class hospital corpsman, who I believe may have been the laboratory duty NCO (possibly HM1 Keys). Dr. J. Thornton Boswell also came into the morgue but left after talking to the first class.

Paul and I began to set up the instruments and label the specimen jars for the tissue samples that we normally took at autopsy. These jars were used to hold tissue samples taken from various organs and areas of the body for the microscopic exams. We were using tape for labels on the jars with the date autopsy number and patient name. After we had finished labeling, we were told to remove all the labels and re-label the specimen jars with only the autopsy number. We were also told not to log the President's name into the logbook. We were to only use the next sequential number for identification. During this time, we were told that the President's body would definitely be brought to the Bethesda morgue for autopsy. Dr. Boswell came in and confirmed that we would be doing the autopsy on the President's body. When I asked the first-class corpsman why we were doing the autopsy instead of Walter Reed Medical Center or AFIP in downtown DC, he said that it was probably because the President was Navy. I later learned that Mrs. Kennedy had requested that the autopsy be performed at the Bethesda Naval Medical Center.

The timeline that I use in the discussion of the following events, was established by Dennis David, the Chief of the Day for the Medical School and collaborated by Sergeant Roger Boyajian, the Marine sergeant in charge of the security detail, in his action report and verified years later by Dr. Jay Cox, the Officer of the Day for the Hospital, in a telephone conversation with William Law. My duties required that I remain attentive to the pathologist's needs and to help meet those needs. It was necessary to be able to hear and see what the pathologist wanted me to do at all times. Paul and I were HM3 hospital corpsmen and were the lowest people on the "totem pole" in the morgue that night. We did what we were told and asked no questions. It was a very intense and sometimes disconcerting situation.

The body arrived in the morgue about 1835(6:35PM). It was brought into the morgue in a grayish-brown shipping-transport casket, not the bronze burial casket that the body was reportedly placed in at Parkland Hospital. The casket was placed on the floor beside the autopsy table, the body was removed and placed on the front table where the autopsy was performed. I did not directly participate in the removal of the body from the casket, because there seemed to be too many helpers already, mostly civilians in suits and maybe a military officer or two. Paul was the only enlisted person I remember seeing that helped remove the body from the casket and he like myself was dressed in surgical scrubs. When the body arrived, I was busy at the front table preparing the instruments for the autopsy. The body was placed on the table in front of me. The body was wrapped in a single sheet and the head was wrapped in what appeared to be a towel and a sheet.

After the body was removed from the casket and placed on the autopsy table, Dr. Boswell thanked everyone for their help and asked everyone with the exception of Paul and me to leave the morgue. Dr. Boswell then told us not to unwrap the body or to let anyone into the morgue and he left the morgue. I assumed that he was going upstairs to the laboratory to coordinate the autopsy procedure with Dr. James J. Humes. After about 15-20 minutes, Dr. Boswell returned, he and I unwrapped the body and covered it with a sheet from the waist down. Dr. Boswell gave me the clipboard with the face sheet, a printed form for entering distinguishing body markings etc., and we started recording the body measurements and identifying scars, marks and wounds, surgical and otherwise. Dr. Boswell examined the body and gave me the measurements and locations and I wrote them on the face sheet. I then gave Dr. Boswell the face sheet and he verified the placement of the scars, surgical incisions and body wounds. During this time, Dr. Humes and several military officers arrived in the morgue and other individuals began to filter in. The military and civilians went into the gallery. Dr. Humes came to the autopsy table and began examining the head. He then removed the sheet and the blood-soaked towel from the head and discarded them on the floor and I thought to myself, "why didn't he use the waste bucket under the head of the autopsy table?" I stood at the right shoulder of the body and looked down at the face of President Kennedy. He could've been sleeping except his right eye was slightly open and the left eye closed, his lips were slightly parted, there was a huge gash in the front of his throat. The hair was bloody and matted together so I didn't see the massive damage to his head at first glance. As Dr. Humes removed the wrappings from the head, the wound gaped open along a laceration that ran forward along the top of the head, but immediately closed when it was separated from the bottom wrappings which appeared to be towels. The first appearance of the head wound was deceiving, as the reader will learn later. I didn't have the time for much thought or feeling, I was on auto-pilot, concentrating on the job at hand. Paul or I later removed the wrappings to the hampers in the dirty linen room. I don't remember which one of us put them in the dirty linen hampers. Dr. Humes, in a later interview, stated that he placed the bloody head wrappings in a washing machine in the morgue. I never saw a washing machine in the dirty linen room. We only had a contamination hamper for bloody and contaminated linen which was to be incinerated and a second hamper to be sent to the laundry. Was he talking about another morgue?

The x-ray and photography technicians had come into the morgue with the people that filtered in after Dr. Humes.

The medical photography technician, a Hospital corpsman, began taking a series of photographs under the direction of Dr. Humes, mainly of the head area and the upper thorax. There were other photographs taken during the autopsy by a civilian medical photographer, John Stringer, who had come into the morgue with Dr. John H. Ebersol. As the x-ray technician prepared, everyone was asked to leave the morgue while the x-rays were being taken. I was given a lead apron, so I could help position the body for the x-rays that Dr. Humes ordered. We took AP's (front), laterals and obliques of the head and upper thorax and neck. After the x-rays were completed, the technician left the morgue to process the film in the x-ray department. When the technician and a helper returned to the morgue with the processed x-ray films, they showed no bullets or large fragments in the body. This seemed to produce tension between the military officials in the gallery and the autopsy doctors, and we were told to repeat the x-rays. The x-ray technician and his assistant repeated the same set of x-rays that we had previously taken. The new set of x-rays also showed no bullets or large fragments. Dr. Ebersol, the radiologist, was then called to the morgue to direct a second re-taking of the x-rays. When these were developed, Dr. Ebersol and the technicians returned to the morgue with the films and a bank of x-ray view boxes, which were set up against the back wall. The doctors and others from the gallery moved to the view boxes to examine the three sets of x-rays. They found no large fragments or partial bullets in the third set. This seemed to intensify the tension between the military officials in the gallery and the autopsy doctors. While I could see the x-rays, now, I have to say that at that time in 1963, my familiarity with x-rays was very limited. I could possibly find a broken bone or cloudy chest, but I would have had to have a doctor verify those finding for me. There seemed to be a lot of frustration and tension in the conversations because the x-rays showed no partial bullets or large metal fragments. After we were finished with the x-rays, additional pictures were taken of the President's body by John Stringer, the civilian photographer that had followed Dr. Ebersol into the morgue. Floyd Riebe, who was the assistant to the civilian photographer John Stringer, had taken the first photographs of the president's head immediately after the head was unwrapped. This was before any washing of the body or any manipulation of the head or scalp had occurred. At some point in the process of taking pictures, I was vaguely aware of some kind of commotion near the back of the gallery. I was later told that Riebe had his camera taken and the film exposed by the Secret Service. After the x-rays were finished, I don't remember much about Stringer taking photographs. I have seen the so-called "Fox" set of photographs, and I do remember that the body was not clean, nor was the back of the president's head intact when Stringer was taking pictures. There were additional pictures taken throughout the autopsy, but the body was not cleaned until it was turned over to the morticians after the autopsy had ended.

Dr. Pierre A. Fink and Dr. Humes started examining the head wounds. They found a small wound on the right side of the head in the temporal area just forward and slightly above the right ear. The small hole (wound) was rounded and about the size of the tip of one's little finger. There appeared to be graying around the margins of the wound, but it was difficult to see because the wound was in the hair line. Dr. Fink speculated that the gray material might have come from a bullet. During the examination of the temple wound, Dr. Humes was called to the gallery to talk to one of the people that had come into the morgue with him and who seemed to be directing the autopsy. I later was told this was Dr. George G. Burkley (Admiral), the President's personal physician. Dr. Humes returned to the table and immediately directed Dr. Fink away from the small wound in the temple to the large posterior head wound. The temple wound was abandoned and never returned to that night. Drs. Humes and Fink turned their attention to the large posterior head wound and began to examine its extent and boundaries. After the examination of the large posterior, occipital-parietal head wound began, Dr. Humes noticed an area of connected scalp lacerations, along the top of the head that extended forward almost parallel to the midline just past the coronal suture. They extended almost to the frontal bone of the skull. They appeared to have been surgically altered. This prompted Dr. Humes to ask someone in the gallery if there had been any surgery done on the head in Dallas. He was told that there had been no surgery on the head in Dallas. Some of these tears in the scalp appeared to be extended laterally along the top of the head. This could have occurred when the bone underneath was fractured and expanded from the force created by the passage of the bullet, but the lacerations seemed to be neater, cleaner, less random and more directional than the other lacerations in the area as if they had been surgically connected. The posterior head wound will be discussed in more detail later.

After the head wound examination was finished Dr. Humes removed the brain by extending some of the lacerations along fracture lines and spreading the fractures in the underlying skull. The traditional skull cap procedure was not necessary for access to the brain cavity. Dr. Humes then handed the brain to Dr. Boswell who motioned for me to follow and we walked to the end of the autopsy table and through the separation between the two autopsy tables to the infusion bucket. I bent down on one knee and was given the brain, which I placed upside down in a gauze sling over the brain bucket. The brain bucket was close to cabinets that were on the wall opposite the gallery. There were two sets of cabinets, wall cabinets with floor cabinets underneath. On top of the cabinets that were mounted on the wall, there was a large glass carboy. A carboy is nothing more than a big glass jar with a spigot at the bottom. It was filled with formalin, which is diluted formaldehyde adjusted to the pH of the body. The carboy had a plastic tube attached to the spigot that came down and was separated into a "Y" to give two tubes. At the end of these tubes were attached needles. Our normal procedure was to take the needles and insert them into the internal carotid arteries. The internal carotid arteries are a part of the brain's vascular system at the base of the brain. Suture silk would be used to tie off the ends of the arteries, and then the spigot would be opened. Gravity would force the formalin to infusion into the brain. After the brain began infusing at the beginning of the autopsy, it would be left until the completion of the autopsy. Then we would remove the infusion apparatus, drop the brain in the bucket filled with formalin solution, put the lid on it, and put it in the brain room. It would sit in the bucket at least 72 hours. Most of the time, brains would sit there until the following Monday. Unless an autopsy was performed on Saturday night, or Sunday then that brain would not have been examined or sectioned on Monday. If an infused brain had been allowed enough time for the brain to be fixed, i.e. the required 72 hours, the brain would be sectioned and examined on Monday. The reason we didn't fix brains by just dropping them into the bucket of formalin was that it would take at least seven days for brain to be firm enough to section versus 72 hours with the extra infusion process.

I was having trouble getting the needles into the carotid arteries because the ends of the vessels had constricted, making it difficult to insert the needles. One of the residents who had come into the morgue to bring something to Dr. Boswell, came over to see if he could help me insert the needles. The fact that the vessels appeared shriveled and had constricted, led me to believe that they had been cut for quite some time and this along with the irregularly cut brain stem and the long laceration of the scalp that gaped open when the head wrappings were removed gave credence to the possibility that the brain had been removed from the head and replaced or substituted back into the head some hours before. In other words, the brain had been removed from the cranium and then replaced or substituted prior to the arrival of the body at the Bethesda morgue.

We did not normally weigh the brain in the morgue before we infused it. This was a normal procedure for the handling of recently removed brains at the Bethesda morgue. The brain would be infused, placed in a stainless bucket of formalin, covered with the lid and placed in what we call "the brain room" for a supplemental autopsy after the brain was fully fixed. The supplemental autopsy was usually done as a teaching mechanism for the residence.

Dr. Fink said that he was told upon his arrival in the morgue that Dr. Humes had only to extend a few fracture lines to be able to remove the brain. This is supported by Dr. Fink's written report to his commanding officer General Joseph M. Blumberg. This report is somewhat suspect because the brain was removed after the head was examined by both Dr. Fink and Dr. Humes. During the examination of the head, the small wound on the right temple just slightly forward and above the right ear was discovered and examined by both Dr. Humes and Dr. Fink while the brain was still in the cranium. Dr. Fink also later testified that he had suggested the taking of some of the x-rays. I don't remember any x-ray being taken after the removal of the brain. I believe the x-ray personnel had left the morgue by that time.

Dr. Humes later told the ARRB Board that he did a skull cap to remove the brain. This seems highly unlikely for the following reasons:

Tom Robinson, the mortician who prepared the President's body for burial, states that he and his assistants closed the head wound by using a small rubber sheet to replace the 3 inches of missing bone and scalp and that the remaining wound was closed by stretching the remaining scalp over the skull fractures and suturing them closed. He made no mention of replacing the skull cap which he would have had to do if the brain had been removed by doing a normal skull cap.

Tom Robinson also stated that he saw what seemed to be marks from a bone saw in the right temporal area. These marks were probably not from a bone saw. We used a Stryker saw at the Bethesda morgue to cut bone and remove the skull cap. This saw has a blade that vibrates back and forth and does not cut flesh. It is designed to cut solid fixed material such as bone. It would have been difficult if not impossible to cut the floating, fractured bone of the skull without first being able to fix each individual piece in a rigid manner. For this reason, it seems improbable that Dr. Humes' testimony, before the ARRB board, that he did a skull cap, is plausible.

Dr. Humes has been inconsistent in his testimony before several government commissions when describing the removal of the brain.

During a normal autopsy, the brain would have been removed by doing a skull cap. This procedure began with a coronal incision from one ear to the other ear and reflecting the scalp backward to the occipital area and forward to the frontal area. We would then remove the skull cap by sawing around the skull leaving a notch in the frontal bone to be able to replace the skull cap in the same position after the brain was removed. Once the skull cap was replaced, the reflected scalp would be brought together and sutured in place. This was not the closure procedure described by Tom Robinson, the mortician who closed the head wounds.

The descriptions of the brain in the supplemental autopsy report is more consistent with the description given by the Parkland doctors than its consistency with the brain that was removed from the cranium by Dr. Humes during the Bethesda autopsy. This points to the credibility of Doug Horns belief that there were two brains. If this is the case, the first brain described in the supplemental autopsy of the official autopsy report appears to be the original brain that was possibly removed prior to the Bethesda autopsy. A clue to the possible truth of the statement is the testimony of Dr. Humes when he said that he took the brain and locked it in Dr. John H. Stover's closet. I guess the remaining question is whether the brain that Dr. Humes locked in the closet was given to him prior to the autopsy or was it the actual brain that was taking during the autopsy?

The brain that was removed at the Bethesda autopsy was apparently the second brain that was autopsied by Dr. Humes, Dr. Boswell, Dr. Fink and an unknown medical photographer.

These descriptions of the brain above cannot be conclusive unless one has the ability to compare the original brain and the autopsy brain, which of course has been made impossible today.

It now seems possible, after reading the original autopsy report statement of Dr. Humes, that he placed the bucket with the brain in Dr. Stover's locked closet. This raises the possibility that the original brain may have been brought to Bethesda separate from the body and was placed in the locked closet prior to the beginning of the autopsy.

If this is the case, then the brain that was removed from the cranium by Dr. Humes and infused by me and Dr. Boswell was a substitute brain. This would've accounted for its appearance and the inconsistency with the amount of damage to the brain seen at autopsy when compared to the damage of the skull and scalp. I believe the damage to the brain described in Dr. Humes' official report would have been more consistent with what one would expect when observing the damage to the skull and scalp.

I further believe this lends more credence to Doug Horne's conclusions of two brains and two brain autopsy examinations.

Since my request for permission to view the original photographs in the National Archives has been denied by Paul Kirk Jr., the Kennedy lawyer who controls the access to these photos and x-rays and I have received no response to an email address that was given to me by my local congressman's aide, I can only rely on the descriptions of the photographs viewed by Dr. Michael Chesser and Dr. David Mantik.

Over these many years, I have been asked if I thought that the brain that I saw at the Bethesda autopsy was the President's brain. I have always said that I had no reason to believe that it was not, even though it looked different from the brains I usually saw at autopsy.

In 2015, I had the opportunity to sit down with William Law, author and researcher, Dr. David Mantik, a noted Pathology-Oncologist with a Doctorate in Physics and Dr. Michael Chesser, a neurologist, both of whom had viewed the photographs of the President's brain in the national archives. Before this meeting, I had made notes on the unusual appearance of the brain as it was removed from the cranium by Dr. Humes during the autopsy. At the meeting, I asked Dr. Chesser to describe the brain that he saw on his visit to the national archives. Dr. Chesser told me that the brain in the archives photograph appeared to have been in formalin for some time. I then asked him to describe what he saw that led him to that conclusion. He described the brain in the archive photographs as being asymmetrical, as if it had been lying in a container of preservative with other brains and it appeared to be flattened on the top of the left cerebral lobe. I then asked him to describe the damage to the brain in the photographs that he saw in the national archives. Dr. Chesser said that the damage was primarily to the rear of the right parietal lobe and that there appeared to be very little discernible damage to the cerebellum. Dr. Chesser also described what appeared to be saw marks along the left frontal area of the left cerebral lobe as if a routine skull cap procedure had been done to remove the brain. This is significant, because there was no saw used to remove the president's brain at the Bethesda autopsy. Dr. Humes only had to extend several fracture lines with a scalpel and the defect could be spread open enough to allow the brain to be removed.

I then described the brain that was removed by Dr. Humes from the head at the Bethesda autopsy. It seemed to be smaller than expected in comparison to the size of the president's head and the damage was primarily to the posterior of the right cerebral lobe. The damage to the brain didn't seem to correlate with the damage seen on the skull and scalp. The damage to the skull and scalp seemed to be much more extensive than one would expect if only determined from the damage seen to the brain. The gyri appeared to be larger and flatter and the sulci seemed to be much narrower compared to the usual brains taken at autopsy. The surface seemed to be smoother and shinier than usual. It seemed to have a pale, whitish color, not the usual gray that we saw at autopsy. I believe this occurred in the area where Dr. Chesser saw the flattening on the top of the left hemisphere of the cerebrum.

There were other anomalies; as we were trying to infuse the brain, there appeared to be no major damage to the underside of the brain. The brain stem appeared to have been severed from two different sides. The cerebellum seemed to be intact with no noticeable damage and the internal carotid arteries were severely retracted and shriveled as if they had been cut for some time, not as expected with a recently removed brain. This retraction of the arteries made it difficult to insert the infusion needles and required the help of a resident, who I later learned was the chief pathology resident.

After my discussion with Dr. Chesser and Dr. Mantik, I now believe that I have answers to the abnormal appearance of the brain that I helped infuse at the Bethesda autopsy. I now believe there is a great probability that the brain we infused in the morgue is the same brain seen by Dr. Chesser in the national archives photograph and is probably not the President's brain. A later discussion with Dr. Chesser concerning the extent of the damage to the brain he saw in the archives in comparison to the damage I observed while infusing the brain taken at autopsy, seemed to indicate a more extensive damage to the brain in the archive photo due to a large laceration that transverses the brain from back to front. This could possibly mean that the President's brain was removed, examined and replaced or substituted before the body was received in the Bethesda morgue for autopsy. I believe there is further support for this conclusion in the description of the brain damage given in the official autopsy report and the Ida Dox drawing. Neither the autopsy report description or the Ida Dox drawing match the description of the brain that was removed at autopsy.

The damage to the brain stated by the Parkland doctors, that approximately one-third to one-half of the brain was missing and the cerebellum was severely damaged and hanging on by a thread would be consistent with the supplemental autopsy report but would not be consistent with the appearance of the brain that was removed at autopsy. This type of damage to the brain would have been more consistent with the damage listed in the supplemental autopsy report and that seen in the Ida Dox drawing opposed to what one would expect from observing the damage to the skull and scalp. The damage to the brain taken at the Bethesda autopsy did not show noticeable damage to the cerebellum or damage comparable to what you would expect when observing the damage to the skull and scalp or to that described by the Parkland doctors.

The unusual appearance of the Bethesda autopsy brain seemed to correlate somewhat with the brain seen in the national archives photograph described by Dr. Chesser, with the exception of the front-to-back laceration described.

When the autopsy brain was placed upside down in the gauze sling to be infused, I noticed that the brain stem appeared to have been severed from two sides as one side of the cut was slightly higher than the other side.

As Dr. Humes was removing the brain from the skull, I heard him say as if to himself, "the damn thing almost fell out into my hands." This led me to believe at the time, that the damage caused by the bullet had somehow severed the brainstem and the brain was unattached in the cranium, but the brain removed at the Bethesda autopsy showed that the brain stem had been surgically cut, as described previously, with minimum damage to the cerebellum or underside of the brain

Doug Horne, the military analyst for the ARRB found evidence of two brain examinations by the autopsy pathologist, one where Drs. Humes and Boswell attended with a medical photographer, John Stringer. Stringer stated that he took photographs of coronal sections of the brain over a viewing plate. Dr. Humes later stated in the supplemental autopsy report that the brain was not sectioned in order to preserve it integrity. Mr. Stringer also stated that he took no photographs of the underside of the brain, yet one of the national archive photographs seen by Dr. Chesser is clearly of the underside of the brain.

Dr. Fink in a later testimony stated that the brain he examined with Drs. Humes and Boswell had flat convolutions, gyri, and narrow sulci, which he attributed to the brain being fixed in formalin. This is an accurate description of the brain's gyrus and sulci that I helped infused at the Bethesda autopsy. This is also a description of the brain photograph viewed by Dr. Chesser in the National Archives.

After the infusion of the brain was started, Dr. Boswell and I returned to the autopsy table, and started the autopsy of the body proper. Dr. Boswell started the autopsy of the body by making the normal 'U" shaped incision from the right armpit across the chest at about the level of the diaphragm to the left armpit. We then folded the flap created by this incision back over the neck and face to expose the rib cage. We then used a Stryker saw to remove the rib chest plate. The chest organs were examined and removed. The chest cavity was then examined for signs of wounds, tears or other indications that a missile had entered the cavity. We found no indication that anything had entered the cavity. There was no large amount of blood or fluid as you would expect to find if an organ had been torn or if the pleural cavity had been breached. The "U" incision was extended from the center of the "U" shaped chest incision to the pubic area.

After tying off the major vessels to reduce the amount of blood draining from the arterial-venous system, the organs were removed, and I placed the dissection board over the body, the organs were placed on the dissection board for examination and dissection. The lungs appeared to be exceptionally pink and healthy with what seemed to be very little fluid accumulation in the lungs, which you often see in massive trauma. This prompted a question to the gallery, did the President smoke? Someone in the gallery, probably Admiral Burkley, said, "he only smoked an occasional cigar." We did not often see healthy lungs at autopsy in those days – almost everyone smoked. After the lungs were removed from the pleural cavity and examined, we found a reddish, almost bluish small area on the right upper lobe just above the apex of the middle lobe at the junction of the upper lobe, the middle lobe, and the lower lobe. It was about the size of the end of the thumb. This reddish area correlated with the approximate level of the probed depth of the back wound.

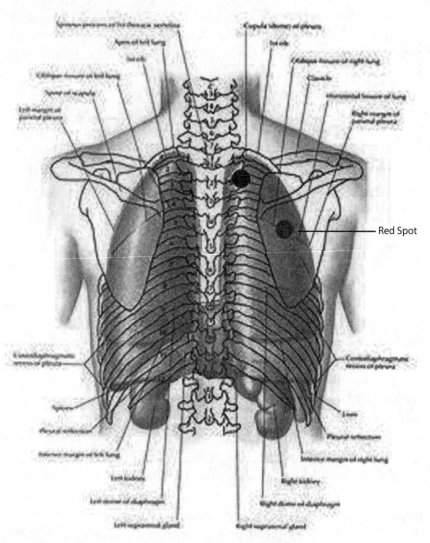

The red dot represents the relative position on the upper lobe of the right lung. While the red spot was described as being located on the upper lobe of the lung at the top of the middle lobe, one must take into consideration that the lower lobe of the lung partially covers the middle lobe and part of the upper lobe in the posterior view. This makes it impossible to precisely locate the reddish-purple spot seen at autopsy on a one-dimensional drawing.

While the purpose of the drawing is to give the reader an approximate location of the contusion (red spot) seen on the lungs at autopsy, the black spot is furnished to reference the relationship of the back wound to the spot on the lungs.

Dr. Boswell took samples from the "red spot" for microscopic examination. Next, we examined the heart. Dr. Boswell opened the heart and examined the heart valves; they all appeared to be normal and healthy. The stomach was opened, and the contents were examined. The lining was examined for lesions, ulcers or other pathology. Dr. Boswell removed the intestinal tract from the stomach and we took it intact to the deep sink, there we took sections and cut the intestines open, cleaned them and examined the lining. This was a normal protocol. Normally, one of the technicians would have done this type of work. We would have taken the intestines and colon, opened them, cleaned them and then the pathologist would have examined them. Instead, Dr. Boswell did all the work. I was there to assist him if he needed help. Once the examination of the intestines was completed, they were left in the deep sink. Dr. Boswell and I went back to the autopsy table and examined the liver. It seemed to be healthy. We took the kidneys, the spleen, and the pancreas and examined them. They all appeared to be normal, there was no cancerous tissue, no ischemia, or other pathology found. Nothing abnormal was found in the other organs with the exception of the adrenal glands. The adrenal glands normally sit on the top of the kidneys and are about the size of a walnut. The President's adrenal glands were almost nonexistent, they appeared to be severely atrophied and wasted. Dr. Burkley didn't want us to examine the kidneys because the Kennedy family apparently didn't want the general public to know about the President's illness. We had to take the kidneys anyway.

There was someone from the Kennedy family, through Dr. Burkley, insisting that the autopsy only consist of the head area but the doctors kept pushing for a full autopsy. We had found no bullets or fragments of bullets and I think Dr. Fink and Dr. Humes worried that a bullet or fragment had ended up in the abdominal area or somewhere else in the body, and that's why they argued for a total autopsy instead of just stopping at the chest. We took tissue sections of the adrenals, but you couldn't really tell if you were in the adrenals or not. We took sections for study from all organs, anything that appeared to be unusual or suspect. Normally, we take a section from a normal area and one from an abnormal area if an abnormal area is found. That way you can compare the tissue within the same organ once you process tissue samples for slides. The organs on the cutting board were weighed and entered on the face sheet. At this time, the internal organs had all been removed and the body cavity was empty. I could see that Dr. Humes and Dr. Fink had started to probe the back wound. Dr.

Humes first probed the wound with a metal probe but later used a round tipped sound (probe) and his little finger because he was afraid of creating a false passage from the back wound into the chest cavity. The impression that his finger made was clearly visible under the pleural lining of the chest cavity. There was no entrance found into the chest cavity from the back wound. The wound seemed to end slightly above the apex of the middle lobe of the right lung. This seemed to correlate with the reddish-purple area found on the bottom of the upper lobe of the right lung. The wound appeared to extend downward from the entrance about 45 to 60 degrees. This back wound will be discussed later.

There was no entry into the pleural cavity, or tear in the pleural lining. The meaning of this will become important later. At this point in the autopsy, more pictures of the head and other specific areas of the body were taken, i.e., with the brain out of the head, a picture of the empty cranium was taken. The photographer took his pictures without any interruption to our work at the autopsy table. As the doctors directed what they wanted to have photographed, they sometimes would hold the head or the body in certain positions. The empty body cavity was examined, and no wounds were found to have penetrated into the chest or body cavities.

After Dr. Boswell and I had finished the autopsy of the body, I saw that Dr. Humes and Dr. Fink had retracted the scalp back away from the head wound, so that the full extent of the head wound could be seen clearly. I could tell the major portion of the area which looked like the wound going forward was not actually part of the original wound of missing bone and scalp. It just intersected with it. It looked as if it was a fracture line going forward slightly past the coronal suture almost to the frontal bone. The coronal suture runs across the skull in front of one ear to the other ear and separates the frontal bone from the parietal bones. You could see that the area where the bone was actually missing was in the parietal-occipital area in the back of the head and extended downward touching the temporal area. The wound was not a totally circular wound. It had a ragged convex top with a rectangular/trapezoid shape tapering off to the right, when viewed from the back of the head, at the bottom was a kind of a tail. There were areas where you could tell that the bone had been chipped out on the surface. When Humes asked about "surgery to the head at Parkland" he was referring to the area on the top of the head where the scalp was holding the fractured skull together, the fractured skull was still adhered to the scalp and there was a laceration in this area that was connected to the top of the wound and ran forward almost to the frontal bone. The laceration seemed to consist of multiple tears in the scalp connected by small neat, clean incisions. The fractured bone pieces that were still attached to the scalp, had separated from the scalp when the scalp was reflected. This made the original wound of missing bone and scalp appear to be larger than when I first saw it. This may account for the differences between the size of the wound seen at Parkland and the size of the wound listed in the official autopsy report. One could take the skull and open it up on the right side. It was as if you could take the skull and fold it down. It was very ragged. Some of the fractures of the skull had actually caused tears in the scalp itself but had not separated from the scalp. This long laceration along the fracture lines seemed to be responsible for the gaping seen when the head was unwrapped. The comments I remember from Humes and Boswell were "the skull is really malleable." You could move the bones on the right side of the head around with your hand. Humes continued his inspection of the head with Dr. Fink.

Late into the autopsy, a man in a suit came into the autopsy room. He had a small plastic bag with a twist tie at the top. The bag contained pieces of bone and bullet fragments. I remember Dr. Humes and Dr. Fink took the pieces of bone out of the bag and tried to fit them into the area of the head wound, but they were not able to make the bone fragments fit very well. There were still two thirds of the open wound visible. The doctors took a flap of scalp that was at the back of the head and stretched it back up to see if it could be used to cover the still open wound in the skull. It could not, as there was still a portion of the wound that was visible with missing bone and scalp. There weren't enough bone pieces to complete the defect in the skull. The last time I saw the bone and metal fragments they were laying on the autopsy table next to the president's head beneath his right ear. Once we finished the autopsy, the small plastic bag had disappeared. The three larger bone fragments that Dr. Humes discusses in the autopsy report, I never saw. The autopsy was finished around midnight and the President's body was turned over to the morticians.

I say morticians, because I understand that there were supposed to be three that did work on the president's, but I only remember one, and two helpers. I noticed him rather late in the autopsy standing by the back, autopsy table, leaning on the rail in front of the gallery. I noticed him because of the way he was dressed. He was dressed in a three-piece suit and wearing a bowler hat, his vest was actually more of a waistcoat than a normal vest, but it was matched to the suit. It was a very elegant tailored suit but the bowler hat he was wearing was what drew my attention and he was carrying an umbrella or cane, I'm not sure which. I assumed he was from Boston or somewhere in Massachusetts, because of the Kennedy's connection with this area, so I assumed they had sent their own mortician. I saw two people bring in embalming equipment; they arrived after I noticed the first mortician. They were not dressed in suits. They were dressed in casual clothes. These two men set up the pump for the embalming process. The mortician that was dressed in a three-piece suit did the main work on the president's body. He warmed the body with warm water which I gave him from the deep sink because there was only cold water available at the autopsy table. He then took what I assumed was plaster of paris and filled the body cavity. The only parts of the internal organs that were returned to the body were the intestine that was cut up into the body cavity to help activate the plaster filler. I understand that this is normal procedure. I stood within earshot so I could help the mortician with anything he might need. All I remember him asking me for was the basin of warm water. There was a spray device that we used at the morgue table but it was only attached to cold water. We used it for cleaning up after autopsies.

There was no longer murmuring from the gallery nor did I feel the extreme tension in the air as I had during the actual autopsy. Now that the autopsy was in effect over and the morticians had begun their work, things had settled down and people began to leave the morgue.

The mortician then filled the body cavity and closed the" U" incision and formed the abdomen, making the president look like he had a six pack. Next, he cleaned and closed the head wound and used a brown rubber material to cover the area he could not cover by stretching the loose scalp over the wound. This was done after the skull cavity was filled with the plaster material. He then put mortician's wax on the small wound in the right temple over the ear, which I believe was from a bullet, and then sutured the wound in the throat and put wax over it, so the wound appeared to be nonexistent. I don't remember if he closed the back wound. The body was cleaned and the hair was shampooed and the whole body was dried and was then moved to the clean back table. I know that there are photos that exist (Fox photos) showing what is purportedly the back of the president's head. The back of the head appears to be intact and the hair looks clean and shiny, freshly washed, but no pictures were taken after the autopsy ended or during the time the mortician was working on the body. After the President's body was moved from the first table where the autopsy had been performed, to the second table, the mortician began working on the cosmetics for the President's face. After the mortician finished the cosmetics, the President looked perfectly normal. I understand that Jacqueline Kennedy when she saw the president's body at the White House later, said something like "that's not Jack" but I thought he looked fine. The only problem the mortician had making up the President's face was that he couldn't get the right eye to completely close. He solved the problem by putting a small suture stitch under the eyelid to keep it closed and make it look normal. Paul O'Connor and I then helped the mortician dress the body. We put socks on the President along with garters, undershorts, undershirt, trousers, shirt, and shoes. Normally, as I understand it, when the body is being dressed at a funeral home, the clothes are split up the back to make it easier to dress the body. This was not done with the President's body. I helped hold the body up to allow the mortician and Paul to dress the body without cutting the clothing. Once the body was dressed, it was placed in a new casket that had been brought into the morgue around midnight by Gawler's Funeral Home. Paul later told me he was handed rosary beads by someone and was told to wrap them in President Kennedy's hands, and he did. I don't remember that, to be honest, I don't remember the rosary beads.

After the lid of the casket was closed a military honor guard came in, picked the casket up and carried it from the morgue. The morgue emptied out and Paul and I were left behind to clean up. We picked up the blood-soaked sheets and towels that the President's body had been wrapped in and took them to the dirty laundry room and placed them in the hamper with the plastic lining, that was used for anything that was contaminated with blood or bodily fluids and would be incinerated, because sheets with blood on them could not be washed and used again. It took Paul and me several hours to clean the morgue. After we came out of the morgue, we were met by someone who told us to report to Captain Stover's office. Paul and I went to Stover's office where we were issued two sets of orders both verbally and written, one set from the Navy and one from the Department of Defense. We stood in front of Captain Stover's desk. Stover then said, "Gentlemen, you are not to discuss what you have seen or heard or participated in the morgue last night. Do you understand the order?" Paul and I of course said, "Yes, sir." What else were two third-class corpsmen who had just witnessed the autopsy of the 35th president of the United States going to say, but "Yes, sir?" We were then asked to sign the orders, which Paul and I did. We were then given copies of the orders and Captain Stover dismissed us. We left the office and started to walk away when a man in a suit that had been in Captain Stover's office when we were given the orders to sign, came out of the office and said that he needed to take the copies and told us that we were not supposed to have been given the copies. We gave our copies of the orders to the man and he said 'thank you" and went back into Capt. Stover's office. Paul and I looked at each other, too tired at this point to be shocked or surprised. I didn't know where Paul went, but I went out to the parking lot where I met my wife and drove home, eager for sleep.

Why did I think the man from Stover's office came and ask for the copies of the orders we had been given, back? At the time, I thought that they did not want any information getting out into the public, especially if they were investigating the President's assassination. That was naïve of me, but that's the way I thought about the circumstances at the time. The orders we were told to sign I didn't feel were out of place; after all, we had just performed an autopsy on the assassinated President of the United States, it was only logical to think it was under investigation. I knew nothing about Lee Harvey Oswald during the autopsy as I had been sequestered in the morgue since 3:30 that afternoon. It did seem a little unusual that Paul and I had received orders from the Department of Defense, and to this day I don't know why, because orders from the Department of the Navy would have been sufficient.

I never discussed the Kennedy autopsy or my part in it. I never talked about it with my wife, or Paul or any of our friends, besides, who would believe me. Instead, I went back to my life as usual. I was stationed at Bethesda hospital for another year. Life during that time continued to be filled with classwork and duty in the morgue.

CHAPTER FIVE

After graduation, my next duty station was a naval hospital laboratory in Philadelphia, Pa. I worked in the hematology department and in pathology processing tissue samples and assisting in the morgue with autopsies, the things I had been trained for at Bethesda. We had students at Philadelphia that would normally do autopsies, but when they were in class and not available, I would assist with the autopsies. At Philadelphia Naval Hospital, it was different. The pathology residents actually did the autopsies but we did very few autopsies, certainly not to the extent we did at Bethesda. But, basically the autopsy procedures were the same. Pennsylvania law was different; for instance, in Philadelphia the organs would have to be returned to the body as opposed to the regulations in Maryland.

While we were stationed in Philadelphia, my wife and I lived in an apartment in New Jersey which was across the Walt Whitman Bridge from Philadelphia. My wife had a job working as a receptionist, in Cherry Hill, New Jersey. Every day she would take me to work, and some days she was able to pick me up after my day was finished. When she wasn't able to pick me up after work, I would take the bus to downtown Philadelphia, and take the subway across the river to Camden and take the bus home. I didn't like taking the subway because it was extremely dangerous being in that area in those days. My wife had developed a friendship with one of the older ladies that lived in the same apartment complex, who also worked in Cherry Hill. She didn't have a car, so she rode public transportation to work. My wife began to ride the same transportation with her, to work. This gave me the opportunity to drive the car back and forth to work. I worked rotating shifts, a month on nights, a month on days. I was part of the staff at the hospital.

There was always some danger for my wife riding the bus and I always worried about that. A woman who lived across from us in the apartment complex had been attacked in her apartment. One night before I had to leave for work, my wife and I were sitting on the couch watching TV and someone tried to break in our front door. Neither my wife nor I liked the cold weather of Philadelphia or the unsafe conditions that we were forced to live in, and we were both miserable.

I decided to ask for a transfer to Florida nearer to my wife's family. There was a billet open in Key West for a second-class hospital corpsman with a certification in laboratory sciences. I made the request for the billet and was assigned to the *USS Bushnell,* which was a submarine tender. It was a large ship. There were 900 sailors stationed on board. The *Bushnell* was actually a maintenance docking for submarines, but it qualified for sea duty. My wife and I moved into a small house which we were able to furnish comfortably. I had some seniority by then. I had received a promotion, so in the squadron, I had more authority on the ship along with a lot of responsibility. Florida was great! We bought a small boat, and went fishing almost every day after work, my wife caught fish but I just drowned bait. My duties included managing the ships pharmacy and laboratory, being responsible for the the needs of the corpsman's medical stations on the nine submarines and the needs of the corpsmen at the dive locker which were assigned to the Subron12 squadron. I had two Submarines that had corpsmen on them that out ranked me, so, I didn't have to do as much for them; they usually took care of their own medical lockers, inventories and turned the reports into me on the *Bushnell.*

I was even the designated career counselor on the ship, which was a joke because everyone knew that I planned to get out and return to college. Everyone ragged me about this assignment so, if you laughed you got appointed the assistant career counselor for your department. This quieted the harassment some. Aboard the *USS Bushnell,* we had about 12 corpsmen, each submarine also had a corpsman assigned to it. We had one corpsman who was a certified diver stationed in the dive locker so, we just let him stay in the dive locker all the time and handle their own medical needs. We had a couple of doctors that were assigned to the ship, Dr. Hodges and Dr. Trevino. Dr. Trevino handled everything that we needed a doctor for on the *Bushnell.* The corpsmen would actually see the people who came to sick bay, and if it was something serious, the corpsmen would refer them to the doctor, and if it was something really serious, the doctor would transfer the patient to the Naval Hospital on the other side of the island. Though Dr. Hodges was assigned to the *Bushnell,* I never saw him during my tour on the ship, but I talked to him on the telephone each morning because I had to attend Officers' call for him. It got so that the ship's executive officer started to jokingly call me Doc Hodges. Dr. Hodges was able to get away with this because he was a personal friend with the base Admiral and was also the private physician for the Admiral's family. Rank has its privileges.

My most memorable time while stationed on the *Bushnell* was the night it caught on fire. On ships in those days, trash was dumped into the bilges. When the boat went out to sea, the bilges were blown out, meaning you would eject the trash into the open sea. The *Bushnell* was equipped with eight diesel engines and, just by their very presence, the engines drip oil into the bilges. Normally the bilges were cleaned periodically because of that dripping oil, but, apparently the diesel engines aboard the *Bushnell* had not been cleaned for some time. A spark from a bad generator start or something had caused the bilge oil to catch on fire. I don't really know, as I wasn't aboard the ship at the time. I was at home, but I was called back to the ship as soon as the fire started. As I approached the ship it was already at "General Quarters." I could see sailors off-loading nuclear torpedo warheads and other munitions from the ship to the pier, they were literally throwing nuclear warheads from the ship to the pier. I was later told that the nuclear warheads that were being thrown from the ship to the pier were not armed, so there was no danger of explosion.

I immediately called back the corpsmen who lived off base and notified the doctors. The single corpsmen that lived in sick bay had already started the emergency setup, under the supervision of the duty crew. This was for the treatment or recovery of the crews fighting the fire. I next went to the engine room to check on the two corpsmen who were already manning the emergency medical station there. Standing on the steel catwalk above the engine room, the heat melted grooves in the soles of my shoes. We had a submarine tender which was a sub-repair boat that was helping fight the fire and a couple of torpedo retrievers alongside pumping saltwater into the ship. There were tugs standing by to tow the ship to sea if she started to sink. One of the ventilation stacks from the engine room went up through the sick bay. It had become so hot that it had turned cherry red and all the paint had burned off. During the crisis, we were always doing something that was essential, which didn't give us much time to dwell on the danger. The fire was finally put out the following afternoon.

CHAPTER SIX

I remained at this duty station in the Florida Keys until 1966, when I left the military. I wanted to go back to school and finish my degree. That was, after all, the main reason for going into the Navy in the first place. My wife and I moved back to my hometown of Summit, Mississippi and rented an apartment from my brother-in-law. It was good to be home and we settled into a hectic but comfortable life. In Key West, my wife had worked for the base as a key punch operator. This experience helped her get a good job with Bell telephone and I started into the second semester at Southwest Mississippi Junior College a local junior college in my hometown. After the second semester, I transferred to a college in Jackson, Mississippi. It was a small liberal arts college, but it had a good academic reputation. I chose the school because my church offered some financial assistance because it was a Methodist supported school, and the University of Mississippi medical school was located across the street there in Jackson.

I ran into a lot of prejudice at the college because of my age and because of my military service. I was 26 years old, which was a bit long in the tooth for some of the liberal professors, to be attending "their" college. One professor told me I was too old and I needed to get a job. I did have a job. I worked at the University of Jackson medical center, working in the clinical laboratory at night. Another professor told me that I would have to make a decision between working or going to school at his college. I told him that if I didn't work I couldn't go to school. I wasn't doing autopsies at this time. I would not do more autopsies until I came back to the Medical Center as a graduate student in the Pathology Department. After the first year at "his college" I soon realized that I had made a mistake in my choice of colleges and I consequently transferred to the University of Mississippi in Oxford.

I commuted from Jackson to Oxford during the week and returned home on weekends. At the University of Mississippi, I worked for the local hospital taking calls for the clinical laboratory at night. The hospital furnished me with a room and meals and paid me a small salary which I used toward tuition and books. During this time, I got to know several of the doctors that practiced at the hospital. Through the encouragement of one of the physicians who was on the medical school admission board, I applied for acceptance to an MD/PhD program at the University Medical Center in Jackson, Mississippi. After graduating from the University in Oxford, I returned to my home in Jackson and entered the MD/PhD program in the pathology department. My first- and second-year academic studies were taken with the medical students, with some additional course-work related to my graduate degree in pathology/immunology. It was here that I once again resumed my work with autopsies. The department had no pathology residents at that time, consequently the graduate students fulfilled the autopsy need, at first under the supervision and assistance of senior graduate students with a review by a staff pathologist. Later the autopsies were done by senior graduate students and presented to interested physicians under the review of a staff pathologist. This was a very enjoyable but intense learning experience.

Despite all my efforts to continue my education, life intervened, which is a nice way of saying that I ran out of money. I then left school and went to work for a company that specialized in the development and sale of hematology equipment. After working for this company for approximately four years, I was able to improve my financial resources and return to graduate school and completed my Master's Degree. I was admitted under the same program that I had previously pursued. Even though the school no longer had the MD/PhD program, previous students could return to the same program that they had left in good standing within a five-year period of time from their departure.

I went back to the same program that I had left four years earlier with the goal of obtaining a MD/PHD degree and become a practicing physician. I began to realize that the intervening years had redirected my interest in medicine. The type of medicine that I wanted to practice no longer existed. The intrusion into medicine by large corporate health care entities and insurance companies was beginning to dictate how a physician could treat his patients. I felt that this intrusion was a wedge between a physician and his patient and I wanted no part of it. Consequently, I directed my education toward the science of medicine as opposed to the practice of medicine.

During the time that I was in graduate school I received a call from Paul O'Connor. Paul and I were students in the clinical laboratory blood banking school at the National Naval Medical Center in Bethesda, Maryland.

Paul, of course, was the other Navy laboratory technician who worked with me during the autopsy of the assassinated President, John F. Kennedy. Paul was not only a good friend but had become a relative by marriage to my wife's cousin. Paul told me he had been interviewed by two men from the House Select Committee on Assassinations concerning his role in the autopsy of the President's body and they wanted to talk with me. In August 1977, I received a letter from the House Select Committee requesting that I be interviewed by two of their representatives. I then received a phone call from a Ms. Bolin, telling me that a Mr. Andy Purdy and Mr. Jim Kelly would be arriving at my home shortly to conduct the interview.

I had not thought about my participation in the Kennedy autopsy for many years and was a little surprised by the seemingly demanding request, especially from people that I had no knowledge of. During the phone conversation, I told the caller that I would not allow people that I did not know to come into my home and that I really wasn't interested in being interviewed by anyone concerning my role in the autopsy of President Kennedy. I was told that this was an official request from the House Select Committee established by Congress to investigate the assassination of John Fitzgerald Kennedy and Martin Luther King. I was given the date of arrival of Mr. Kelly and Mr. Purdy. After concluding the phone call, I called the local office of Thad Cochran, one of Mississippi's senators, to verify that the House Select Committee was a legitimate federal entity and explain my concern to one of his aides. Cochran's aid called me back and told me that the House Select Committee was a legitimate Congress-mandated committee to investigate the assassination of the President and Martin Luther King. He also told me that Sen. Cochran had suggested we hold the meeting in his office and to have the credentials of Mr. Kelly and Mr. Purdy verified by phone with the committee by his secretary. The arrangements were made, and I agreed to meet with Mr. Kelly and Mr. Purdy.

CHAPTER SEVEN

I met Mr. Purdy and Mr. Kelly on August 29, 1977 at Senator Cochran's office where we were greeted by his secretary and introductions were made. Mr. Purdy and Kelly presented their credentials and Senator Cochran's secretary made a phone call to verify their authenticity. Previously I'd been told that Mr. Purdy and Mr. Kelly were counsel for the assassination committee but when the credentials were checked I learned that Mr. Kelly was an FBI agent. This was a little disconcerting to me because I had been told that this was to be a normal interview to acquire information and now apparently one of the interviewers was an FBI agent. This fact pretty much set the tone for the "interview." From the very beginning, I felt the interview was directed more toward having me confirm facts that they already had a formed an opinion on as opposed to gaining any new or additional information. They would ask me questions and when I gave an answer they would tell me that couldn't be right because of such and such.

They began asking me questions about the Warren Commission conclusion and about the drawings that were presented by the autopsy doctors. I told them that I had not read any of the Warren Commission conclusions or seen the drawings that they were asking about. They then took me to the local law library and showed me the Harold Ryberg drawings and again asked me questions. They showed me a drawing that seemed to have a flap standing up on the top of the head. I told them that I didn't see a flap like that on the top of the head and then they tried to shift my opinion as to the location of the head wound to the top of Kennedy's head. They next asked me about the location of the back wound and I told them that the wound was in the upper back not in the lower neck as seen in the drawing. I was then asked if I could have missed the wounds because I was busy doing something else at the time. (*Note: if the flap had been present on the top of president Kennedy's head I would've had ample opportunity during the taking of the x-rays and the examination of the body to see it. I was also sure of the location of the back wound because I HAD PLACED IT ON THE "FACE SHEET"*).

Purdy and Kelly were continually questioning my answers by saying things like, "Are you sure you saw that?" or "Maybe you missed it because you were distracted by something else," or "That's not what another witness told us." They questioned me about the differences between my description of the brain that we removed at autopsy and Paul's description of no brain being present. I had no answer for them because that was the first time that I became aware of Paul's statement that there was no brain. There were other times when they would tell me "You couldn't possibility have seen that" or "You didn't see that did you?" I told them that my primary focus at the autopsy was directed toward the large posterior head wound. They came back to me with "We interviewed this other individual who was there" (who I knew was Paul O'Connor) and he said that the whole back of the head was blown out and the brain was missing." I told them again that I was not aware of Paul's testimony and that I had seen the wound after the scalp was reflected from the skull and that I did not feel that the entire back of the head was blown out.

I was asked if I had any notes or pictures that I took from the autopsy. I told them that I had nothing of that nature. "Surely you have notes," was their response and again I told him that I took no notes or pictures or anything else concerning the autopsy. I really don't know why Purdy and Kelly thought that I would've taken notes or pictures at the autopsy. In retrospect, I probably should have written notes about my experiences that night after I arrived home the following Saturday morning, but I'd been given orders to not talk about or discuss what happened in the morgue that night and I was concerned about the consequences of putting my experience on paper. The discussion continued, and they asked a great deal about the head wound and the body wounds, but they never asked me to describe the wounds to them. They asked me where the head wound was located, and I told them it was located on the right posterior portion of the head in the occipital- parietal area. As the interview continued, the questions became more redundant and condescending. Finally, I told them I had nothing else to offer and the interview was ended.

I left the interview feeling that it had been a waste of time because Purdy's and Kelly's interest was directed more toward confirming their preconceived opinions that the Warren commission was correct and that I was wrong.

Years later, I was sent a copy of the Kelly/Purdy report as presented to the House Select Committee and a copy of the notes that they took from the interview. The report seemed to be a composite of things that I said intermingled with those that Paul O'Connor had said. It seemed to have no congruence of thought or form. I felt that the material in the report was presented in such a way that sometimes it was misleading and often times seem to support conclusions that it was not meant to support. It often avoided or ignored material that appeared to be controversial.

Below you will find a copy of the official report of my deposition presented by Andrew Purdy to the House Select Committee on Assassinations.

August 29, 1977

Re: interview with James Chris Jenkins (*James Curtis Jenkins correct name*), 9:30 AM central time, August 24, 1977 room 316 federal building in Jackson Mississippi.

Mr. Jenkins was interviewed because of his participation in the autopsy of President Kennedy.

Mr. Jenkins currently resides at 210 Flagg Chapel Dr., Jackson, MS 39209 (home phone: 601-922 – 6866). (See memo from Colin Boland to Jacqueline Hess, August 17, 1977)

Mr. Jenkins told Ms. Bolin in their phone conversation of August 17 that he was very hesitant to talk over the phone because he had information which was controversial (*Note: add in statement not mine*). He indicated to us that he will be applying for a government insured loan for his graduate medical education. Mr. Jenkins was in the service just over five years (serving between 1960 and 1966). Mr. Jenkins began his service in San Diego in 1960 and went on to Balboa Hospital. Mr. Jenkins made no mention of any service in an area near Lee Oswald. Mr. Jenkins was present in Bethesda in 1963 attending lab technician school there. At the time of his training, Captain Stover was head of the Medical School, Dr. Humes chief of the Laboratory and Dr. Boswell was assistant chief of the Laboratory.

Mr. Jenkins immediate superior on the night of the autopsy was a pathologist who had the duty (*Note: my immediate superior was an NCO HM1*) that night (he can't remember his name).

Mr. Jenkins was a student lab technician (H. N. 4). He had been serving approximately six or seven months in that capacity, during which he had autopsy duty every fourth night. He said his duties include the admission of the bodies to the morgue and the discharge. He said it was normally in charge of most of the paperwork including the body description which consisted of filling in a free-printed sheet which had the body diagrams (the front on one side and the back on the other) and the blanks for the weights and others notations. Mr. Jenkins said he participated in two or three autopsies each time he was on duty, and he usually finished about 3 – 4 AM. Jenkins said the individuals who outline standard operating procedure to him were probably Chief Ewald bacteriology and or Chief Norman who dealt with the academic part of the school. Mr. Jenkins said that two people pulled duty together. He said they usually wore scrub clothes. He said his usual partner was Stanley Miller who was not present that evening for some unknown reason. He said that on that night he was working with Paul O'Connor (O'Connor later married Jenkins wife's cousin). He said that Mr. O'Connor is presently attending college in Florida. He said he thought he was at the University of Gainesville studying either sociology or psychology. (At this time Mr. Jenkins gave no indication of knowing exactly where Mr. O'Connor was or that he had been in touch with him recently). On the day of the assassination Mr. Jenkins learned of the death at approximately 3:30 PM while in class. He said classes were subsequently dismissed. He was told to prepare the morgue at approximately 4:15 – 4:30 PM, his orders come in from the duties section chief he said he got there about 30 or 40 minutes before the autopsy.

Note: I believe the above statement concerning my arrival 30 or 40 minutes before the autopsy was either a fill-in statement or misinterpretation of Mr. Purdy's notes. As I've previously stated, I first arrived in the morgue between 3:30 and 4 :00 PM. The President's body didn't arrive in the morgue until approximately 6:38 PM.

Mr. Jenkins said he logged the autopsy number in the ledger book but did not put a name in there. Mr. Jenkins was told not to put the name in the log. Mr. Jenkins noticed that later that someone had written the initial "C" or "CNC" where the name would normally be. Mr. Jenkins said that subsequent to the present autopsy and Air Force Col. and a child were autopsy that night and would have been logged into that ledger book before it was "retired." Mr. Jenkins said that when the funeral home came in he had to identify the body. He first said he put a tag on the wrist but later said he put it just on the big toe.

Note: The above statements concerning the Air Force Col. and the child being autopsied prior to that of the President is totally erroneous. There was a second casket in the morgue that was pushed up against the morgue cold boxes. I had been told that this was an Air Force major that was to be buried in Arlington Cemetery and that the casket had arrived too late to be received at Arlington and that we were to hold it in the morgue for burial the following day. *The statement concerning the baby also is erroneous; sometimes late in the evening there was a stillborn admitted to the morgue but it was not autopsied.*

The discussion concerning the admission and tagging of bodies into the morgue and their identification for release to the funeral home was a discussion about our normal protocol and was not related to the admission of the President's body into the morgue.

Mr. Jenkins said he entered all information that he was supposed to on the autopsy form, except for the name. He recalls that he was told to omit the name by either the pathologist or a lieutenant. He recalled that Dr. Dixon came into the autopsy room once but doesn't believe he participated other than that. He believes its pathologist was ("... A new man"). Humes!!! (*Note: this statement makes no sense, because I knew Dr. Boswell and Dr. Humes.*)

Jenkins says he helped put the body on the table (*Note: I did not help remove the body from the casket and place it on the table. Paul O'Connor was involved in that procedure.*) and started making the regular markings on the sheet. He recalls describing the scar on the back and the chest incisions on either side. He said "... he only remembers a throat wound which looked like a tracheotomy." He said he thought it was a tracheotomy "... Because it looked like a surgically made incision." He said he saw a head wound in the "... Middle temporal region back to the occipital the occipital region. (*Note: The original statement by me was a description of a small wound in the temporal area just slightly above and forward of the right ear. This statement is misleading; it seems to insinuate that there was a large wound starting at the middle temporal region going back to the occipital area*). Mr. Jenkins described the back wound as being "... Just below the collar to the right of the midline." (*Note: this statement is also misleading in that it seems to place the back wound higher into the neck area as described in the Warren Commission report as opposed to its actual location at the top of the right scapula midway between the scapula and the vertebral column.*) Mr. Jenkins indicated that he was "... Not sure if I finished..." Filling in the markings.

Mr. Jenkins said he located marks on the body before any weighing was done and "... As soon as he came in." Mr. Jenkins says he believes Dr. Humes attempted to probe the back wound. He said he didn't believe that Dr. Humes found that the probe "... Penetrated into the chest." Mr. Jenkins said he believes the organs had already been taken out he said the body was "... Repeatedly x-rayed because they felt there should be a bullet or something there" Mr. Jenkins recalls writing down the weights but doesn't "... Believe he actually weighed them." He said the doctors did not redo the sheets that he had prepared to his knowledge.

Mr. Jenkins is "... Unsure who did the incisions... He believes Commander Boswell" ... Did most of the work." Mr. Jenkins was not clear as to who may have been giving the autopsy doctors their orders. He said "... A lot of people were making suggestions." Mr. Jenkins appeared very uneasy about the subject. specifically, he said he "... Was very uneasy about this...." He said he wished someone had "... Talked with me several years ago when this was fresher." He said that "... With the Warren Commission findings you can understand why I am skeptical."

Mr. Jenkins said that he doesn't specifically recall any photographs been taken of the interior of the chest. He said he believed that full body x-rays are taken including the extremities. He said he "... Saw them do them." He said all were taken at the autopsy. He said that whole body x-rays are normal at legal autopsy. (*Note: I don't believe that is my statement. I would not have made a statement like that because at that time I had no experience with or knowledge of legal autopsies.*) Mr. Jenkins said that the only thing he found impressionable was that Drs. Humes, Boswell and the Captain of the Honor Guard seemed to be the only officers not of flag rank."

Mr. Jenkins said he was told subsequent to the autopsy by an admiral not to discuss the autopsy. He said he later learned this man was the Surgeon General. (*Note: after the autopsy, Paul and I were given orders by Capt. Stover, commanding officer of the medical school. I never had a conversation with an admiral that night and I had never met the Surgeon General.*)

While Mr. Jenkins recalls no comment regarding the tracheotomy, he said he saw the "... Natural assumption was that it was a tracheotomy, because it was a natural procedure." He recalls the doctors concern about not being able to find any metal fragments. He said repeated x-rays were taken by a "... Third class x-ray technician." (Custer) he remembers that if anyone left the morgue they did so with a Marine escort. He said food was brought in. He said he didn't leave during the autopsy. Regarding the autopsy descriptive sheet, Mr. Jenkins recalls that he "... Put in the chest incisions and tracheotomy." That he doesn't think he drew the back wound. He said it was possible that Dr. Humes added to the sheet. Mr. Jenkins said that five or six years later he saw the publication which included an autopsy description sheet which he "didn't feel was the same one he wrote on." He said this made him very uneasy specifically, he "... Didn't believe it was my handwriting." He is sure it may have been Time or Newsweek but he cannot identify he "... wrote at least some of the informational sheet." He said his recollection was "very striking." He said it was a situation where you look at something and "knew" it was wrong.

Mr. Jenkins believes that he wrote on the sheet in pencil. He said it was "... A requirement that it had to be done in pencil." He said the sheet was on the clipboard which had a string with the pencil attached. He recalls that the backside of the figure was on the back of the sheet and said he had no recollection of a drawing of a head on the sheet anywhere (*Note: This statement refers to the drawing of the head wounds by Dr. Boswell on the back of the "Face sheet"*). He believes the writing on the sheet would have had to have been Paul O'Connor's or one of the doctors or himself.

Mr. Jenkins said he had no information concerning the destruction of any film during the autopsy. He said he does remember an incident which was probably that. He said it was "... A brief flareup." He said there was a lot of incidents like that where examined people were "curt" and specifically remembered that the "... Gallery was very impatient." They seem to be "... Mad about the doctors not finding a bullet."

Regarding the head wound Mr. Jenkins said he was "... Surprised that the conclusions the doctors reach." He said he was previously at Cecil Field where he saw a person who had been shot in the side of the head. He said this wound seemed to come in the right side above the ear and out the top left. He said the visitors were "... So intense about finding the wound in the back of the head. He said he had a "... Vague recollection of the doctors trying to fit the bones in the head...." He said he thought the bones were already there and not the bones they brought in. Mr. Jenkins recalls Humes trying to probe the wound with his finger which enabled him to reach the end of the wound. He said that around the time of the probing they repeated the took x-rays of the area. He said he believes they examined the organs for any trace of the bullet are bullet fragments. Regarding the possibility of the chest having been open, and face blood or fluid present, he said "... I should remember... It would be my job to suction that."

Mr. Jenkins was also present for the embalming of the body. He said the embalmers replaced some of the tissue and used some type of plaster molding to close the head wound. (*Note: Paul was the one who discussed the use of plaster in the repair of the head wound. The wound was closed by stretching the scalp over the wound and use of a rubber-like material to cover the remaining opening which the hair was combed over*). He said there was a problem with the right eye because it would not remain closed. He said this was one of the reasons the body was not viewed in an open casket. He recalls mortician trying to arrange a small skull fragments in the head and believe some of them were put in a small jar during the autopsy. (*Note:*

the morticians were not the ones trying to fit the small bone fragments that we received in a zip tie bag, it was the pathologist performing the autopsy that did this.) Mr. Jenkins says he couldn't recall whether or not the brain was removed but said that "… It is normally my function to remove the brain and infiltrated it." He says brain is possibly put in a glass jar. However, he then said the brain is usually first put in a fusion bucket (crock or porcelain) before his foot in and the glass, usually about 24 hours later. (*Note: I believe these discussions of the brain are attributed to Paul O'Connor and not to myself. One of the most lasting memories that I have of the autopsy is the removal of the brain from the cranium by Dr. Humes and his giving it to Dr. Boswell and my attempts to place infusion needles in the internal carotids and the problems that we had doing this. The brain was infused with formalin during the autopsy procedure and after the autopsy was finished it was dropped in a stainless bucket and covered. I have no memories of the disposition of the brain after that time. The usual procedure was to place stainless bucket in the little specimen room off the corridor in the morgue for further examination.*)

Mr. Jenkins remembers the doctors examining x-rays on the viewing screen to try to find fragments but couldn't remember where they found any of whether they removed any from the body are the head. He recalls "… A lot of little jars…" But can't remember the fragments. (*Note: these statements are not even related – "a lot of little jars" relates to the initial set-up when we were setting up specimen jars for tissue samples before the autopsy ever began. The reason for the multiple sets of x-rays being taken was that there were no fragments of bullets being found and consequently we were told to repeat the x-rays*). Jenkins does not remember whether any agents were present; he recalls a number of civilians there and he knew that the Secret Service was there but he didn't know who they were. Mr. Jenkins said that the cleanup of the autopsy normally entails a proper labeling of the organs. He said this would have been done under Boswell's direction. He recalls that the body was put in a different casket and the sheets were put in the laundry basket. He said that he and Paul O'Connor were the last ones to leave the morgue. Jenkins was later told that the paperwork was "retired." He had the feeling that some of it was put in Galloways hospital safe. Jenkins recalls giving a face sheet to Boswell. He is not sure if Paul or he wrote the numbers but he believes one of them did as the organs were weighed he said that the face sheet probably had blood on it. Mr. Jenkins said that the whole attitude in the autopsy room change when Dr. Humes came in. He had a sense that it was very restricted and that he had to watch what he said. He said the whole thing became a "… Guarded type of thing." Jenkins had the distinct impression that someone in the gallery loss "... Telling them what to do."

Jenkins recalls Humes discussion with someone the problem of finding the bullet. He said this discussion amounted to a "disturbance." Jenkins had the impression that everything "... Seem like it was pretty designated... Seem they had an answer and wanted to prove it." Said he doesn't remember any phone calls being made out does remember a phone call by phone being on the wall. Jenkins said that "... A lot of people were taking notes in the galleries... Some in suits some in uniforms. He said that "... Possibly Humes made recorded notations (*Note: there was no dictation, only hand-written notes taken by the pathologist*) ..." Of what he saw. (*Note: there were no recordings made that night in the morgue that we were aware of.*)

Jenkins said the back wound was "... Very shallow... It didn't enter the peritoneal (chest) cavity." He said the wound to the head enter the top rear quadrant from the front side.

Approximately 11:45 PM we accompanied subject to the garden justice building the law library to examine the version of the autopsy descriptive sheet contained therein he examined CE 397, volume 17, page 45 – 46. While examine the front page of the autopsy descriptive sheet, Jenkins said that it "should have a Navy number on the top left." As he was examining this sheet which had a lot of blank spaces, Jenkins said "... All the top would have had to be filled in." He said the numbers looks "... Like my handwriting...," Referring to the numbers on the top part of the page. The numbers at top left of the page was stamped or typed in and Jenkins said "... It would be written in." Jenkins says he believes he hand wrote in the number on the original autopsy descriptive sheet.

Re: the writing concerning the head wound on the diagram itself, Jenkins said that it was "... Not mine." Jenkins said he would have labeled the back scar (it is labeled); but he said it was "... Not his handwriting." Regarding the marking the location of the throat will, Jenkins said the slit he drew was "... Not crescent – like..." Like the one in the Warren commission volumes. Jenkins added that was normal for the pathologist to sign the description sheet which was not done on the version in the report. Jenkins said all the heights and weights "... Would be filled in..." But said he could "... Not remember specifically" writing them in.

Jenkins said the notations regarding the lungs, spleen and kidney looked like his handwriting. He said that the "... Date did not even look like... His handwriting. He said that "... Possibly the rest is Paul's."

45

Jenkins said "... We would write the starting time in." Starting time blank was not filled in. Regarding the diagram, Jenkins said "... None of that handwriting looks like mine." He said that the autopsy descriptive sheet in the Warren volumes does not look like the one he saw in the publication five – six years after the autopsy.

Jenkins did not recall a small hole in the head as drawn on the descriptive sheet; he said that the big hole would have covered the area where the little old was drawn on the sheet. Regarding the back wound he said that he "... Thought it was a little higher up, underneath the collar" he said wound itself was "... Below the collar at an angle, and a downward trajectory." (*Note: it seems like they're trying to move the back wound up into the neck area, in order to validate the Warren Commission's single-bullet theory, because if the single bullet theory is valid the bullet would have had to travel upwards from the location of the back wound in order to exit at the throat wound.*) Jenkins had no information regarding the changes in the numbers in the top part of the sheet. Jenkins recalled that the doctors extensively attempted to probe the back wound. He said they probably use was a metal one, approximately 8 inches long. He said that "... Most of the probe one in... Between the skin..." And not into the chest cavity he said Humes could probe the bottom of the wound with his little finger and said that the metal probe went in 2- 4 inches. He said it was quite a "... Fact of controversy..." That the doctors "... Couldn't prove the bullet came into the cavity."

Jenkins said he "... Possibly drew the back scar..." But "... Doesn't think so...." He said he is "positive" he did draw the head wound.

Jenkins said the number of the patient on the log and on the descriptive sheet would be the same. He said he thought they may have been a stamp for putting the number on the log but didn't for the descriptive sheet. Jenkins believe he would have filled in the physical description where the descriptive sheet is blank regarding the color of the eyes the race the hair color and the heights. Jenkins says the chest measurements or the location of the chest incisions were not made by him and were possibly made by Paul regarding. Regarding erasures generally, Jenkins said they must be initialed. When asked about his recollection that the drawing of the front of the body was on one side of the sheet in the back on the other, he said it was "... Possible is recollection from another morgue."

Regarding the autopsy descriptive sheet that he saw in the publication, he said the other one was neater and he "... Couldn't be sure that the numbers in it were his." Jenkins says he has no recollection of the drawing of the head on the back side.

Re: CE 386 (volume 16, page 977), Jenkins said the wound at the top part of the head look familiar but said he had no recollection of that little bullet hole in the head. Jenkins placed a major defect in the head a little lower than the schematic drawing. He said that the neck wound he recall was lower and more to the midline than that drawn in the drawing. He reiterated his belief that the wound in the back was "... Below the collar line which is what the picture shows."

Re: CE 385, Jenkins said he didn't see the possibility that it was accurate. He said he didn't remember whether anyone look to see if the trach was torn. He said that the probing of the back wound was attempted toward the center as indicated in the drawing, said that in actuality only way the probe was able to go and was at a "... Fairly dramatic angle downward so as not to enter the cavity." He added that he thought the entry wound in the back was lower than that shown in the drawing. He said he didn't notice any bruising at the tip of the lung. He said that according to his recollection of the location of the back wound the bullet would have been going upwards through the body to have exited in the front of the neck. He said he was basing his impression of direction on the fact that the probe did not enter the body cavity. Jenkins said he believed the autopsy face sheet was essentially accurate regarding the location of the wound in the back.

As one reads through the above report you get the impression that it was not of importance to the interviewers. It is fraught with careless errors and it is obvious that there is a lack of knowledge concerning medical nomenclature and procedure. It also is obvious that the notes from which this report was written are inconsistent and incomplete. It seems that when there is an unsure meaning of a statement the fill-in interpretation is always biased toward the conclusion made by the Warren Commission. There are many erroneous statements attributed to me in this interview. I have tried to make the reader aware of the missteps by the interviewers. Whether this was due to bias or due to a lack of experience with medical evidence terminology I can only speculate. I can only say that something as important as the assassination of a president would deserve more attention to detail.

The above is a direct copy of the original report to the HSCA. Please don't hold me responsible for the spelling and grammar.

In June 1978, I received a call from Mark Flanagan concerning my involvement in the autopsy. The contents of that call are listed below.

I do not remember this telephone call but after my name was released to the public by the House Select Committee on Assassinations, I began to receive phone calls from many unknown persons.

After reading this outside contact report, I find it has some of the erroneous statements attributed to me that are in the Purdy-Kelly report. Some of the language seems to come directly from the Purdy-Kelly report. It erroneously states that I normally pulled duty with Paul O'Connor. My normal duty partner was Stanley Miller. It also implies that I helped remove the body from the coffin. Paul was the only one of the two of us that helped remove the body.

The outside report by Mark Flanagan is presented on the next two pages. This report is fragmented and seems to be done as a required afterthought. It is presented as I received it with my apology to the reader.

KENNEDY

OUTSIDE CONTACT REPORT   009526

DATE _6-27-78_ TIME _3:15_

I.   Identifying Information:

       Name _James Curtis Jenkins_   Telephone _(601)373-7568_
       Address _Jackson, Mississippi_

       Type of Contact: ✓ Telephone
                         __ Person

II. Summary of Contact:

       contacted re: autopsy (previously interviewed) – Jenkins
       said he had been present in the morgue for several
       hours before the President's body was brought in.
       He was on ~~this~~ his normal duty which included
       admitting a body into the morgue and the discharge
       of the body. He ~~normally pulled duty with~~
       ~~Paul O'Connor.~~ Jenkins said he recalled that
       the President's body did not have any
       clothes on; it may have been wrapped in
       only a sheet.
       ~~Jenkins said he and several others~~
       ~~moved the President's body from the~~
       ~~coffin to the autopsy table.~~ At this time

III. Recommended Follow-up (if any):

       _____

       _____

       Signature: _Mark Flanagan_

an examination was conducted to discover all the wounds and defects of the body. Jenkins said he would then document these wounds and defects on a body description sheet.

~~When the body was brought in~~

During the time the body was brought into the morgue, moved from the coffin ~~in~~ to the ~~table~~ autopsy table, and initially examined, Jenkins could not recall any foreign objects being discovered or discussed. He specifically could not recall any missile or fragments of a missile falling out onto the autopsy table or onto the floor.

Jenkins emphasized that it was Paul O'Connor's and his duty to place the body on the autopsy table and to conduct the initial examination of the exterior of the body. Although he could not be certain, Jenkins could not recall any clothes being on the body. Jenkins was certain, however, that no missile or foreign object was discovered at this time.

Jenkins could not remember who Captain ~~Bob~~ Osborne was. *who is this*

CHAPTER EIGHT

I returned to my graduate studies and relegated John Kennedy and the assassination to the past. After receiving my graduate degree, I again went to work for the same hematology equipment company that I had worked for before returning to school. The company moved me to Texas in 1980. Shortly after my wife and I had settled in our new home, the company downsized and restructured my home office in Houston. I worked for a subsidiary of the company for a short period of time. I had always wanted to see if I could run my own business, so I set up a clinical laboratory consultation and supply business. The second year we were in Texas, I received a call from an individual that identified himself as David Lifton. Mr. Lifton told me that he had been trying to get in touch with me and that he had gotten my phone number from Paul O'Connor, a friend and my counterpart during the JFK autopsy. Mr. Lifton proceeded to tell me he was working on a book about the John Fitzgerald Kennedy assassination. Mr. Lifton asked me if I'd let him come to my home in Texas and interview me. I told Mr. Lifton I didn't really care to relive my experiences of that night and besides I didn't know who he was. But I said I would call and talk to Paul and ask Paul to call him with my decision. Paul recommended that I talk to Mr. Lifton, so I agreed. David Lifton called me back and we set up a time for the interview. I was expecting a simple one-on-one talk with Mr. Lifton, but he showed up with and elaborate entourage of cameras, lights and sound equipment and people to operate the equipment. Mr. Lifton had not told me that he was bringing all these people and equipment. It was a little unnerving to have this many strangers in my home, as I was discussing such a controversial and tender subject.

My wife and I were living, at the time, about 30 miles north of San Antonio in the country.

Mr. Lifton arrived at my house in the early evening with approximately four other individuals and equipment. He was a pleasant man, average height, slightly balding and wearing glasses. After the introductions, the people with him begin to set up their equipment. Mr. Lifton asked me if had followed anything about the Kennedy assassination in the ensuing years since the autopsy. I told him that I would occasionally see something in the paper or TV but that I had no interest in reading other materials; therefore I knew very little other than what I remembered of the autopsy.

My wife was nervous about Mr. Lifton's visit, because by this time she knew of my involvement with the Kennedy autopsy, but I had never discussed it with her. I tried to get her to go to a neighbor for safety, as we were not really sure of these people, but she refused and chose to stay in a back room with a phone. My concern for her safety made the situation more fraught.

My interview with David Lifton lasted approximately three hours. It seemed to be a typical information-gathering interview. He started the interview by asking what I'd seen on the night of November 22, 1963 during the autopsy of John Fitzgerald Kennedy. I answered the questions he asked but didn't volunteer a lot of information. I wasn't really sure what type of information he was interested in. He seemed to be trying to corroborate certain information that he had received from others. To this day, I have never received a copy of the filming or of the dialogue from that interview, even though, unbeknown to me at the time, such seemed to be an established courtesy in the industry, to the person being interviewed.

Later, I received a couple of phone calls asking a few questions and a brief handwritten letter requesting permission to use a photograph. I have had no further communication with Mr. Lifton since that time.

After David Lifton's book *Best Evidence* was published, I received a complimentary copy. After reading the section that pertained to our interview, I was surprised about the amount of the interview that was left out, my description of the brain that was removed at autopsy, and the misinterpretation of the story that I told him about a previous experience with a head wound similar to that of the President's. The book stated that the right side of the head and face of the individual shot by his brother-in-law was completely missing or blown away, which seemed to imply a shot from the rear. As I related to David Lifton, the individual was shot from the right front while butchering his brother-in-law's cattle, which took out the back of his head. I perceive this as the lack of my credibility with Mr. Lifton or misinterpretation of the material discussed in our interview. It was very disconcerting for me and I resolved to limit or avoid any future interviews.

Harrison Livingstone

Once again, I received a call from a man by the name of Harrison Livingstone, telling me that Paul O'Connor had given him my contact information, and once again, I went through the same dance I had with David Lifton at Paul's urging. I contacted Paul and he told me that Livingstone was a "good guy and I'm working with him." I then received a series of phone calls from Harrison Livingstone. Even though I had been decidedly uncomfortable with my meeting with David Lifton, I decided to grant Mr. Livingstone an interview at the urging of Paul, with the hope that I could get my information and the intent of that information to come through accurately. I did more with Livingstone because Paul and I worked together with him. My contact with Mr. Livingstone was always congenial, he was always willing to share information and allow me to review the information given him before it was printed. This is not to say that all information shared with Livingstone was always presented as intended, but there seemed to be little or no slanting of the information toward personal agendas. Most of the mistakes were honest mistakes due to the interpretation of what was said or what was understood. If we talked on the phone, and Livingstone wanted to use that in a presentation or otherwise he would always follow the phone call with a letter stating his understanding of our telephone conversation and asking for confirmation.

At one point he asked me to go to Dallas and meet with Dr. Robert McClelland, who had worked on the President's injuries in trauma room one and with nurse Bell and others from Parkland Hospital associated with the treatment of the wounded President in trauma one. I agreed to attend the conference in Dallas at the request of Harry Livingstone and the urging of Paul. The conference was an attempt to get the Bethesda witnesses who were present at the JFK autopsy and the Parkland witnesses who were present in the emergency room when the president was brought in. The goal of the conference was to be able to compare and discuss what each group had observed and the differences between their observations.

Present at this conference was Dr. McClelland, Dr. Philip Williams, ambulance driver Aubrey Rike and nurse Audrey Bell, who were all present in the emergency room during the attempt to save the President's life. The Bethesda witnesses were medical photographer Floyd Riebe, medical technicians Paul O'Connor and me, James Jenkins.

My interest in attending this conference was to discuss the wrappings of the President's head at Parkland Hospital. When the head was unwrapped by Dr. Humes at Bethesda, the secondary wrappings after the sheet was removed appeared to be towels and I wanted to see if the towels that I saw could possibly have been placed there as the body was being prepared for transportation to Bethesda.

My discussion with Ms. Bell led me to believe that the towels that I saw could not have possibly come from Parkland Hospital. Ms. Bell said that the towels that were in the emergency room were green and that the towels used in the operating rooms were also green, though the towels used in ER were in the process of being changed. Ms. Bell asked me if what I had seen could possibly have been surgical drapes used to maintain a sterile field around a surgical incision. While the off-white or light-green appearance and woven texture of the towels removed from the head does somewhat resemble that of a surgical drape, the blue stripe down the middle of the towel did not resemble any surgical drape that I'd ever seen. It seemed apparent that the towel or towel-like material that I saw wrapped around the President's head did not exist in the emergency room at Parkland Hospital. However, Aubrey Rike the ambulance driver, said that he saw someone give Mrs. Kennedy a light-green towel which they took from a room across the hall, to wipe the blood from her clothes and hands. Mr. Rike didn't know if the towel had a blue stripe are not.

The conference was very informative in that it gave me an opportunity to hear the description of the wounds from the people who directly observed them during their attempted resuscitation of the President. It also afforded me the opportunity to compare the differences between the wounds that the Parkland witnesses saw and the wounds we saw in the morgue at Bethesda. My discussion with Ms. Bell about the wrappings that were removed from the head of the President at Bethesda and the absence of availability of that particular towel material at Parkland seems to lend further credence to the possible examination of the President's wounds prior to being received at the Bethesda morgue.

That was the first personal contact I had with Harrison Livingstone. He seemed astute and intelligent and not possessive of his materials like the previous researcher that I had dealt with. At the time of the meeting in Dallas I didn't know anything about the people I was to meet. I knew very little about the Kennedy assassination outside of the autopsy and only a little that I had read from David Lifton's book, the letters written to me by Harry Livingstone and the news blurbs one sees on television news programs. Consequently, the people at the meeting were a mystery to me. I came away from the Livingstone meeting in Dallas realizing there

were many conflicts in the evidence that had been presented in the Warren Commission's report, and what the public had been told versus what
had actually happened to President Kennedy.

At the press conference, after the Dallas meeting, I began to notice an
almost manic intenseness when Livingstone would talk about what he believed had happened to President Kennedy and who was responsible for
the assassination. This behavior only intensified with my further contacts
with Livingstone until I finally decided to break all contacts with him.
This was not a lightly taken position, Harrison Livingstone had always
treated me fairly and respectfully. It was sad and tragic to see such an intelligent rational individual who had invested so much of himself into the
Kennedy assassination that it had begun to take a toll on his health and
create a fissure in his personality.

I still have great respect and admiration for Harrison Livingstone and
the tenacious effort that he put forth in his quest for the truth concerning
the Kennedy assassination and its dissemination to the public. As previously stated, I always felt that Harry tried very hard to be fair with me,
even though at times I had a slight feeling that our conversations were being pushed toward his personal conclusions. His efforts were more directed toward proving that the government was responsible for the Kennedy assassination and those involved should be prosecuted for treason, as
opposed to the David Lifton theory that everything was directed toward
evidence that there had been illicit surgery done on the President's body
prior to the autopsy, where, how and why the surgery was done.

I again vowed that I would never become involved with researchers or
writers concerning the assassination again. But then came the inevitable
phone call from Paul Kelly O'Connor. This time Paul said that a researcher by the name of Rick Russo was not writing a book, but wanted Paul,
Dennis David, Floyd Riebe and me to meet in Pittsburgh, Pennsylvania
and talk about what we remembered from the Kennedy autopsy. Russo
had said he just wanted to capture what we remembered for posterity on
film. When Rick contacted me, he said that his anger had been aroused
by Jim Humes' interview with the *Journal of the American Medical Association. JAMA* had done interviews with Drs. Boswell, Fink and Humes
and Rick didn't think that they had been truthful. Paul was so enthusiastic about going to Pittsburgh that I really couldn't say no, so December
1992 found me, Paul, Dennis, Floyd Riebe, Rick Russo and a doctor by
the name of Cyril Wecht, who was the head forensic pathologist for Al-
legheny County and one of the best internationally-known and respected

forensic pathologists in this country. The meeting was conducted as others which I had attended, "Tell me about what you saw and did November 22, 1963 during the Bethesda autopsy of John F. Kennedy?" There was a question and answer session after our discussion. I had a brief discussion with Dr. Wecht, concerning the wounds, but he seemed dismissive of my answers. It was also the first time that I had met Floyd Riebe, the military photographer. During the review of the Fox photographs, Floyd had made a comment to Dennis David, "Did I take these pictures standing on my head?" Floyd Riebe thought that the cameras had been turned off and was a little frustrated with the purported authenticity of the photos. Floyd Riebe had taken the first photographs of the head immediately after Dr. Humes had unwrapped the head. Some of the photos appeared to have be taken at seemingly improbable angles. Floyd did not believe that the photos were the ones he took in the morgue that night. While most of the other information discussed at this meeting was information that I had heard before, Floyd Riebe's revelation concerning the photos was new and interesting information to me. It gave me a different perspective on the Fox photographs. I had briefly viewed these photos before and couldn't quite bring myself to believe that all of the photos were taken in the morgue during the Bethesda autopsy.

Chapter Nine

After the meeting in Pittsburgh, I didn't talk to Rick Russo again until July or August 1993. Rick told me that he had taken Dennis David to New York to see a psychiatrist-hypnotist by the name of Dr. Herbert Spiegel. Dr. Spiegel had great success in placing Dennis under hypnosis and allowing him to recall things from his past involving the JFK autopsy at Bethesda hospital in 1963. During this session, Dennis was able to recall the names of the two FBI agents James Sibert and Francis O'Neill among other previously lost memories of that night.

While I felt this was a little far-fetched, I must admit that while I lived in Texas, I had entertained the idea of regression hypnosis to resolve for myself the haziness and and differences of some of my memories of my participation in the autopsy of President Kennedy as opposed to those of other witnesses. For this reason, and my own curiosity, I agreed to Rick Russo's request.

I will say this, it was an interesting experience. My wife and I were in the middle of moving to Mobile, Alabama from San Antonio when Rick contacted me. My wife was still in San Antonio trying to sell our home there and orchestrate the move to Mobile and I was living on my boat at a marina in Mobile while working for the University of South Alabama Medical Center.

Being a little skeptical, maybe even a little mistrusting, I asked a friend who was a professor at the University and lived on his boat in the Marina, to accompany me to New York for the session with Dr. Spiegel. He jumped at the chance to visit New York City as opposed to any interest in what I was going to do for Rick Russo.

It was a bad time to visit New York. It was cold, and it was also Black Friday, the day after Thanksgiving, when people go shopping for special bargains. The hotel that we were booked to stay in, for some reason which all these years still eludes me, was not available for the night that we arrived and was not going to be available until the next day. This probably had something to do with it being Black Friday. As it turned out, the only reservation to be had was a Ramada in Queens. This turned out to be quite an adventure. We were picked up at the airport by the hotel shuttle service, and as we begin the ride through Queens the driver stopped at every red light and he would turn on the interior lights of the van; after about the third time the driver did this I asked him why, he told me, "There are gang members who control this turf and they want to see who is in the van." I wished I had not asked.

What I remember most about the hotel in Queens is it was across the street from a massive cemetery. After we got to our hotel, the desk clerk, a large friendly, bubbly, black lady with a very pleasant, outgoing demeanor, alleviated some of the apprehension of being in this area of New York. As we settled into our room, a group of young people checked into the room across the hall and started an open-door party. It made sleep impossible and my friend wondered why we hadn't been invited to join the party. I decided to watch TV, possibly get some news or weather. As I was watching the news, I noticed a slight movement on the table next to the TV. It seems that we had a small furry visitor that was sitting up on its hind legs and watching us. I called the bubbly lady at the front desk and told her that we had a mouse in our room. She told me not to worry, "Honey, we don't charge for pets," and we both had a good laugh.

The next morning, we were picked up and taken downtown to a nice hotel off-Broadway and were checked into our rooms. Rick had not yet arrived. My friend wanted to go ice skating so we walked to Rockefeller Center where I spent a lot of time laughing at him trying to stay upright on the skates. It seemed to be taking a marked toll on his rear end. I'd wanted to see the rock opera *Tommy*, which was playing in town. But as we walked back up Broadway to the hotel, I was a little surprised to find that the theaters were closed on Sunday. After all this was New York City.

We arrived back at our hotel and by that time Rick Russo had arrived and took us to dinner around the corner from the hotel to a small restaurant. It was reported to be famous as a place where movie stars could be seen. With my shoulder length white hair, jeans, cowboy boots and London fog trench coat, I seem to fit in well. No one seemed to notice two Alabama boys and a Bostonian. I guess it was just New York City.

The next morning, we went to see Dr. Herbert Spiegel. We were greeted by a pleasant friendly receptionist and ushered into Dr. Spiegel's office. After introducing himself Dr. Spiegel began to explain to me what he intended to do. He directed me to a very comfortable chair and began what he called a "relaxation session." This seemed to be successful, under Dr. Spiegel's direction I could achieve a slight sensation of floating and my memories would come and go but there was no clarity, there was a sensation that I was an observer and not a participant.

Dr. Spiegel started asking me questions and the session began.

Spiegel: If you get absorbed in a play and it's a good movie or play, can you get so absorbed that when it's over you are surprised to find that you are just sitting there?

Jenkins: No.

S: As you perceive time, do you focus more of your time on past, present, future, or all three?

J: I would say probably present.

S: How would you put that in a rough percentage off the top of your head - past, present, future?

J: I would say probably 60% present.

S: And how much on past and future?

J: I would say 30% future. 10% past.

S: Okay. Pascal, the French philosopher, once wrote, "The heart has a mind which the brain won't understand." Of these two minds, which do you give priority to? The heart, the mind, or the brain?

J: Probably equal.

S: Equal. Exactly equal? It doesn't veer more to one side or the other?

J: Well, of course, probably the mind, I would think, is the dominant part of it.

S: Okay. When you relate to people in general, do you prefer to control the interaction, or do you prefer to let the other person to take over if they wish?

J: I prefer the control.

S: When it comes to trusting others, would you say, in general, you are trusting, very trusting, or not so trusting of others?

J: I think I judge my trust by individuals.

S: Overall would you say you're average, below or above in your tendency to trust others?

J: I guess average.

S: And when you are learning something new, do you tend to critically judge it at the time you learn it, or do you tend to accept it and perhaps judge it later?

J: I think I judge it as I am learning it.

S: When in the sense of your feeling responsible at what you do, how would you rate yourself on a scale of average or below? Feeling responsible for what you do?

J: I would say above.

S: When you are learning something - and if you know in advance that you can learn it equally well by either seeing it or by touching, which would you prefer - to see or touch?

J: See.

S: When coming up with new ideas, there are two parts to that. Think up the idea, then figure out how to do it. Which gives you a bigger sense of fulfillment - to dream it up, or to figure out how to do it?

J: Probably to figure out how to do it.

S: Why you are figuring it out, do you find it necessary to write notes, or do you figure it out without writing notes?

J: I take very few notes.

S: Are you right handed?

J: Yes.

S: In everything?

J: Well, I eat left handed.

S: Were you forced to write right-handed when you were a kid?

J: Yes. Probably in first grade.

S: They forced you? So, your tendency was to be left handed. How about in sports?

J: Not really. No tendency either way. It's according to how I learned the sport.

S: Okay. Now, what kind of work do you do?

J: Currently, I am a supervisor in a hematology laboratory.

S: Where, in a hospital?

J: Yeah, a clinical laboratory. A clinical pathology lab.

S: Okay. That's down in Mobile [Alabama]?

J: Yes, University of South Alabama.

S: Have you had a psychiatric treatment in the past? Psychotherapy treatment?

J: No. Nothing - I have had sessions with psychologists to see if I can improve things I wanted to improve.

At this point in the session, Spiegel attempts to put Jenkins under hypnosis.

SPIEGEL: Alright, please take your glasses off. Look toward me. Now, without moving your head, look all the way up to the top of the ceiling. Straight up, as far as you can. Higher, higher, higher, now look up slowly, close your eyes, it's fine. You're looking up now, take a deep breath. Exhale. Let your eyes relax, let your body float. Imagine yourself floating right through the chair. There will be something pleasant and welcome about this imaginary floating. As your concentrate on this floating, I am going to concentrate on your left arm and hand. In a while, I am going to stroke the middle finger of your left hand. After I do, you will develop movements. Sensation to that finger, then the movements will spread, causing your left hand to feel light and buoyant, and let it floats upward. Ready? First one finger, then another finger, you will have these restless movements develop, your left hand will lift upward, the left elbow bend, your forearm moves into an upright position. Just permit your hand to feel like a buoyant balloon, and just let it float up there. You have the power to do it. Higher and higher. All the way - higher and higher and higher. All the way. Now, I am going to position your arm in this manner. And your forearm will remain in this position even after I give you the signal for your eyes to open. In fact, after your eyes are open, and I put your hand down, it will float back up to where it is now. You will find something amusing about this sensation. Later, when I touch your left elbow, your usual sensation and control will return. In the future, each time you give yourself a signal for the self-hypnosis, on the count of one, your eyes will roll upward, by three your eyes will close, and you will begin to relax and find yourself in the trans state. Each time, you will find the experience easier and easier. Now, I am going to count backwards. At two, again, your eyes will roll up and with your eyes closed and at the one, you'll let them open slowly. Ready- one, two, three. With your eyes closed, roll up your eyes and open them slowly. Open all the way. Open them further. Open them completely. Now, stay in this position and describe the physical sensations that you're aware of now in your left arm. Is it comfortable?

JENKINS: [Unintelligible]

S: Does your left hand feel as if it is not as much a part of your wrist as your right hand?

J: [Unintelligible]

S: Does your left hand feel as connected to the wrist as the right hand feels connected to the wrist? Do they feel exactly the same or is there a difference?

J: No difference.

S: No difference. Now, turn your head, look at your left hand and what is going to happen. as your concentrate on your left hand, imagine it to be a large buoyant balloon. And as you imagine it to act as if it were a balloon. Be bigger, just like a balloon. Let it go, all the way. Now while it remains there, by comparison, raise your right hand up. Now put your right arm down. Now, are you aware of a difference in your right arm, going up and comparing it to the left? For example, is one lighter or heavier on a relative basis?

J: It's a little lighter.

S: Were you aware of a relative difference in your feeling of control in one arm as one of compared to the other, on a more or less basis? Did you experience relatively more control in one arm one of compared to the other.

J: More than the right.

S: Okay. Now do this. Make a tight fist. Open. Open. Are you aware of a change in sensation now in your left arm? Lift them both up together. Now, put them both down. Now is there any difference in control, or is the control becoming equal?

J: Equal.

S: Is there anything that I said, or did that might account for that?

J: No.

S: When your left arm went up before, did you get a physical sense of lightness or buoyancy?

J: A little lighter.

S: Did you get a feeling of any other part of your body, like your head, neck, chest, abdomen, thighs, legs, all over your body, or just in your left hand?

J: Just in the left hand.

S: Okay, now you're learning how to identify hypnosis. You were just in and out of hypnosis. You didn't go to sleep, you didn't black out, it's a method of concentration, a more accurate way of describing hypnosis, is you develop parallel awareness. It's like being here and there at the same time. For example, you were there paying attention to me while you were, something happened to your left arm, and you were aware of that, too. That's what hypnosis is. The value of it is, it makes your mind most receptive to your own thoughts and makes you receptive of your own memories. Now, the strategy that we do to get to those memories is what we're going to do next. But, before we get to that, I want to point out something. I didn't tell you that you have more control, one arm control to the other. You described that. People who have natural hypnotic ability discover that difference in that test.

But I did tell you what will cause a control and become equal. Now, even though your arm knew what to do, you now have an amnesia to what I said about it. Now that amnesia is part of the hypnotic experience. I asked you to control it. Why did your control become equal, and you said you didn't know? Now, you really do know, but right now you have an amnesia to it. I repeat what I said, but the memory doesn't return. I said later when I touch your left elbow, your usual sensation will return to your left arm and hand. Does that ring a bell? Now, Jim, remember this: did I touch your left elbow? Are you envisioning I did or do you remember I did?

J: I remember you did.

S: How many times?

J: Once, if I remember.

S: Well, it was twice. Now, that amnesia is part of your test. I'll repeat what I did and see if your memory doesn't return. Your arm's up like this, and I said to you; "Now note this," I did this, I said "make a fist, open fist." Then I did two and one down like this. It shows that your mind is so organized that your head [unintelligible] up here they have many subsystems all the way down the line, they go once, more or less independent but still be partnering [unintelligible]. It's fact that you have an accumulation of layer upon layer upon layer of things all kinds of circuits in there, that we can now use that knowledge as a way of having access to some of the early circuits that haven't been activated for a long time. It's within that spirit that we are going to now help you. Some of that old circuitry that were operational years ago. Hold that concept?

J: Yes.

S: Okay, we are going to go back into - now is there a special screen you want to set up or is it at the very beginning?

At this point researcher Rick Russo enters the discussion.

RUSSO: When he is asked to - were you already there?

JENKINS: I was there around 3 o'clock in the afternoon or something.

R: You were called over to the hospital?

J: No, actually I was in a - I think at that - time I was told to go to the morgue, somewhere around that period of time. I had the duty that night.

SPIEGEL: Have you already been over this with Jim to see what he can remember so far?

R: About a year ago we did it?

S: And you have a record of that?

R: Yeah. We didn't cover the experience that I am sure we'll try to address today, but we covered certain points and there are other things that I think Jim, you know, might not remember that - he'd like to come to terms with. One of the questions that came up before we started, he's wondered and I was curious, too, he's not like a lot of other people, even though he experienced something 30 years ago, some other people who had a similar experience at that point in time have read a lot of books, film, and documentaries, things like that, which it may have brought in outside information that may have affected their perception.

Jim isn't so much in that category, as much of a student of the topic, yet he can't help but overhear certain things over the years. How much of that memory merge, information that came from secondary sources from the outside that unintentionally infiltrate his data if you may.

S: Yeah, alright.

R: Would that be a problem?

S: No, no.

With that, Dr. Spiegel proceeds to try to put Jim Jenkins under hypnosis. The next sounds on the tape that is heard:

Spiegel: .... straight up as high as you can. Now, as you look up, slowly close your eyes and take a deep breath, deep breath. Exhale. Just relax and let your body float. Imagine yourself floating, floating just like a balloon, and as you concentrate on this imaginary floating, at the same time, you permit one hand or the other to feel like a buoyant balloon and let it float upward. As it does, your elbow bends, your forearm floats to the upward position, just like a balloon. This is a conscious decision. That's right, just like a dancer, let it float up. Now when you reach this upright position becomes your signal to enter a state of meditation - just let your elbow rest like this - and this is like a - imagine yourself floating just like a balloon, imaging you are like an astronaut floating above the field of gravity. At the same time that you do that, visualize a huge movie screen or a TV screen or a clear blue sky that acts like a screen. And on this screen, you project your thoughts, ideas and feelings way out there on the screen while you float here. This is like setting up a private theater which you are viewing the drama of your own life. Your floating here, your thoughts and feelings are there. By distancing yourself from your thoughts and feelings, you are now positioned to get a perspective on your past memories that you ordinarily don't have. It's like setting up a private theater where you are viewing your past memories this way. As you sit in the chair, here and feel yourself floating and you view what is coming out on that screen, we are going to ask you to report to us what you see on the screen. You are the only one that is seeing it, and we are going to ask you to report to us and let the camera record what you are viewing on the screen. Now, you can get started if you wish, by placing yourself somewhere back in 1963. This is the November 22, 1963. You get a call. You are a student. You are in the Navy, something is happening. Give a starting point there and let us hear what see on the screen.

Jenkins: Okay. I just had a break in serology lab, talking to a friend of mine. Bill was kind of a jokester and comes back into the lab and tells us that the President has been assassinated. The people around me thinks it's another one of Bill's jokes. It's not. [unintelligible].

S: What's your feelings when you hear the news that the President has been assassinated? What's your feelings?

J: At this time, I don't have any. I don't have any feelings.

S: You don't believe it though.

J: Everyone in the classroom is talking. There is a feeling that they don't really believe it either. They're waiting for Bill to finish the punchline, or something. No one else in the classroom, just us.

S: Who else is there now?

J: There is a guy named Pace. A guy named Willy. A female in the class whose name is Donna Duffy. Metzler. Jim Metzler. A guy named Leach. Cordova. Paul is there. Stanley and the Chief are coming back. The instructor, actually he just came back. He is in front of the board and he is telling us that class is dismissed. The President has been assassinated.

S: Go ahead.

J: [long pause] Someone just came in. The duty people are going to tell me to report to the morgue.

S: And you are part of the duty people?

J: Yeah. Paul and me.

S: Paul and you. Okay. Go ahead.

J: Nothing's really [unintelligible].

S: Alright.

J: [long pause] Paul and I are going. We met with the senior staff petty officer that's on duty. Now, we are going down inside the morgue. We're preparing the jars and the labels. I can't really get a clear picture of who is there. I know that Paul and I are there. I know the first class is there. There are people in and out. I can't - can't -

S: Okay, just report what you see.

J: I am standing at the counter. Someone is writing numbers on a label, and I am posting them on jars of formaldehyde. Just [unintelligible] pasting them on a stainless steel pail and the number. The number is the number that we - the next number that we place in the log in the autopsy in the [unintelligible] that is where we get the number that we just used. We're uh basically waiting. We haven't been told whether the body is going to come in to us.

S: So, you are just waiting there?

J: Yes.

S: Are you standing or sitting?

J: I changed clothes and uh, we've got preparations there. That's - we are just waiting.

S: Alright, are you talking to anybody?

J: No one that I - just waiting. People are coming in and out of the lab and I am not being told much of anything. Paul is being sent on some errands. I've been told to stay there [unintelligible]. Dr. Boswell is coming in.

S: Dr. Boswell. Who is he?

J: Dr. Boswell was the assistant pathologist in charge of the laboratory. He came in and asked the first class if everything was ready. It was. There are some people with him, I am not sure who they were. And they left. Beginning to see people come in - I don't know who they are. Or why they are there. [long pause] There is a lot of commotion in the hall. By this time, we really hadn't been told we are going to do the autopsy.

S: But you suspect it?

J: Yes [Long pause] The door to the - the double doors to the morgue open. It's the casket being brought in. It's on a folding type of gurney. I go to help them bring him in. I'm told that this is not the President's body. This is an Air Force Major that came in too late to be buried.

S: What time is this now?

J: I really have no time frame.

S: Is it morning, afternoon, or nighttime?

J: It's afternoon, it is after 3 o'clock. I think it my perceptions that is around 5 o'clock.

S: Around 5 o'clock. Go ahead.

J: I am told that this Air Force Major is to be buried the next day at Arlington.

S: Who tells you this?

J: The First Class [Officer] and because I asked him [unintelligible] I asked him if we had to log him in and he said "No." I thought that was very unusual because, you know, it was always an emphatic type thing that whatever we received in the morgue be properly labeled and was a specific matter. The casket was pushed against the - alongside the cold boxes. It was left there. Not much more attention was paid to it. [unintelligible]. Getting some other things, details. I got the clipboard with the face sheet ready. Lay them on the counter next to the deep sink. Still people in and out of the morgue. Basically, I think for - I have a feeling for curiosity they were there. People from the class, people from pathology, Jim Metzler, Stan comes in. Most of these people are being ushered out. Especially if they didn't have any reason to be there.

S: Are they in uniform?

J: Yes.

S: Where is the body now?

J: I don't know, it hasn't arrived.

S: Well, what's in the casket? You said the thing in the casket -

J: There was a casket there - I don't think it was ever opened, at least in my presence, but I was told there was an Air Force Major's body in it and it was destined to be buried.

S: This body in the casket, it's not to be autopsied, is that what your…

J: No, it's … my understanding was it's already prepared for burial.

S: Then why is it brought into the room now?

J: I have no rationale. I have asked and accepted what I was told. Actually, it never came into the morgue proper.

S: Where are you standing now in relation to the casket?

J: Now, I am inside the morgue.

S: Now where is the casket again?

J: The casket's out in the atrium.

S: In the atrium? Now, can you put yourself back into the atrium where the casket is and describe what it looks like?

J: It's a mahogany type dark - not dark - a mahogany color - maybe dark oak casket. It has brass - instead of having a chrome handle, it has a brass rail on the side of it. There is a dome shaped lid on it with brass trim on the corners. I don't see anything remarkable about it or distinguishing about it, it's just very ornate, expensive casket.

S: And do you see any connection between the presence of that casket and the perceptions for the autopsy?

J: No.

S: Okay, is this unusual to have such a pressing event?

J: Yes. I have - it's struck me as being very much. And being [unintelligible] I am doing what I am told.

S: Yeah. Okay. Now you are coming back from the atrium to the autopsy room again. Could you describe what you - what the autopsy room looks like. Where is the table, where is the headrest? From the atrium, the atrium is at the foot of the tables? Yes.

J: The entrance of the morgue, the two tables, they are lying one in front of the other. One at the other end of the room, one directly behind it. There is an autoclave in the back of the room. In the back being the part by the atrium. There is a gallery to my right.

S: As you are coming in the Atrium?

J: Right. And there is a door at the other end to my right that goes into the hallway. There is a - I don't see the X-ray machine. There is normally a portable x-ray machine that sits at the end of the morgue. Most of the time it is covered by a sheet or something. There are x-ray view boxes on the other side of the [unintelligible] wall. There is a - on the left side there is a passageway, a short hall, that goes into three rooms. As you go into a small hallway, passageway, there is a room to the left. This room to the left has a - actually jars with brains in them. This is where they do brain conference. The one to the right has a dirty linen hamper in it. The one on the end is the locker room with lockers for clothing and it has a shower [unintelligible] I am not seeing it very clear, but I do see the lockers. As you come out of the hallway to the immediate right, there is a deep sink. Immediately after the deep sink, there are counter spaces. [unintelligible] that presently have jars with autopsy [unintelligible] on them.

S: Alright.

J: Above that, there is a cabinet that runs the length of the counter to the back of the morgue. There are various things in the cabinet. Chemicals, jars of tissue, organs, on the top of it, there is a large glass carboy of formalin, about two thirds of the way down that has tubing from it. It's the tubing we used to infuses the brains with. As I turn away from the counter there's the autoclave. Immediately to my back is the second autopsy table. Immediately after that is the entrance to the atrium where the cold boxes are. Cold boxes are immediately to the right and the double doors to the left. There is a kind of podium stand that has the autopsy book in it. To the right of that, is a thing that has tags in it. Body tags, used to write the autopsy number and place it on the left toe [unintelligible] where the bodies are placed in the cold boxes. Also used to identify them as they take them out for autopsy. [Long pause] seems to be commotion again in the hall.

S: Go ahead.

J: I am walking back into the morgue to the front table. There are people coming in. There is a - they are bringing in a casket. [sounds a little surprised - W.L.] The casket is being put down at the end of the morgue.

S: You say there were two tables, two autopsy tables. You -

J: Yes.

S: Which, where - does the - placed?

J: The body has not been removed from the casket, really. It hasn't come in to the morgue proper. It's still in partially in the atrium. It's a rather plain casket. Grayish. [unintelligible.] There are some military people with it, dressed in dress uniforms. At this time, I can't tell whether they are army, marine corp. I am not familiar with dress uniforms, formal dress uniforms. Caskets -

S: What time is it now? Would you say?

J: I think it is ... 7 o'clock.

S: About 7 o'clock.

J: Or after 7 o'clock.

S: After 7 o'clock. Alright.

J: They are taking the body out of the casket. [long pause] It's being placed on the - in front of me on the first autopsy table. The one at the other end. Where - Dr. Boswell I can't place, Dr. Humes and the Army-Colonel Major - I think they have come in - only Dr. Boswell. The body is being placed on the table - Dr. Boswell leaves. The body is on the table. No one in the morgue except myself, Paul, the first class [officer] and I think there was a chief named Mason. [long pause]

S: Boswell was there? And then he leaves?

J: For a small period of time. I don't know if he went into the hall and came back. But Dr. Humes, Boswell, and Dr. Fink - Dr. Boswell, Dr. Humes came back in with some people.

S: They're there now?

J: Yes. We have taken the sheets off before they came back, we unwrapped the body from the sheets. We'd been told by Dr. Boswell not to unwrap the head. The body, once we removed the sheet, was covered again with just a sheet over it.

S: Are you removing the sheets?

J: Yes, we were.

S: Who else was removing the sheets? Who was helping you?

J: Paul. There was a third party there. I think it's the first [unintelligible].

S: Corpsman?

J: Now, there seems to be just Dr. Boswell and me. We are doing the face sheet. I am doing what he tells me. He tells me to write on the face sheet, which is a little unusual because [unintelligible]. He is basically examining the body for reference points. The body is turned up, and the scars being measured by Dr. Boswell, the back, the other [long pause] points of reference *the line is mentioned (?) I, uh, since became aware - I realized that these scars and injuries was a result of World War II.

S: Where do you see the scars?

J: Scars on his back. Along his spine and [unintelligible] he is extremely muscular. Dr. Humes and Dr. Fink are back and are presently at the head of the table. The general condition of the body [unintelligible] as if he had worked out and kept in shape. That's [unintelligible] Dr. Fink is beginning to look at the head, bending down, pulling the sheets away. From this angle at this time, you can't really see a lot except bloody sheets.

S: Where are you standing now in relationship to the body?

J: I am standing at the right elbow. At the table.

S: And who else is standing around the table?

J: Dr. Fink is to my left shoulder. Dr. Humes to his left, to the right of the left shoulder. Dr. Boswell is standing across the table between the left shoulder and the elbow.

S: Okay. Now, go ahead.

J: They're taking, actually, they are looking at the head wound without really removing the sheets this time. Dr. Humes is beginning to unwrap the sheet, there is another wrapping underneath the sheet - looks like something absorbent. It looks kind of like [unintelligible] bath towels. It's white material - it's rather bloody. It's hard to tell what it is. It is really soaked with blood.

S: Where's this come from?

J: It's coming from the wound in the head. The wound in the head is really, really macerated. Some of the scalp is sticking to the wrapping. Dr. Humes is separating it from the towels, because he is afraid some of the scalp wound came off on the towels. There is two pieces of very small tissue that remain on the towels from the blood. The blood is still not dry. (Jenkins sounds a little surprised.) It's coagulated, but there's not dried blood. It's almost like a seepage. The head now - the right side of the head - is odd shaped almost like... it's kind of symmetric. From where I am standing, [unintelligible] from the top of the head, I don't see any holes or anything. I just see tissue and scalp, actually scalp that looks like it's intact - It's kind of pressed in. Right in front of the ear, back toward the back of the head, Dr. Humes, Dr. Fink are standing at the head of the table. Now, they are lifting the body up for - I can see the wound on the side. It's fairly extensive. It's fairly high in the back of the head. Really the gaping starts toward the center, back behind the ear. It's a lot of scalp and tissue. It's being held together by - a lot of the bones were held together by scalp. The scalp is ragged and the bones in that area .... it's exposed the brain. The brain's exposed [unintelligible] like it is macerated. The skull is exploded [unintelligible] the tissue and scalp are kind of laid back.

The head is being placed on the [unintelligible] x-rays and photography. People are beginning to come into the gallery - actually, it's filled about maybe [unintelligible] the media photographer coming into the door from the hallway, I can see a guard, military guard as he enters the door from the other hallway. He comes in and he is taking photographs.

S: And where is he in relation to you while he is taking the photographs?

J: He is at the head of the table. And I am helping Dr. Boswell turn the body. Actually, Dr. Humes is directing him, the photographs of the body. They're taking photographs. The photographer is going around us, actually to the left of Dr. Boswell. He is taking the face with the head slightly rotated, the head and shoulders slightly raised. [Unintelligible] the photographer's finished with the films. He has x-ray people coming in again. They have a portable x-ray, there is really only one technician with the x-ray. They're taking x-rays of the chest, and the stomach area. They had to raise the body up to do that. The body's raised, the head has to be supported. Now, they are taking x-rays of the head, the cassette is underneath. (heads out?) [Unintelligible] we are lifting, the body, cassettes are underneath the body, to get the cassettes out from underneath him. Taking pictures... put the smaller cassettes on the right side of the head and the x-ray machine is on the left side of the head. The head is turned slightly, x-rays are taken [unintelligible].

S: Can you estimate what the time is now?

J: I would say the time must be (long pause) between 8:30 and 9 o'clock.

S: 8:30 - 9. Alright. Would you just hold now until we have changed the tape? Alright now, go ahead. Just continue that sequence.

J: Dr. Humes and Dr. Fink are still working with the head and examining it, but they are not doing anything with it, other than [unintelligible] with their hands, by pressing on the scalp, skull. There is a discussion between Dr. Fink and Dr. Humes - about an area, right ear. Skull seems to be shattered underneath the skull. There is a ragged tear in the scalp. [long pause] Dr, Fink's pointing to an area - looks like it has some gray substance on it. Dr. Fink was speculating with Dr. Humes [unintelligible] or a bullet fragment. It's hard to make out anything definite - structure of the ear (?) with the [unintelligible] hole. The hole is just a break in the bone [unintelligible] the scalp, whether it's jagged part of the fracture or whether it is round. It's very difficult. Also difficult for me to determine whether this gray material is [unintelligible] it's darker and seem to be metallic. Extremely difficult to determine. So much disruption in the whole side of the head. Lifting the body and so forth you could feel the head and support the neck as you support your thumb, you can actually move the bones on the right side of the head [unintelligible].

S: And now come back to the sequence. What follows?

J: They came back with the X-rays. They are going to take more X-rays. Seems like they are taking the same X-rays they were taking before. Chest, neck and head.

S: Can you tell if the body has been opened up yet?

J: No, the body hasn't been opened.

S: Describe any other parts - the face, the neck, what do you see?

J: The face still has blood on it. There's still matted hair on the fore-head. The right eye is slightly open. It's seems to be (long pause) open on the [unintelligible]. You can see the white of the eye but seems to be kind of pushed in [unintelligible] but the damage doesn't extend that far.

S: Can you describe the throat?

J: Well, the throat has a trach, it runs across the throat, it's rather ragged. It's like [unintelligible] a tracheotomy, very sloppy.

S: Is it cut horizontally or vertical?

J: It's horizontal. It's across the throat.

S: Do you know how long?

J: It's probably long enough for me to put my two fingers in. Nothing really unusual about it. It's very sloppy. Very little blood there. It seems to be in relative comparison to the head, virtually no blood. It's a trach.

S: Can you describe the top right front of the head, around the temple area?

J: Yes.

S: What's it look like to you?

J: Follow the ear, it looks like it's to intact. You can tell that it's depressed and it's not round, it's not [unintelligible]. It's just not round. The tear in the scalp seems to have stopped slightly forward of the ear. You can see the extent of the scalp is [unintelligible] and then laid back and then [unintelligible] with fingers probing. The brain's still - seems to be… first seems to be gelatinous. Mass. But you can see - you can actually see solid, undamaged brain tissue. Probably about a third back from the laceration. Toward the head. A major laceration that seems the brain was lacerated. Jelly. The brain at this point in time, nothing was seen [unintelligible].

S: Did you hear any conversations going on between Dr. Humes and anybody else in the room?

J: There's a feeling in the room. The tension is really high. They're not happy with the X-rays. They are not happy with the examination. There is a direction from someone in the area of Dr. Galloway to Dr. Humes. Dr. Humes goes and talks to someone.

S: Can you hear Dr. Humes making any comments about the head area? Has he said anything after you've seen him?

J: Not at this time, no. He and Dr. Fink are still examining the head area [unintelligible] at this point in time just separating the tissue and looking into the cranium and examining the back of the head. Dr. Boswell asked me to help him with the body, to do the "U" incision that starts at one shoulder, comes down two-thirds of the chest cavity, I guess, to the other shoulder. Second incision from the back of that down to the pelvis and beyond all the way down to the pubic area. We're laying the flap back over the face, tying off all the major blood vessels in the area of the shoulders, tying off the aorta, (* the radius?) the lower area. We're taking the organs out in masse, they are being laid out on the cutting table, which I placed over the autopsy table.

S: Can you describe this cutting table?

J: The cutting table is table that fits onto the autopsy table. Has cork-type surface on it [unintelligible] autopsy knives on one side. Dr. Boswell separated the organs [unintelligible] give him the weights. The heart is being opened, which is the usual technique for what we've done there. The heart was opened a little more, *the linings of the vessels [unintelligible] actually with the opening of the heart. He's cutting it in [unintelligible] the aorta [unintelligible] heart seemed to be shiny. The heart's placed in a formalin jar and set aside. The next thing is looking at the kidneys. The kidneys are just being described out of [unintelligible] the only that seems to be unusual, there is no extensive dissection of them that I can see there. It's a little different in the fact is that usually we open up a kidney and look at the chamber of the kidney, there are no nodules or anything on the surface, seemed to be a nice red healthy color, with the fossa? * around the [unintelligible] trach, and so forth. I don't see anything unusual. There are comments made by me that are [unintelligible]. The intestinal tract being removed and placed in the deep sink.

S: Did they examine the adrenals?

J: No, the adrenals were almost non-existing [unintelligible] placed in formaldehyde.

S: Okay.

J: The - Dr. Boswell's coming around to the deep sink. He is opening up the intestines, washing them out and looking at [unintelligible]. He's on my side of the table now at the deep sink. The other organs are lying on the cutting board. [unintelligible]. I've turned back to the body, the autopsy table. Dr. Humes is – he and Dr. Fink are probing the wound in the back. Dr. Humes is trying to put his little finger in the ... I can see the end of his fingers are moved down through the chest... I can see the wall of the mucosa on [unintelligible] of the plural area of the back wound. They're trying very desperately to find the passageway to the chest cavity. There's no excessive blood in the chest cavity. What we thought was [unintelligible] was in the organs. Dr. Humes now has a probe he is using. The probe is about four or five inches with a flat end. It has an eye(?) at the other end that is a sharper area with a rounded ball tip. He is using the flat end to - almost seems like to me, he is trying to tear into the chest cavity with it. It's going downward, behind the pleura. It extends maybe four or six inches. Dr. Humes - I am kind of impressed by the size of his hands. About him being able to get his little finger into that cavity. There seems to be some desperation about not being able to find an entrance wound into the chest cavity. Dr. Boswell is back from the other side of the table and examining the wound and examining the lungs. Seemed to be a nice pink color. Someone asked a question: "Did the President smoke?" and [unintelligible] said "He occasionally smoked a cigar." The lungs are really unusually pink for a man [unintelligible] with healthy lungs. The trach seems to be healthy, the esophagus is - has a good tone, seems to be no abnormalities there. Dr. Humes and Dr. Fink, they're all concentrating on the [unintelligible] head. Dr. Humes, Dr. Fink are still in the same positions looking over the right shoulder into the pleural cavity. There is a purplish spot on the lung, the back of the lung, almost on the upper lobe and partially on the middle one, but it's not a - kind of a dark purple. It's kind of intermediate, a reddish purple. There's a lot of tension coming from the gallery. There's the discussion between (long pause) two admirals. I'm not - I don't know either one of them. The only admiral that I know in the gallery, is Dr. Galloway. He's the commanding officer of the hospital. Now we have two men in suits that are at the head of the table behind Dr. Humes and Dr. Boswell. They're taking notes. The organs have been finished, now they're beginning to - Dr. Humes and Dr. Fink have gone back to the head. Dr. Boswell has followed the cut edge of the trach up by the esophagus. The trach he has followed it up with his hand, kind of lifted up the flap and looked in the area. Now everybody has come back to concentrating on the head. Dr. Humes and Dr. Fink continue with the brain (?) they're looking at the wound again. They're spreading it apart, they're looking at the tear, the scalp and the fracture lines about half-way about the middle of the head on the right side, about half-way back from the forehead. Dr. Humes has asked someone in the gallery if there was any surgery done at Parkland. The shorter of the two admirals - I don't know who they are, said: "No, there was no surgery."

S: Why would he have asked that question, Jim?

J: I really don't know. He seemed to feel there was some trauma force or something there that looked as if it had severed or extended the scalp. In fact, that is how they removed the brain - Dr. Humes brought the brain out, [unintelligible] "It fell out in my hands," or something similar to that. I don't remember them ever cutting the brain stem, the idea had always been in the past to try and remove the brain from the spinal cord as much as you can, intact. It very rarely ever works. [Unintelligible] is try.

S: Did they attempt to do a craniotomy?

J: There was no cutting part of that. Sawing the head. There were no skull caps done, it wasn't necessary.

S: How did they remove the brain?

J: Through the incision. Through the hole in the...

S: Through the wound?

J: Yes.

S: So, they didn't have to do any additional cutting. So, from what you can see, no one has to do any further examination of the wound to remove the brain?

J: All they were doing was - all they've done is separating the wound - you know, they're - stretched the wound.

S: They use instruments?

J: No. With their hands.

S: Does this seem unusual to you?

J: Gives me the impression that the wound's very large. The brain is taken out, Dr. Humes has given it to Dr. Boswell, and Dr. Boswell is being followed over to the bucket, and I am going with him.

S: Why did you do that? Why do you follow him?

J: Because my responsibility is actually to assist them in whatever they need. If they need something, if they need someone [unintelligible] that's my job to be close enough to hear what they want. In some sense to anticipate [unintelligible] I know that in order to infuse the brain, we have to connect the needles into the blood vessels at the base of the brain. They have to be tied off and that is what I am going to assist with.

S: Can you describe the brain? How much do you think it weighs?

J: I really don't know about the weight. Seems to be – I have an impression the brain is small. I have an impression the surface of the brain where the damage is seeming to be smooth. The ridges of the brain seem to be [unintelligible] in fact, I have a flash impression that it is a woman's brain. I don't know why.

S: Does the brain seem to relate to the nature of the wound that you saw in the head itself?

J: Yes. The damage to the brain in the general area, I would say, probably no more than a third of the right hemisphere, cerebral hemisphere is damage. It is macerated. It has kind of a gelatinous consistency there. You can tell that there is a certain amount of it gone, but not to a great extent. Dr. Humes is carrying it - or Dr. Boswell's carrying it. Dr. Humes is [unintelligible] put the brain in a gauze sling. We are supposed to turn it upside down. We're having problems getting the needles into the vessels. The vessel's retracted, kind of damaged to a certain extent.

S: Is there a name on the bucket?

J: No. We've been told, we have been told to take all of the numbers off the vessels.

S: So, there's no identification on the bucket?

J: No. The gauze or the tape that had the number on it's been removed, and at this time it's been removed from all the jars.

S: Is that unusual?

J: Yes, very.

S: Can you go back to the brain stem? How do you know that Dr. Humes did not have to sever the brain stem before he removed the brain? Did you see it?

J: No, I only, you know, from basically the brief comment - I never saw him use a scalpel really inside the skull to take the brain out. In fact, the brain stem had been cut.

S: Did you see it?

J: Yes. As we turned it upside down, we could see that it looked as if it had been cut two-thirds of the way through on one side, and about a third of the way through on the other side. Both sides. The short side, the third(?) side was a little higher than the other one.

S: Do any of the Doctors Humes or Boswell or Fink, make any comments about–

J: Fink never really came over. Dr. Humes never came that far. There was another resident that came in at that time, bringing something they had asked for. He was trying to help get the needles in the vessels at the base of the skull. At the base of the brain, there is a kind of an "H" shaped ring of vessels. They seem to be retracted. I - we had a fairly hard time - getting the needles in. The needles are - it's hard to find the wound to put the needles into. The doctor - the resident is [unintelligible] into the vessels and tying it off. The vessels are [unintelligible].

S: Where are you when he is lifting the brain out?

J: I am at the right elbow, between the elbow and the shoulder.

S: And it's clear to you that he is not cutting the cord?

J: I don't remember him cutting into it.

S: Does he remark - make any remarks at all about the fact that the brain it's been out that easily?

J: He made a comment that it virtually fell out in his hands. I don't exactly remember what the comment was, it seems like it was "the damn thing fell out in my hands." Or "it definitely fell out in my hand."

S: And he said nothing else?

J: Nothing else.

S: Before this was done, can you describe the headrest on the autopsy table for me?

J: The headrest is a block.

S: It's not connected to the table, it's removeable?

J: No - it doesn't really fit under the head itself. It fits under the neck. We also had a metal rest of this type that was - that had - looked like an "X" that we used for smaller individuals.

S: But that wasn't used tonight?

J: No, the wooden - the wooden block was being used because it's not under the head, it's under the neck.

S: I see. You mentioned earlier the table with the instruments that was over the President's body at the time of the "U" incision. Would you tell me before that, before the "U" incision was made, but during the autopsy photographs, was the table still resting on the President's body.

J: No - the table was - I put the table on after the incision was made.

S: You yourself put the table on him?

J: Yes, it was a table that clamped onto the autopsy table.

S: I see. At any time, once the autopsy began, even before the photographs, was any part of the President's body covered with a sheet or a towel - specifically in the groin area?

J: Not that I remember. I know that while we were waiting for - to start the autopsy, the body was covered with a sheet, but after that, there was really no reason.

S: Once the photographs - once they started to take the photographs, there was nothing covering the nude body of the President?

J: No, the photographs were taken in the head area. They were, you know, there would have been - everything was focused on the head as far as the photographs were concerned, from different angles, different aspects. Once they did come back, they came back several times - for photographs, because they apparently had run out of film or wanted other things taken, but sometimes it was specific areas. At one time, Dr. Humes and Dr. Fink had some photographs of the head wound taken. That's really kind of all I remember about the photographs. It was after the brain was removed, there [unintelligible] the cavity was examined, the brain other than the area that was damaged was probably all intact. In looking down into the skull, there was nothing obvious, other than the damage to the top of the skull. You could tell where the fractures radiated out of the floor of the skull is shiny. The fractures became invisible there. (?)

S: Can you still see the two men who were standing behind Dr. Humes? Are they still taking notes? Plain clothed? Men dressed in plain clothes?

J: I can still 'em, I am not -

S: Can you describe what they look like with these [unintelligible] being distinguishing?

J: They were both dressed in dark suits. They're both between medium height. One is a little shorter than the other. Neither one of them are slender, they're just [unintelligible] only one of them is really writing. He is writing on kind of a flip top notepad.

S: Can you see what color hair they have, or do you remember?

J: No.

S: Do you know who they may be?

J: No, I have no idea.

S: Okay, well right now, let's proceed. What comes next?

J: Dr. Boswell comes back to the table, they begin looking at the chest cavity, at the end of the back wound - where it seems to end, and they begin to examine the chest walls to see if there is an entrance wound into the - I think that they've concluded that there is no entry wound! The focus goes back to the head. [unintelligible] looking in various areas. Then again, we set the body up, they examined the base of the neck in the area of, kind of separating the hair and looking through it, they're setting the body back down. There is discussion in the gallery between Dr. Humes, and Dr. Fink has been asked to come over. They come back to the table and there is a man in a suit that comes in from the end of - comes into the morgue from the atrium. He is carrying something and gives it to Dr. Humes. It seems to be a small specimen bag that - metal fragments and bone fragments in it. Dr. Humes looks at it, holds it in his hand, kind of rubs his thumb across the outside of the bag as if he [unintelligible] sits it down by the right ear of the President's body. They came back to combing the head again. Now they're beginning to put the scalp and the bone back in place as best they can. Everything seems to fit back except for the area of about not larger than a silver dollar. It's about I'd say [unintelligible] maybe two inches of the occipital area on the parietal side in the area [unintelligible] kind of standing looking at the head, it would be the upper left of the wound in the area of the wound. It doesn't cross the midline. The scalp's being pulled back up, the bone that is attached to the scalp goes back in there. They're taking some of the fragments out of the back of the skull, small fragments, and are trying to see if they fit into the absent area that's close to the center line. It seems to be a long "V" shaped piece of bone from the edge of the wound - edge of the scalp of the skull. [Unintelligible] the atmosphere in the gallery at the end of the gallery part where we are, the tension seems to have eased some. Cause there's not discussion and no direction aimed at, you know, the doctors on the floor.

S: Did you [unintelligible] this atmosphere, was there one person that seems to be "in charge?"

J: Not so much one person, most of this seems to come from two admirals.

S: In the gallery.

J: In the gallery.

S: And is it your feeling that the doctors doing the autopsy are subordinating themselves to the admirals?

J: My feeling is that they are not finding what the admirals want them to find. They are not doing what they should be doing. It's almost as if they are not doing it correctly. A lot of tension, there's a lot of feelings. You can almost see it directed toward the three pathologists.

S: As far as you know, have the three of these pathologists done this work before?

J: Dr. Humes was more of an administrator. I never saw him do - he certainly didn't do any of the autopsies. Dr. Boswell only - he was teaching pathology for residents. I never did an autopsy with Dr. Boswell. I do know that he did the brain conferences on Mondays. But I never did any autopsies with him, and neither did any of the other students, but I don't really know anything about the other autopsies that were done during the day.

S: How about Dr. Fink?

J: I knew very little about Dr. Fink. I was told that Dr. Fink was a battlefield wounds expert from downtown.

S: A what expert?

J: He was an expert on battlefield wounds. [Unintelligible]

S: Was he a Navy officer?

J: No, he was Army.

S: What time in the evening is it right now?

J: I think it is in the morning.

S: In the morning? What time in the morning?

J: It's probably one or, two o'clock.

S: Do you mean to say that you were here from three in the afternoon until two in the morning?

J: I think I have been here since three o'clock and in the morning.

S: No leaving, no food?

J: I had a sandwich, a couple of bites from the sandwich. I am not exactly sure what the time frame was. It was prior to [unintelligible] the body. Dr. Stover had moved in behind me. He had changed into scrubs. I thought that maybe he was going to get involved in the autopsy at one time, but he never did. He sat in a chair behind me, he told me that they had brought some sandwiches, and told me to go get one. I walked [unintelligible] took a couple of bites out of the sandwich.

S: What has been Paul been doing all this time?

J: I know that he has been leaving the morgue.

End of Tape #1

Start of Tape #2 (background noise, Jenkins voice is lost amongst it)

JENKINS: I have no real significant awareness of where Paul is. I can't tell you where he is right now.

SPIEGEL: Once the autopsy pictures and X-rays have been taken, have those men been asked to the leave the morgue? The autopsy?

J: They left, the radiologist and Dr. Humes and Dr. Fink view the X-rays on the viewing lights or the tables at the end of the morgue. They've left. The radiologist stays for a short period of time, and he's gone also. This time, there's only Dr. Stover behind me that I am aware of. Dr. Fink is to the left of me, Dr. Boswell's back again across the table, closer up to the head, along with Dr. Humes, and Dr. Humes, Dr. Fink and Dr. Boswell are kind of crowded at the head.

S: Alright, we're going to take a rest. I am going to... before we make the rest at this point, I want you to keep this point in time in mind, so we can go back to this as we resume, but for the present, bring yourself out of this transconsiousness, three get ready, at two, with your eyes closed, at one make your eyes open slowly.

Taping resumes after rest break ... ...

SPIEGEL: Again, look up at the top, higher, higher, as you look up, slowly close [your eyes] a deep breath, three exhales, let your eyes relax, let your body float, and again, let one hand float up like a balloon. Now, when it's upright position, your [unintelligible] to shift gears again, just let yourself float, imaging yourself floating away, an astronaut above the [unintelligible] craft. It's the same time again. Just imagine this movie screen or TV screen or a clear blue sky that acts like a screen and again, you're viewing this out there, and reporting it as your view it out there on this imaginary screen. Now, let's go back to the same place, now, and that's somewhere around one o'clock in the morning. Fix an event around that time, and proceed from there and when you are ready, go ahead.

JENKINS: (Long pause) I think it's later - it seems to be later -

S: Go ahead, it's alright.

J: Dr. Humes and Dr. Fink and Dr. Boswell standing at the head. Dr. Boswell has a clipboard and making some notes – can't see what he is writing on the face sheet and what he is doing and Dr. Humes is taking another [unintelligible] on the man standing now – they seem to be reviewing these. It's not very vocal and not very loud. I am not getting any real specifics. Even though they're within touching distance. I think they are concluding the autopsy. There is an individual that is coming into the laboratory, an unusual individual [unintelligible] bowler hat and a waistcoat carrying an umbrella, very sharply dressed. He's being told to start preparing the body. He is giving the bowler, and the umbrella and his coat to someone and is taking a plastic apron out of one of the pockets of the waistcoat, putting it on. He's coming over to the table. Someone's brought in a pump. He's sliding the pump into the chest cavity, hooking up the pump to one side. The vacuum pump is [unintelligible] he's [unintelligible] the container on the other side. He's changing (?) the vessels that we've tied off to begin to pump in the embalming fluid through the body. He is cutting up the intestines, back into the body with the plaster - material that he's filled the body with. He has a [unintelligible] that he is injecting the embalming fluid into - back into this mixture, tissue and plaster stuff that he's placed into the chest. He's filled the chest cavity now, he's replaced the breast pump just laying on top of the plaster. He's pulled the skin flap down and he's suturing that. After he's finished that, he' molding the body. Meanwhile he's continuing the - it seems like the body has been moved to the other table or the body is higher than it was originally. Now, he is working on the head, he has filled the head cavity with the material he used on the body. Closing the scalp as best he can, he is putting a piece of the same type of material over the area [unintelligible]. All this is sutured up, he is washing the hair.

S: What part of the head can't be covered, what part of the head–

J: It's the area in the back of the head, a little high, it's right above the occipital area. Part of the parietal through occipital it's kind of in that area. He just seems to have put a mesh or something over it.

S: How big of area is it?

J: It's a little larger than a silver dollar, it's kind of hard to say how large it is, because it is not round. At one end there's a sliver, seems to be a sliver of bone, it covers all of this back plate, there is material underneath, scalp, and all this scalp coming back and then securing it with sutures. Then, he is washing the hair, and he's actually shampooing the hair. Now, he is molding the head by pressing on the head, on the [unintelligible] of the head. He's looking at the face, holding the head in his hands and looking at the face. He's got a suture, a small suture kit, [unintelligible] he is sewing the right eye in the corner. He seems to be using his hands to mold the head. Now, he's combed the hair back to see - seems like he's testing it to see if it will cover the patch he's made. He seems to be satisfied, now he has a makeup kit and is making up the President's face.

S: What kind of makeup is he using?

J: It's just cosmetics. It's seems to be, similar to the ones makeup [unintelligible].

S: Is that the only thing he puts on the face?

J: Just seems to be a base, nothing structural. The - seems now, he is washing the body with a hose, sponge. He hasn't closed the throat wound. He's finished washing and drying the body, and we've turned the body over and removed the blood from the back of the body. By now this time, the area of the body, the body has become relatively rigid. He's begun [unintelligible] right on the table, the buttocks and the shoulder area. He doesn't seem to be concerned about that. (Long pause) he's pulling something out of a tube into the area where the throat wound is. Seems to be masking it together, filling it in. He doesn't take any great care doing that, just closes it. He asks someone about the clothing. Someone brings in a suit, shoes, socks, shirt, tie. He starts dressing the body - he's actually dressing the body [unintelligible]. We help him set the body up [unintelligible] the shirt, he doesn't dress - there are no underclothes. He's just dressing the front. Suits, the tie, the shirt-coat are all placed on the body as if it is being dressed. The shoe for the left leg is - the comment is made about … "is it a special shoe?" and so forth. I never really heard an answer to that. The body has been dressed and placed into the casket. The casket is very plush. It seems to be really large.

S: Is this the same casket that [unintelligible] brought him, or is it a new one?

J: It's a new one, it's another one. This one has a [unintelligible] - is more of a rose colored, or a red.

The one that was brought in [with the president's body in it] was a grayish silver type, not silver but grayish, metallic. It's very plain. This one has brass rails and handles and the top on it is a double type top. But it's – it has a kind of a shiny brass, highly polished, metal golden colored, metal around [unintelligible] around the lid. There's a lid and the lid are the main part of the casket. It's also not - you know, it's not a "box" type, it seems to be [unintelligible]. Undertaker is now arranging and placing the body in the casket, arranging the [unintelligible] on the head. Placed the pillow under the head, and subsequently the neck.

S: Can you describe how President Kennedy looks now that the makeup has been put on his face, does it look like him?

J: Yes. All the pictures that I have seen.

S: So there really wasn't much difference between when the body arrived, and when you finally see the body being put in the casket? There wasn't much makeup needed in other words?

J: No. There was the difference being when the body came in, it was [unintelligible] a lot of blood, that kind of ... this looked like a photograph, actually it looked like the President. I'd never seen him in person before. It did look like the photographs I'd seen, I remember specifically seeing close on TV [unintelligible].

S: Since you are watching the undertaker doing his job, how many people are in the room with you? Do you know?

J: Most of the gallery is still there.

S: Really? They're still there watching this?

J: Dr. Humes, Dr. Boswell, Dr. Fink are still there.

S: Are they watching or helping?

J: No, they are just kind of standing to the side, you know, at some time, you know, when we raised the body, Dr. Boswell helped with that.

S: How long does it take for the undertaker to do his job?

J: It seems like forever, he seems to be very meticulous and thorough.

S: Were the men in the dark suits that were behind Dr. Humes still in the room?

J: They are up in the gallery part. People [unintelligible] the gallery.

S: But you don't see them?

J: They're not on the floor?

S: They're not on the floor?

J: No.

S: As a student, you've watched other autopsies before this?

J: Our duty sections did the autopsies at night with the residents.

S: Well, from a student's point of view, did you have any observations about the professionalism or the competence of the people doing this autopsy, compared to the others you observed?

J: I didn't, you know... this autopsy was done as systematic for thoroughness as the other ones I participated in. There are certain things that we as the students, or as the duty corpsman had to do, was to get things, like remove the skullcaps, like remove the brains. We stripped the intestines, cleaned these, we - there were certain residents where we opened the body up, took the organs out for them. It didn't seem to be as systematic. There was not as much time devoted to the organs that came out. Normally, we would have normally taken the kidney and sliced them to look at the [unintelligible] and tissues that type of stuff, see if there were any tumors or that type of stuff. We would have opened the adrenals, they were never removed. I really didn't think anything of this, I ... again, my impression was do what was told to do. My impression did not matter. The other thing, our duty was to store the jars and I have no memory of what we did with them, other than they were still on the counter. I think we were told as we left the morgue, to leave them as they would be taken care of. That's all after the body - my last memory of the brain was in a bucket. It had not, at that time, been dropped into the bucket. The procedure was to infuse it for several hours and drop it in the bucket until the brain conference came, which came a week or several days. My last memory now, is that I see the bucket sitting by - next to the autoclave, and it goes up on the counter. The casket, (phone beeps, Spiegel takes a call, background noise cuts into what Jenkins is saying.) people, people are gone, it's just myself and Paul. First class is back. We are cleaning up. We clean up the autopsy table and floors [unintelligible] someone comes down and tells the (unintelligible) "you need to meet in Dr. Stover's office." Paul and I... Dr. Stover's office. He's sitting behind his desk; some other people are there. I don't know who they are. They're coming...orders were not to be discussed though, with anyone for any reason, and we are also given written orders [unintelligible] officially, I guess. It's stamped at the top [unintelligible] we're asked to give them, and someone else signs, then we leave. (Long pause) Dr. Stover has thanked us.

S: He what?

J: He thanked us, said we'd done a fine job.

S: Can you see on the sheet where the orders came from?

J: My - it's the Department of the Navy. At least the one on top is. It has the Department Navy seal at the top.

S: Can you read, though? Can you see it, what it is that you are signing? Can you read what it says?

J: No.

S: Put your psychological zoom lens on and see if you can pick up the words.

J: It's a full sheet of paper filled. Space at the bottom right for signatures. There's the Navy seal in the middle of the file. Small "pc" on there. There's is date on the top right-hand corner, I really can't make out.

S: Right now, in a short while, I am going to ask you again to open your eyes. Staying in the same state of physical relaxation while your eyes open, I want to show you some pictures. Now, 3, get ready, 2, with your eyelids closed, roll up your eyes, and 1, let your eyes open slowly.

Rick Russo remembers:

The reason I asked Jim to go under hypnosis is I had already done so with Dennis David sometime before and had wonderful results. Jim, if I remember correctly, wanted to come in a day early to see the city or a show. Unfortunately, the only room I can get him, and his friend was in Queens it turned out to be some god-awful place. I'm sure Jim had some recollection that were memorable. The second night was a much better hotel. I think I came in right around then. I can't remember if I met him as we were going over the over to the psychiatrist office or I met them there if I met them at the hotel. I can't recall. I'm unclear about what happened prior to the sessions with Herbert Spiegel. I think we all walked over to Spiegel's office together. Spiegel was the best in the business Spiegel he was a very nice person very professional. Spiegel had his precursor to the process. Just to see how susceptible you will be to the process of being put under, the right arm is extended and as you fall further under hypnosis the arm rises. I think we realized Jim did not have susceptibility to hypnosis. I think Jim wanted to do it really badly, so he closed his eyes for the initial process and entered an increased relaxed awareness state which clearly allowed Jim to remember in some detail that night in November, but I think he knew he wasn't really in a hypnotic state but just being in the relaxation state allowed him to recall things in greater detail than ever before.
The above transcription was taken from a 30 plus year old recordings on microcassette tapes. The tapes are of poor quality and often are unintelligible and the voice quality is only legible with good earphones. It is presented here only for completeness.

Note: Jenkins comes out of relaxation state. What follows is an analysis of the Fox set of Kennedy autopsy photographs. For a good discussion of this, see William Law's book *In the Eye of History* and companion DVD.

CHAPTER TEN

After the session in New York I returned home to Mobile and to working for the USA Medical Center Hospital. I had a brief contact with Rick Russo a few years later asking if I would consider a filming with Nigel Turner, a British film maker. Turner wanted to film me in my laboratory and after getting the administration's approval, Turner promised the PR department a copy of the filming to use as publicity. The filming was done in the special coagulation laboratory. The incident was a disaster. After the completion of the filming, the PR department never received a copy of the film nor did I, which put me in a little hot water with the administration.

Over the ensuing years, I have kept in occasional contact with Rick and he has given me invaluable help in writing this book, as have many others.

In 1998 I once again agreed to meet with a researcher named William Law. I really wasn't interested in rehashing the same experiences that I had gone over with previous researchers, but as a courtesy and because my wife and I were passing through New Orleans on a trip, I agreed to briefly meet with Mr. Law. The interview lasted two hours. My next contact with Mr. Law was in 2002, when he invited me to participate in a meeting of the Bethesda witnesses in Fort Myers, Fl. My interest was piqued when I was told that Jim Sibert, one of the FBI agents present in the morgue, was going to be present.

My wife and I decided to make a much needed mini-vacation of the trip. Since Paul O'Connor and his wife were going to be at the meeting, it would give my wife an opportunity to visit with Paul's wife, her cousin. At the meeting I was introduced to Mr. Sibert. He was a pleasant, likable, older man. During the meeting, I listened intently to Mr. Sibert's relating his experiences of that night in the morgue, but came away with the feeling that what he was telling us had been heavily influenced by his following the case over the many years. It seemed as if he was relating a blend of his own experiences and what he had read intermingled with the government's official line. I understood that Mr. Sibert had been an avid reader of the case. In spite of these personal misgivings, I found Jim Sibert a very amiable and personable man, someone I would have liked to develop a friendship with if given the opportunity. [1]

---

1. The text of these meetings can be found in William Law's book *In the Eye of History*.

After the Florida meeting I continued my contact with William and in 2013, I finally succumbed to his constant requests to attend the JFK Lancer Conference in Dallas, Texas. It was the 50th anniversary of the assassination. I encountered an unexpected wealth of interest which totally surprised me. I was asked to take questions, which I was totally unprepared for. I left the conference with a new perspective. As I traveled home, I thought about the sincere interest that I had encountered.

Two years later in 2015, I again returned to Dallas and was invited to speak at the Lancer and Judyth Baker conferences with William Law. At these conferences, I found the same enthusiasm that I had encountered two years before. As I was flying home I again had the feeling that maybe I had been selfish because I had refused to share my experiences in the Bethesda morgue during the JFK autopsy with these passionate people.

After sharing my thoughts with William and with his enthusiastic encouragement and offer of help, I decided to write this book.

The commitment to this decision I must admit was a little frightening. I began to read about the assassination because I knew very little about it other than what I had seen and participated in during the autopsy. I soon stopped reading books on the assassination because I felt that it might influence my memories of that night. I began to focus on the attempt to clarify some of the differences between other people present at the autopsy and my own recollections. To this end I began to limit my endeavors to only these witnesses.

Thomas Robinson

Thomas Robinson was the mortician that prepared the President's body for burial. I first became aware of Thomas Robinson during the latter part of the Bethesda autopsy. Toward the end of the autopsy I noticed a rather dapper young man standing against the galley rail. He was dressed in a three-piece suit and was wearing a bowler hat and carrying an umbrella or cane. I was told that he was the mortician, who was to prepare the president's body for burial. His manner of dress stood out in the sea of dark suits and military uniforms present in the morgue that night.

I have had no further contact with Mr. Robinson after that night. Some years later I read an interview that was given to a Swedish or Danish author/filmmaker and was interested as to how close Mr. Robinson's interview followed my own memories of the autopsy wounds.

I decided to try and contact Mr. Robinson and see if he could help me clarify some of the gray areas in my memories. I obtained a possible telephone number and address in Winter Haven, Florida but I was unsuccessful in my many attempts to contact him by phone. The internet search of his possible address showed that the property was in foreclosure.

In the summer of 2016, my wife and I had planned a mini-vacation to visit her cousin, Paul O'Connor's wife in Gainesville, Florida. After our visit, I wanted to go to Winter Haven and see if I could find Thomas Robinson or at the least maybe find someone who knew him.

I talked to current residents of the several addresses that I was given by the Winter Haven clerk's office and the property assessor's office. At the last address I visited, I found a young man who was clearing his late mother's estate. He told me that Mr. Robinson had worked with his mother in an antique store and at one time lived at the present address but he had not seen him in over 10 years, and the last time he heard of him he was living in a converted hotel downtown. The young man offered to look through his mother's address files from the business. We only found the phone number for the young man's present address listed in his mother's files.

During our conversation I asked several questions about Thomas Robinson. The young man said that he thought that the Mr. Robinson he knew was about his mother's age. His mother had been in her early 70's ten years ago. This would put Mr. Robinson currently in his early 80's. If he was 26 years old at the time of the Bethesda autopsy, the age would be somewhat correct. I asked if he knew if Mr. Robinson had ever lived in the DC area or if he had ever been a mortician. The young man said that he only knew Mr. Robinson through his mother and did not know a great deal about him.

I decided to see if I could find the converted hotel and see if I could get further information on Mr. Robinson. I found that the converted hotel had been torn down some years back and I could find no further information concerning the whereabouts of Thomas Robinson.

We returned to our motel and I used the motel's computer to check the local newspaper's archives for the last 10 years for possible stories or obituaries mentioning Thomas Robinson. I found a current obituary for a Thomas Robinson in a nearby town, but he was 53 years old and his middle initial was not 'E' for Evan. While I was unable to find Mr. Robinson, I gained a little more information even though I could not be certain it was the same Thomas Evan Robinson that was in the Bethesda morgue during the autopsy of the President's body.

We arrived home several days later and I moved on to other things.

Several weeks later I decided to try and trace the origin of the cell phone number that I had, supposedly that of Thomas Robinson. The area code led me to Lexington, Kentucky. After using the computer to find Thomas Robinsons in Lexington, I found several and chose those in their late 60's and early 80's. I made several calls and was only able to leave messages; I received no return calls. I have recently been told that Mr. Robinson has passed away in Maryland. I don't know but if this is true, it is truly a great loss for myself and others in history. The people of this nation have lost another person present at the JFK autopsy and his first-hand knowledge of what the wounds truly looked like and I have lost the ability to clarify some of the gray areas in my own memory concerning the wounds that I saw that night.

Dr. Michael Chesser

At the 2015 convention I met Dr. Michael Chesser, a neurologist from Little Rock, Arkansas. Dr. Chesser had been allowed to visit the National Archives and view the original autopsy photographs and x-rays. Dr. Chesser and Dr. David Mantik approached me to ask if I would take questions about the brain that was removed at autopsy. I agreed and we met for a filmed session and discussed the brain photos in the Archives and the brain that was removed at autopsy. I for the first time was getting answers to the peculiarities I saw with the brain we removed at the Bethesda autopsy. This meeting is discussed in detail elsewhere in this book.

In 2017 I was invited to attend a Neurology-Radiology conference where Dr. Chesser presented the x-rays of President Kennedy's autopsy. He like Dr. David Mantik has been allowed to review the original x-rays and photographs that are in the National Archives. Dr. Chesser's presentation was before an audience of Radiologists and Neurologists and their residents and fellows. After the presentation Dr. Chesser asked for comments on his presentation and some of the peculiarities seen on the films. The following are some of the answers to that request:

> 1. The appearance of a large amount of brain missing from the frontal area in the right lateral x-ray. The chief of radiology said that it was probably air, due to the body resting on its back for a long period of time. The brain had probably moved backwards due to gravity, trauma and the malleable nature of the skull.

> 2. Another discussion was directed to the fracture lines and how some of them would abruptly stop and disappear and then reappear after a short distance. A radiology fellow said that fractures

usually continue in a straight line unless stopped by a suture or another fracture line. I found this interesting because if you could determine which fracture lines formed first that could possibly indicate if the first fractures formed at the front of the skull or the rear of the skull. That might offer a clue to a frontal or rear entry.

3. The questionnaires did seem to have a consensus as to the marks that Dr. Ebersol said he created by hold the film too close to a spot viewing lamp. The only verbal comment was made by the chief of radiology, was that it must have been a very hot lamp.

4. The general consensus was that the faint fragment trail probably indicated a frontal wound, because as it progressed posteriorly the trail spread out. Dr. Chesser feels that there was an entrance wound high in the frontal area. I did not see a wound in that area at the autopsy but it would have been in the hairline and the focus of my attention was on the posterior head wound. The only frontal wound that I saw was the one found by Drs. Humes and Fink slightly above and forward of the right ear.

Most of the young radiologists and neurologists knew very little about the assassination and displayed only a cursory interest. Their interest seemed to be focused on the interpolative and technical aspects of the x-rays themselves.

I had a short discussion with three of the older staff neurologist/radiologists who seemed to be very interested and at times shocked by the description of the wounds that I saw in contrast to what the x-rays showed.

I gained a better insight into the x-rays from Dr. Chesser's presentation and discussion. I now understand that in the AP x-ray the angle at which the x-ray was taken was not a true AP of the head, causing the apex of the arch of the lambdoid suture to appear in the lower third of the x-ray and not directly behind the nasal bones. This leads people with little experience in interpreting x-rays, like myself, to a possible erroneous conclusion when trying to correlate what I saw and what the x-rays are showing.

I felt honored to have been invited to this meeting and I gained a lot of insight into the x-rays and the information they contained. I have been honored that Dr. Chesser has agreed to further discuss this matter in a chapter of this book.

Chapter Eleven

Bethesda visit with Bill Lynch

In April 2017 I decided to contact a longtime friend, Bill Lynch, who was a fellow student in my Bethesda laboratory and blood banking class. Over the years I'd lost contact will Bill but had recently re-established contact through email and telephone conversations. During these conversations Bill told me that he had made contact with a Navy doctor at Bethesda through his involvement in the yearly local fair. This Navy doctor told Bill that he could get us permission to visit the morgue at the Bethesda Naval Hospital. I contacted William Law and William was elated with this opportunity. Bill told me that the Naval doctor had told him that when we came to Washington, Bill was to call him and he would make the arrangements necessary for us to visit the morgue. This was to be a great adventure, it had been over fifty years since I had been a student at Bethesda and I was eagerly looking forward to the visit. I hoped to be able to answer some of the questions I had in relation to the relocation of the morgue and to see what improvements had been made in the morgue over the years.

It was my intention to visit Bill in May but due to William being unable to travel until later we finally were able to make the visit in July.

My wife and I drove to DC at the end of July. We traveled through the Blue Ridge Mountains sometimes taking the scenic routes, but primarily traveling on the interstates. It was a pleasant and relaxing trip for us. It had been some time since we had been able to take a long trip together. My wife, an ex-history teacher and current history buff, was looking forward to visiting some of the historical sites in the DC area.

We met William Law and his wife Lori in Gaithersburg, Maryland on the 30th of July. They had arrived a day early and had taken a trip to visit Edgar Allen Poe's grave site in the Baltimore area. That evening we met with Bill and his wife Diane and made plans to have breakfast the following morning. At breakfast we got acquainted and Bill and I tried to catch up on the last fifty years. William asked Bill if he would be amicable to doing an interview with us, Bill agreed, and we established the time for the interview.

A Conversation with Jim Jenkins and Bill Lynch

We sat down with Bill Lynch at our hotel in Gaithersburg, Maryland. What follows is a transcript of that meeting.

LAW: First, Bill, tell us who you were and your duties at the hospital when you were at Bethesda that day.

LYNCH: I was a student at the naval medical school command. I went to what we refer to in the Navy as '417 school', or clinical lab and blood bank. That afternoon, our day was in serology, performing surgery on guinea pigs to remove their kidneys to make guinea pig antigen for the mono test. As a student, you get to do the lovely job of doing all that, but we made our own reagents to do our own testing with, which I always thought it was a great thing. I had to do it at Montgomery College, to make your own reagents, if it doesn't work that's your problem, you screwed up. But I was also that the morgue watch that day [November 22, 1963] and they came to me sometime around 3'o'clock - I am trying to think - I think it was Key that came down [or told me] "Get down to the morgue and get it ready, they are bringing the President's body in." I'd already known by that time because I had heard it somewhere that he had been assassinated or shot in Texas. I saw - I mean there were already people gathering in the hospital, I mean people running around - it looked like a circus was getting ready to hit town.

LAW: How did you feel when you heard the news?

LYNCH: Well, I was kind of shocked that somebody had shot the President, but when they told me I had to go to the morgue and get ready, we were on a "port and starboard watch," which meant we were there from 7 in the morning like on Monday and our watch ended at 4PM on Tuesday. We went to school during the day, and I was on the end of my watch. It was 3PM, I was getting off at 4, and when I saw all the crowd and saw what was going on, and they wanted me to go to the morgue. I said... "I think it is time for the oncoming morgue watch to get to work, so... "

LAW: And who was the incoming morgue watch?

LYNCH: The incoming morgue watch was Paul O'Connor and at that time was Curtis Jenkins as he called himself (Bill smiles)

JENKINS: I didn't call myself that (amusement in Jim's voice).

LYNCH: Everyone called him Curtis Jenkins but - (Jim laughs). I gave the keys to Paul and told him: "You guys have the next morgue watch, they're bringing the President's body in and they want you to get down there right away and get the morgue set up and get prepared for the autopsy of Kennedy."

LAW: Now the way I understand it, the reason that they got the duty, was that you wanted to go home.

LYNCH: That's exactly right.

LAW: And so, you are the person who said: "They want you to go to the morgue." because you wanted to get the hell out of there.

LYNCH: I wanted to get the hell out of there, because I knew the way things were building, it was going to be no fun and no party there. It was one of the advantages of being a little older than the rest of the crowd.

LAW: So, in essence you changed their lives forever.

LYNCH: Yes.

LAW: You made them part of history by not taking the duty yourself.

LYNCH: That's true, and I have not heard from them until Jim called me, how many months ago? (Bill looks over at Jim sitting on a couch next to his chair.) I figured they were both still mad at me, so I hadn't heard from them in over 50 years! (laughter from Bill and Jim.) We finished up our tour at school until we graduated. And to be perfectly honest with you, we just went about our business. It was just like it happened last week, and that's it.

LAW: So, tell me about that day. You just left and that was about it? But you had to hear things after the assassination.

LYNCH: Well, I didn't "just leave." (Bill puts both of his hands up and makes air quotes) When I gave them the keys, I had to stay there until 4pm and we had to clean up our lab area. We got everything finished, and went about our routine and (Bill crooks a thumb at Jim) they took off for the morgue. My car was parked - the way I orientate was on the dental end of the building, so I went up to the lobby, like I always did, took a right to the parking lot and that's when I saw the crowd of people in the lobby, and that's when I departed, it was 4:30 - quarter to 5. The crowd was already starting to build outside. There were people climbing all over the -

there was like a 3 foot fence in front of the naval hospital at the time - they've taken it down and replaced it with a barrier fence - but people were climbing over the fence, on the grounds, coming to the hospital, cars parking on the shoulder of the road out there, and I kept looking at that and saying "Take me home, country roads." I wanted to be out of there. I just had that feeling that it was not going to be fun there. It was getting crowded, going crazy.

Law: So, you left and went home at that point.

Lynch: Yes.

Law: And when did you come back to Bethesda?

Lynch: Was that on a Friday? I was off Saturday and had duty on Sunday, I believe. We were doing port and starboard.

Law: Did you watch television during that Saturday?

Lynch: We did. We watched everything on TV.

Law: And what did you think while you were watching that footage, knowing you had skated yourself out of the duty?

Lynch: Hallelujah! (laughter from Bill) I just kept saying, "I am glad I am not there."

Law: So, Sunday, the next day, you had to come back. What was it like at that point?

Lynch: Oh, well, we did our routine, there were people in pathology doing some tissue work, still, I think the atmosphere was difficult. I think on Sunday, and the chatter that went around, was like they had to process the tissue from the autopsy, like on Saturday and then cut the ribbons I guess Saturday night, or whenever. And the chatter about the secret service being there - when you cut tissue on a microtone, then you run what they call "a ribbon" and then you float this ribbon on a warm water bath and eyeball the ribbon with sections of tissue and you find one that is more perfect than others and you stick your little glass slide underneath it and lift it out of the water bath and it adheres to the slide imbedded in a very thin 13 micron piece of tissue imbedded in paraffin. [The] secret service was standing right there as they were working and literally swept up every scrap of ribbon that wasn't being used on a slide and bagged it up and took it.

Law: Were you familiar with autopsies?

Lynch: Did a number of them, yes.

Law: So, tell me what a typical autopsy would be like.

Lynch: A typical autopsy the navy did - that we did there, was once we opened the patient with what they call the "Y" shaped incision, we removed the entire visual block of organs which is from the throat to the rectum, pull the organs out in one big piece, as the technician we removed the entire section of intestine. We would go over to the deep sink and with scissors, run the entire length of the intestine, open it up, rinse it out, and like movie film, we used to go like that - (Bill takes his hands and holds them like he is looking up and down at movie film.) looking for abnormalities, ulcerations in the intestines. And the pathologists he would repeat it if we found anything. We'd show him if we found an abnormality and we would take a small section of the colon, the ascending and descending colon and the duodenum and put them in formaldehyde, you know, the little jars we had with formaldehyde for tissue and as the technician, our other job was to remove the brain and spinal cord from the individual. And for that, we had a stryker saw, which was a vibrating saw, and we would cut across the crown of the cranium and pull the scalp forward and back.

Law: Did you have a particular way you sliced the [scalp]?

Lynch: From ear to ear, just behind the ear, from one ear to the other. First, we would cut the scalp and then once the scalp was pulled back, and then we took the stryker saw and buzzed the skull. We went around the skull and the forehead, and we made a cut with the stryker saw in a "V" shape basically as an orientation and to keep the skull cap from sliding around when we returned [the skull cap] back [to the head] and sewed it up. We would remove the brain.

Law: Tell me what that would entail. Do you remember?

Lynch: Yes, basically, you would cut through the dura which is the covering for the brain, and get down to where the brainstem was, cut the brainstem, lift the brain out very carefully [because the brain] is like a bowl of jelly. We had a sling that we made in a bucket, made out of cheesecloth. We lay that brain inside, upside down, and go to the cranial arteries, we had a needle on a carboy, the carboy contained formaldehyde, we put that in the artery, tie it off tight, and start a drip of formaldehyde and that just ran until it firmed up - well preserved - then we went inside the body to remove the spinal cord and I remember we used to cut a "V" shaped cut down the spinal cord, and lift up the vertebrae, and a cord lay in there just like a telephone cable, and it was messy also. We had to be very, very careful lifting that [out.]

LAW: What was the purpose in taking out the spinal cord?

LYNCH: They took everything. They examined every piece of tissue in there, plus, if my memory is correct. NIH used to literally send us requests for various parts. I remember removing some things from bodies, because NIH was discovering something to do with the tongue and all that stuff.

LAW: There has been much made of the fact that during the autopsy, that President Kennedy's testicles were removed. Is that standard procedure on a male body?

LYNCH: They studied every piece of tissue. I would imagine that they took the testicles also, because when the pathologists took the slides to read to give a report on the liver, everything, and I am sure the testicles were part of that. I don't recall myself, taking any out.

LAW: I always know, that this is unfair to ask, because at this point, it's been 53 almost 54 years going back a way, do you remember any of the scuttlebutt that was going around the base at that time, as far as Kennedy goes?

LYNCH: There was a type of scuttlebutt going on around there, I don't remember anything specific, you know, there was chatter, most of it had to do with how, I think the secret service swept in there and took everything with them - out the door they went. Some of the information I got came from a [former] secret service agent that used to work for me at Montgomery College. He didn't know very much about it, as a matter of fact, he was down at the Kennedy house in Middleburg, wiring it for alarms and stuff like that. And when he got the call that said, "You can stop, the President has been shot."

LAW: I know some of those secret service agents. Do you remember his name?

LYNCH: John Brophy, he was a captain. He came to work at Montgomery college after he retired, and then he was an electronics guy. He was a super-duper guy. His son became a secret service agent.

LAW: Did he give you any opinions on -

LYNCH: No, he did not. He was very cautious about what he talked to me about.

LAW: You stayed at Bethesda Naval Hospital [after the assassination].

LYNCH: After graduation, I stayed at the hospital and became [part of the] staff in the microbiology department.

LAW: Earlier today, we had a nice breakfast together, and Jim and you were talking about Humes and Boswell, and what I wanted to ask you, but I am glad I waited until now, what kind of characters were Humes and Boswell, if you recall. What kind of guys were they?

LYNCH: They were - Boswell more so that Humes, was a real personable guy. And he was - you could talk to him about anything you wanted to talk about. I worked with both Humes and Boswell. They part-timed at Suburban hospital in the pathology department on weekends. We all worked together, it was a small operation.

LAW: Would you say you got to know them fairly well as people?

LYNCH: Yes, and I admired both of them. They were both - I think they were both maligned in what the reports put out about this [JFK] autopsy. They were in the military, and a lot of people don't understand that part. They were career military. One was a captain and one was a commander. That's a lot riding on the line. And I think Jim and I have talked about this before - if either one of them had their druthers, they would have done the same thing I did, [laughs] get in the car and get the heck of out dodge. But, being in the military, they followed orders. They had orders, they had people way above their pay grade.

LAW: If they were given an order - I keep hearing this over and over [that] - they were military. If they were given an order - and I am not saying they were part of anything - this is why I do this kind of work, I try to explore all of the options, and if an answer to a question is not possible, I don't really care what the answer is, I care about the truth of the situation. So, I am asking you - you know Humes and Boswell on a personal basis, not only in a work environment, you got to know them pretty well. Say there was some sort of scenario from people above their pay grade, so to speak, and they said "We need to do this, for this reason, you will do it." Would they do it?

LYNCH: I believe they would, because we are talking 1963, the military was a lot different back in 1963. Today, 2017, the discipline – I am trying to figure out how to word it and be kind, these folks – today – you know, everybody has got their rights. They got this, that and the other, I don't think the military people today wouldn't hesitate to talk back to their superiors. In my time, in the military, if a corporal told a private to jump, he jumped. He wouldn't question it.

I wouldn't have questioned it. I think with the atmosphere that was probably in that autopsy room, and the people that were above them, they had a lot riding on it. I mean, like I say, they were both career officers, they were both high grades in their grade, and they were close to their retirement dates, plus the fact that they knew – I keep using the word military – I guess, but if the Admiral told them to jump, they jumped. I don't think they would do anything illegal or improper, but they followed their orders, whatever they were told to do, I am sure if there was a cover up or whatever, I wouldn't want to be either one of them.

LAW: Well, let me ask you this question in this way. If you were told by your superior officer "the President has been killed, there is a little scenario that needs to be played out here." and they tell you it's for national security and the good of the country, would you do it?

LYNCH: Back then, yes. And the word back then was "if you don't like the order, you do it anyway and complain about it later."

LAW: Jim brought up something to me that I've never thought about as much as I think I know of this kind of thing, now as long as I've been studying about it, Jim said, "Say that Humes and Boswell found themselves in the position of "you will do things for national security," even if they didn't like it and didn't want to do it, who were they going to tell? Where were they going to go if they had done [whatever they were told to do] chances are they might be disciplined or in the extreme might lose their pensions, worse, -

LYNCH: They could be court-martialed.

LAW: They could be court-martialed. So, when people think, "Oh Humes and Boswell, they were not great guys, simply because they did not come forward and say 'We were told to do this,' they really had no options available to them." Would you say that's true?

LYNCH: I would say that's true.

Jim then proceeded to describe some of the things to Bill that went on in the autopsy room on the night he had chosen to turn over the keys to the autopsy room to Jim and Paul O'Connor. Then, at my request, Jim took the Kennedy autopsy photographs out of a folder and began to show them to Bill Lynch.

LAW: I just want Bill's opinion on if it appears to be the morgue or not.

JENKINS: Bill, I don't know if you saw this one or not. (Kennedy on back with small metal table over chest.) It has this holder here (Jim points to head holder).

LAW: Do you remember that holder?

LYNCH: No, we had a block. (Jim picks up photograph showing Kennedy's left profile with his head in a "head holder.")

JENKINS: This one is the one I asked Bill about the phone on the wall, and he doesn't remember the phone on the wall or this headrest.

LAW: Why don't you?

LYNCH: I remember the phone on the wall, but it had a huge long stretchy cord.

LAW: But it wasn't on that particular section of the wall, was it?

JENKINS: No, it was back over here near the deep sink.

LAW: So, Bill, what do you think about looking at that picture?

LYNCH: It was done somewhere else.

JENKINS: This picture (Jim holds up the picture with the back of Kennedy's head intact) not so much of what it depicts, but because of this (Jim points to the object above the gloved hand in the photo) but because this is the head block we used

LAW: Do you agree with that Bill? Do you think that looks like the head block that was used at Bethesda?

LYNCH: Yeah, that is the block we had there.

LAW: Now, just for edification, you don't remember any kind of head holder ever being used [in the morgue] and you've been in the morgue [for autopsies]?

LYNCH: Besides being in the morgue for autopsies, after I was staffed there, they assigned me a new job while I was working in micro, somebody came up with the brilliant idea of using cadaver skin for wound dressing. They didn't know what they were going to do with it, or how, but the Navy felt more comfortable with me working with deceased people than live ones! I spent a lot of time down in the morgue doing autopsies as a student.

LAW: Do you remember what the loading dock looked like?

LYNCH: The loading dock was just steps away from the double doors into the morgue. Because sometimes the undertakers that came to pick up remains asked for help. Once they loaded them into their body bag, and loaded them on their little gurney, I helped them out the door and loaded them in their hearse. So, it was just out the door to the right, and there was a loading door. So, they brought Kennedy's body in and just backed up to the loading door and backed it right in.

Jenkins: As you came in the doors from the loading dock like you came in, you're going down the hall, the morgue is right there on your left. You went into the cool room, and then there was a door from the cool room into the morgue proper.

Law: I know this is a silly question, but there is a reason I am asking it. Do you remember what color the tiles in the cooler room were? Or the morgue itself?

Lynch: They were a light color, I don't exactly remember what color they were. I remember they were a tan or a white color, and I think the morgue [floor] itself was like tile terrazzo something like that. And then in the cool room area were like asphalt tiles. I don't recall a 100%, but they were a light color, I do remember that, and they had to be waterproof, because we had to hose the place down. We had drains in the floors.

Jenkins: I don't specifically remember the tiles, that is one of the reasons I wanted to go back to [Bethesda] see if the tiles really correlated with those in the [autopsy] photographs. I remember there was kind of a wainscot of tiles up - probably ⅔ up the wall in the morgue itself.

Lynch: The wall had ceramic tiles on it.

Jenkins: Yeah, right. Ceramic tiles. And I don't remember a lot about the cool room, other than where the little podium - they had a little box -

Lynch: Yeah

Jenkins: For toe tags -

Lynch: Well, that's where the log book was - when you received a patient in the morgue, you had to sign them in, and if they were new to the area, you put toe tags on them. If they were being discharged, you filled out the log book with time and date you discharged them, and [who] had discharged them, and to whom you discharge them [to]. Like for example, Gawlers. Back in those days a lot of our patients went to Pumphrey's (another funeral home in the area].

Jenkins: Like I said, one of the only things I remember is, we had the log book, and I remember looking at the log book sometime during the autopsy. The blank was there [for the autopsy number] of course we had stamp numbers - we had a little stamping machine we stamped toe tags and the paperwork with the autopsy number. And then it rolled over to the next number. But there was no name in the [space for the name] only the autopsy number was there. And somebody had just put CNC, and of course, the next morning when Paul and I left the morgue, the log book was gone. The morgue log book was gone, the casket that had been rolled up against the cold boxes was gone, and the casket that the body had come in was gone.

Jim takes a picture out of a folder that contains the "Fox" set of Kennedy autopsy photographs and holds up a photograph that shows the back of Kennedy's head.

> JENKINS: See, this one is the only one that I feel like is authentic, and the reason I say that is because it [shows] the block-it's got the head block.
>
> LAW: You see there that there is a towel if you were ever to do an autopsy Bill, would you put a towel under the head?
>
> LYNCH: No.
>
> JENKINS: We never did. But I think the towel may have been placed under there for the photographs.
>
> LYNCH: For contrast.
>
> JENKINS: The others [autopsy photographs] we didn't ever get a good picture of the [autopsy] table itself in any of these.
>
> LAW: Well, the reason I am asking that, is there has been speculation that the animal hospital behind the main building was used [to take the autopsy photographs].

I then asked Jim to ask Bill questions.

> JENKINS: The real reason, the thing that would have been great for me, because all those questions that I have when I saw these pictures, I wanted to confirm. See, first of all the morgue was still the same morgue. After 50 years I think there would be some differences, equipment and so forth. I also wanted to see if it is the same morgue, they probably would not have - when they renovated it, they probably would not have taken up the floor in it, you know, that type of thing. So, that would be some type of confirmation as to whether these photographs show what we remember about the photographs - and see if I remember the same thing Bill does. And

Paul remembers the same thing, Jim remembers the same thing about [it] you know. None of us have ever seen a head rest like that and we have done a lot of autopsies in there during the time, the period I was there and you know that was pretty much my main focus. Plus, the fact is, I don't know anything that happened outside the morgue, because I never left the morgue. Once I went in the morgue, I didn't come out until the next morning when Paul and I finished cleaning it up.

LYNCH: I talked to Paul on Saturday morning, Paul and I matter of fact, we weren't event thinking of length of time as he and I had talked and he wanted to go fishing, and my folks had a boat, and I was going to go fishing with him Saturday morning, and he never showed up, and I called him and they had to wake him up and bring him out and he said, "We didn't get out of the morgue until 7 o'clock." He said, "I am going back to bed, I am not going fishing today." And that was the last time I had talked to him at that time.

LAW: So, you never did get to talk to him about anything he may have experienced?

LYNCH: No.

JENKINS: When we finished that morning, we were told to go directly to Stover's office, and he thanked us for the job we did and so forth and he says, " I have a couple sets of orders for both of you." and I thought I was being transferred, but anyway it was a set of orders from Naval department and from the Defense Department, and it basically was a letter telling us that we were not to discuss anything that we had seen that night in the morgue with anyone without authorization. The letters were from the Department of the Navy, and the another from the Department of Defense and they were both pretty much the same, except terminology was a little bit different. And we were to sign them, and we signed them, and there was somebody else there that had witnessed them, and these things had the official US Navy seal on one, and the Department of Defense on the other, and they gave us copies of them. There were a couple of suits in there too, so, Paul and I left and we get outside of Stover's office, and we started down that little area right there, and this one guy in a dark suit comes out of the office and says "Guys, wait a minute," so we stopped. He said "I need to take those copies" and ... I wasn't going to argue with him, so he took both of the copies and went back into Stover's office. I never heard anything from anyone about that, until some lady called me, I was in grad school. She calls me and I was in my office, she told me that Kelly and Purdy were going to be at my home on such and such a date. And I said, "No you are not, nobody is coming to my home." and I said you know, "I have orders against this, and I am not discussing this with anybody." So, she says, "Well they will be at your home." and I said, "No, they are not." So, I got off the phone and I called Thad Cochran in Jackson at that time senator for Mississippi and I went over it with his aide and he said, but have the meeting in my office." He said, "What we do is when you go to the office, tell my secretary that she has to clear their credentials." So, I went to his office and they met me at his office, so I walked in and the secretary said, "Now when you go in the office, sit in his chair and have them sit in the chairs across from you.

LYNCH: And so, who were these people?

JENKINS: Well, Kelly was an FBI agent, and he told me initially he was an attorney for the House select committee. Now Purdy was a lawyer for the House Select Committee and what they did was, they did depositions for various people. And at that time, I was leery about what was going on and so forth. And I had a tape recorder and I asked them, "Can I tape this?" and they said, "No, you can't tape this." But yet Purdy put a tape recorder on the desk so I put my tape recorder on the desk, and I think it was Kelly who said, "You are not allowed to do this." and I said, "Well, you're going to tape it, then I am going to tape it." And then I looked over at the little intercom box facing me from the reception and the light was on… so, anyway we started talking and they asked me to describe to them, and I started to describe it to them, and they - every time - said, "Oh, that can't possibly be, you know, that's not what we know really happened." So, at that, I would get really irritated, and all of a sudden, they said, "Well, have you seen the Warren Commission set of photographs?" And I said, "No, I haven't." So, they said, "Alright." Well, they called the Law Library there in Jackson, we went down and they showed me the drawings, the Rydeburg drawings and they said, "Well, does this look like what you saw?" And I said, "No." and they said, "Well, what's this flap?" and I said, "The flap wasn't part of any - and the flap in the Rydeberg drawing was not here." (Jim puts his hands up by his head) and so we went back, and they were asking me all kinds of questions, and by the questions they were asking me, I knew that they had already talked to Paul. They were saying, "Well, this witness says this and so forth." and I told them, "Well, I am telling you what I remember and how I remember it." I am standing there at the table across the table from Boswell and Fink at the right shoulder and I am working with Boswell, and the other doctors, you know they were engrossed and I said, "Well, that's what I saw." I described the wound on the side of the head and I told them the comments I heard from Fink and Humes and then I described the wound I saw in the back when the scalp was reflected. They just kept saying, "Well, you know, that's not right." So finally, I said, "You know, I don't understand why you are talking to me, and I am tired of this and this is over with." And so, at that time, Kelly started backing up, saying "Oh well, we didn't mean to be offensive," and so forth, and I said, "Well, the interview is over with." I said, "Well, you know do I get a copy of this?" They said, "Well, we'll send you a copy." – which I never got. And then I found out, the interview with me and Paul, was placed under the 75-year deal, well there was an act passed by Congress that allowed access to that and someone sent me a copy of it.

Law: The records review board 1992.

Jenkins: Well, no, I had gotten a copy of it before then, let's see that was '77.

Law: That would be '77, that was when they were delving into it and that's when the gag orders were released or were taken away, and that's when your name became public, because it was on a list of people that had been inside the autopsy room.

Jenkins: So anyway, I got a copy of it, and I looked at it, and it was just - it was a real mess. There were statements in it that were attributed to me, that I knew that Paul had said it, because Paul had said them publicly. They had me removing the body from the casket - which I did not do – and I told them I didn't. There were a lot of things in it. So then later on, I saw Purdy's handwritten notes – and I mean, the notes didn't even correlate with the deposition that they presented to the House Select Committee and I feel like it kind of made Paul and I look like a bunch of idiots... but anyway, I didn't hear from anybody after that – I did get letters rescinding the orders, but they were specific from my testimony to the House Select Committee, that I still have a copy of these somewhere. But in '81 or so, I talked to – I agreed to an interview with Lifton. I spent a long time with him Then when he published the book, and he had selected things that supported his scenario and his agenda for how the assassination had happened. Which ticked me off a little bit, but you know...

Lynch: I think that's been the quirk of the whole thing, everybody that reports on it. #1, they weren't there, #2 they make it so that it's their agenda or what they'd like it to be.

107

JENKINS: Bill, see I found that too, because you know, I have really only talked to maybe three authors: Lifton, Livingstone and yourself [Law]. And the reason that I have worked with William is because from the very first time that I met William and we talked, he's never put a spin on anything. I mean he doesn't have this scenario that he's developed of how it happened to meld and shape everything. The meeting that we had with Sibert in Florida was kind of refreshing in the fact that when [Sibert's interview] it was published it was what we talked about at that point in time.

LAW: Right, right.

JENKINS: And at the 50th, I became aware, you know, how many people not just in this country, but worldwide are interested and still interested 50 years later.

LYNCH: I looked up on the internet because after you and I started to communicate, because before that, knowing what I know, I guess from the scuttlebutt down there, I do recall asking Paul about what went on and his words to me were, "They told us that if we saw or heard anything in that room, they'd have to mail sunshine to our next duty station." (Laughter)

JENKINS: Actually, and truly, that was the threat. The threat was that we would be prosecuted and be court-martialed and we would spend some time in -

LYNCH: The grey bar hotel!

JENKINS: Yeah, you know, I look at that scenario, to expand a little bit on what Bill was trying to say about Humes and Boswell, you know, you and I have talked about this before, they really had no choice. I mean, they were both career officers, they were getting close to retirement, they had families to support and they needed that retirement. Plus, they needed the job that they had. But, I don't think it was the whole story. I think it's - if you stop and think, if they wanted to talk to someone about it, who would they talk to? Because we know that Johnson was controlling everything. It's quite evident with what he did with Oswald in the OR in Dallas.[1] He put in a personal call to the surgeon and told him that he wanted a deathbed confession. (Jim and Bill look at each other with amused looks on their faces)

LYNCH: Confession.

JENKINS: Confession.

---

1. Charles Crenshaw's book, *Conspiracy of Silence.*

Law: Do you think that is something that Johnson would do? You know him more than me.

(looking at Bill Lynch) You met him, I never saw him.

Lynch: Well, he never picked me off the floor by the ears. (laughter from Jenkins).[2]

Lynch: You know, I think that back then, I really had no interest in politics. It's not that I don't like politics, I just don't like politicians. The way things were going and the [unintelligible] down there, I have my own personal theory, but I wouldn't put it past him.

Jenkins: And see, you're talking about two people that controlled [everything]. You've got Johnson, the new President and you've got Hoover, who is head of the FBI. So, where would you go? There is no place to go. And plus, the fact is if - as I read the autopsy report and go through the testimonies of especially Humes, but also from Dr. Boswell, it's apparent like he's put a big spin on it to entice somebody to look into it further.

At this point in the interview with Bill Lynch, Jim talked about the head wound and the brain, which is discussed in depth elsewhere in this volume. In further discussion by Jenkins to Bill Lynch about what took place in the Bethesda morgue, Jim brought up the subject of President Kennedy's kidneys and adrenal glands.

Jenkins: There was some contention about taking the kidneys and the testicles, they were both taken. The consternation with the kidneys were the adrenals. They were almost non-existent, there wasn't very much there.

Lynch: Well, Boswell told me - we were working together - he was working at the hospital Suburban [hospital] one weekend shortly thereafter and - I don't know what the conversation was about, or what we talked about, but I guess he was saying something about what a tragedy, and all this stuff, and he was killed and was assassinated and Boswell said, "His adrenal disease was so advanced, he probably would have died in office." And I still remember that.

Law: Was there anything else he said to you over the years?

Lynch: No. That's about it. It was like the conversation we were having about the fact that he was killed or shot or something, and I don't remember the whole thing, but it still stays with me all the

2. Lyndon Johnson came under severe criticism from the public when during a press conference he picked up his dog by the ears and held him aloft.

time [Boswell] said, "His Addison's was so advanced, he probably would have died in office."

LAW: You mentioned Burkley. What do you remember about Burkley?

LYNCH: I didn't know him personally. I have met him two or three times, because he was the Presidential doctor. I guess we got to know him more when Johnson became President. They would come out - they would do the Presidential physical at the Naval hospital. In the Presidential Suite, I guess it was an annual thing that all the Presidents go through. If they are Army or whatever related, they went to Walter Reed. I knew Dr. Burkley through the fact that he was there and we got the orders to run specimens, various specimens from the White House from the Kennedy's. They were cultures primarily, but I always got a big kick that they came from the White House marked 'Mr. and Mrs. X, White House.' You know, like we wouldn't know who these people were. I guess we were dummies or something. But when Johnson was President, I was on night duty and would have to do and H&H on Johnson following his post-op for his gallbladder.

LAW: What's an H&H?

LYNCH: Hemoglobin and Hematocrit. They do that to check - just a quick check if there is any bleeding - internal bleeding and stuff like that. Johnson wouldn't let me touch him, because I wasn't a doctor - he used some choice words. He wanted Burkley. He told a secret service agent to get Dr. Burkley. He said to get Dr. Burkley in there, and I had to call him. [I] met him there that night. I guess that's the only time one on one with Burkley. I hope I heard him, because he said - it was 2 o'clock in the morning or so and he said, "I haven't drawn blood in over 30 years." (Lynch laughs at the memory) He said, "You're a lot better at it than I am."

LAW: Now you told a couple of funny stories about Johnson [during dinner]. One was when he was in the hospital and he walked by you. Relate that story again.

LYNCH: When they took him to the O.R. for his gallbladder surgery, he was on the lab floor where we moved the Presidential Suite, and the secret service and locked us all in our labs when they were wheeling him to the O.R. like we were going to jump out of the lab and hurt somebody. The week that I was on night duty - we did 30 day stints on nights during that period- he came down the hall with a secret service agent and I was waiting on the elevator to go up to do some lab work upon the tower, and as a courtesy, since he was standing there, I just said, "Good Evening, Mr. President," and he never replied, never acknowledged that I said anything to him, and a night or two later, he was walking the hall, there was some reporters with him, I - guess they were reporters - some folks. I was assuming they were reporters, because when I said, "Good Evening, Mr. President," it was as like I was his long-lost cousin that was standing there by the elevator. And you know, "How are you doing?" yack, yack, yack. I thought, you know, "Hypocrite." (chuckles from Bill and Jim shakes his head.) But, you know, the word's out of him, he wanted to know if I was a doctor, he didn't want anybody but a doctor to touch him - you know - Dr. Burkley had to come in at 2 in the morning to draw blood on him for a simple little test [on him].

The conversation then switched to Jim talking about the story of an Air Force major's body being brought into the morgue already prepared for burial on the following Monday at Arlington.

LAW: Bill, did you ever have any kind of experience where you held a body over four...?

LYNCH: No. Something's wrong there. If they are going to Arlington, Arlington has a place to put them. I guess even the funeral home wherever [the body] came from, if there was such a body there, they would be in the funeral home. They wouldn't just park them.

LAW: You don't remember any experience...

LYNCH: Never. Never. We were strictly an in and out operation - bring them in, do our thing, and send them out. Undertakers would come in to pick up remains, process them, they would load them up in their bags and put them on their cart and out.

LAW: Did you work in the morgue that day at all?

LYNCH: No, not that day, no. I might have been in there the night before.

A range of subjects were talked about at this point, from the stillborn baby being brought in and logged the night of November 22, 1963, to the President's brain. I then turned the conversation back to Humes and Boswell and Bill's knowledge of the two men.

LAW: It's been said that Humes and Boswell, by the time the President's [body] had been brought in [to Bethesda] were administrators, paper pushers, in effect, would you say that's true?

LYNCH: Well, basically, you know, that's their position. Humes was the director of pathology and Boswell was the director of the lab. At this stage in their life, they were both pathologists. The residents did all the autopsies. They were like the CEO of General Electric. For example, he might not even know how to change a light bulb, much less how, you know, how they made a big jet engine and the same way with Humes and Boswell. At this point in time, and when you become a Captain or Commander, you are rarely on the front line. They were responsible for all the residents we had there. It was a teaching place.

JENKINS: And Boswell, did most of the teaching.

LAW: Humes and Boswell, you wouldn't have picked them to do the autopsy on the President of the United States, would you?

LYNCH: Well, no… that's… I had the greatest admiration for the both of them. I thought they were great people, they were smart, smart people and I think that left alone without all the brass and the hoopla and all the stuff that surrounded them, they would have come to a conclusion that would have been acceptable to just about anybody. You know, I think of the story of a church that had an old priest and a young priest, and the older priest was a golf fanatic. And it was about a week or two downpour of rain and this guy couldn't play golf for two weeks and he was going nuts. Then Sunday morning he woke up and it was a beautiful day, the sun was shining, temperature was cool, the sky was really blue and he wanted to go out on the links, so he thought for a minute and went to the young priest and said "I am not feeling well, you're going to have to do all the masses today." So, the young priest says, "Alright, I'll do it." And the old priest got his got his golf clothes and golf bag and headed out the door and St. Peter and God are sitting on a cloud up in the sky and St. Peter said "Did you see that?" and God said "Yeah, I saw that." St. Peter said, "What are you going to do about it?" And God said, "I am not going to do anything about it." So the old priest went out on the links and teed up his ball, and he had a pretty good round on the first two or three holes and then he came to a par 5 hole, teed up his ball and the green was like a dog leg left behind a bunch of trees and he hit the ball and the ball took off and started flying through the air, went over these trees, and dropped into the cup. A hole in one. Almost impossible. St. Peter said, "Did you see that?" God said, "Yes, I did."

St. Peter said, "And you let it happen." And God said, "Yes, I did." St. Peter said, "What are you going to do about it?" God said, "Nothing. Who is he going to tell?"

CHAPTER TWELVE

After spending a day with Bill doing his interview. We were looking forward to visiting Bethesda morgue but Bill was unable to contact the Navy doctor who told us that he would be able to get us permission to enter the morgue. Bill was to continue trying to contact the doctor and William and I decided that we would make a road trip to see the National Naval Medical Center Hospital, which is now called Walter Reed National Military Medical Center. The Bethesda Naval Hospital had grown considerably in the 50+ years since I went to school there in 1963. The hospital complex now encompasses the entire area previously occupied by the golf course and other open spaces and new construction is still going on. Since 9/11 it is difficult to get onto the complex without an approved reason.

William, through one of his many contacts, had been told that the clandestine surgery suggested by David Lifton and Doug Horne to have been done on the President's body prior to our receiving it in the morgue at Bethesda, was performed at Forest Glen Annex. Forest Glen Annex is a large area close to Bethesda Medical Center which has been used by Walter Reed for medical purposes since before WWII. This hundred-acre plus site was donated to the Army in 1923 and was used as a convalescence facility for injured soldiers by Walter Reed Medical Center during World War I. It was later used during World War II for wounded soldiers returning home from the war. Over the many years it has remained under the control of Walter Reed Medical Center and is presently utilized as an Army-Navy research facility. This facility is approximately 8 to 10 minutes from the back gate of the Bethesda Naval Center by Jones Bridge Road. William and I actually located the complex and timed the travel by GPS from the complex to the back gate of the Bethesda Naval Center. Dennis David, the first-class hospital corpsman who supervised the removal of the casket from a black hearse, said that the driver of the black hearse said they came in the back gate from Jones Bridge Road. This could feasibly be the location where the body was examined prior to it being received in the Bethesda morgue. It was a location that could be controlled by the military. The same as Bethesda Naval Hospital, its existence was not well known and it was only about eight minutes from the back gate of the Naval Medical Center

We also wanted to check on the feasibility that this clandestine surgery/examination could possibly have been done at Gawler's Funeral Home. After locating Gawler's Funeral Home, we measured the distance from Gawler's to the front gate of Bethesda Naval Hospital. The distance traveled by GPS was approximately eight minutes.

Sometime later I ran across an interesting article written by M. A. Crouch. It was an interview with a Reading, Philadelphia undertaker by the named of Terry Starr. Starr said that in 1964 he was transporting a body to Arlington for burial and as usual had to employ the aid of a local funeral home for assistance. The local funeral home was Pumphrey's Funeral Home in Bethesda, Md. Starr states that during his brief layover at Pumphrey's, an employee showed him the JFK Dallas Casket. Starr also said he was told that Thomas Robinson was an employee of Pumphrey's and not Gawlers. This story has some credibility because Pumphrey's was under contract with the Bethesda Naval Hospital at that time and the Dallas casket was missing when Paul and I left the morgue the next morning.

This contract with Pumphrey's may explain Thomas Robinson's reluctance to grant interviews and his difficulty in being located.

Does this raise the possibility of a third location where the pre-surgery/examination could have been performed?

I have no first-hand knowledge of where the clandestine surgery was done or who could have performed this surgery.

I will now leave the discussion of where the clandestine surgery was done to those that have much more information in relation to this subject than I do, and to the reader's cognitive reasoning.

The above discussion is presented here only in relation to the differences between the wounds as described by the Parkland doctors and those wounds that we saw during the autopsy in the Bethesda morgue. I believe that the clandestine surgery/ examination, first described by David Lifton and later by Doug Horne, resulted in the longitudinal scalp laceration that has previously been described in the original autopsy report.

While this is outside my sphere of direct knowledge, it does however lend some credence to Lifton's and Horne's belief of clandestine surgery/ examination on the body before it arrived in the morgue for autopsy.

This working trip for William and me, and a mini-vacation for the wives, was disappointing in that we were unable to visit the Bethesda morgue and consequently confirm or dispel the rumors that the morgue had been completely renovated and relocated. We had been confident that the morgue remained in the original location but were unable to verify this belief. We have been led to this belief by the description of the present-day morgue location, to Bill, by a local mortician who picks up bodies from the Bethesda morgue for burial. The mortician was told by a military escort that "this was the morgue were the autopsy of JFK was done." This location was also described to Bill by a friend, a nurse, who works at the Bethesda hospital.

Even though we were unsuccessful in visiting the Bethesda morgue this trip was quite productive in our conversations and the information that we gained from our discussions and interviews with Bill Lynch and it was good to visit again with an old friend and his wife.

CHAPTER THIRTEEN

Official Autopsy discussion and comparison:

The following is presented as a discussion of the contrast between the official autopsy report findings as presented to the Warren Commission and my memories of what occurred in the morgue on November 22, 1963.

The body is that of a muscular well-developed and well-nourished adult Caucasian male measuring 72 ½ inches and weighing approximately 170 pounds. There is beginning rigor mortis minimal dependent lever mortis of the dorsum and early algor mortis. The hair is reddish-brown and abundant, the eyes are blue, the right pupil measures 8 mm in diameter, the left 4mm. There is edema and ecchymosis of the inner canthus region of the left eyelid measuring approximately 1.5 cm in greatest diameter. There is edema and ecchymosis diffusely over the right suborbital ridge with abnormal mobility of the underlying bone. [The remainder of the scalp will be described with the skull.] There is clotted blood on the external ears but otherwise the ears, nose, and mouth are essentially unremarkable. The teeth are in excellent repair and there is some pallor of the oral mucosa membrane.

Situated on the upper right posterior thorax just above the upper border of the scapula there is a 7 x 4 mm oval wound. This wound is measured to be 14 cm from the tip of the right acromion process and 14 cm below the tip of the right mastoid process.

The general description of the body presented in the official autopsy protocol prepared by Dr. Humes seems to correlate with what we saw as we prepared the face sheet. The above description of the position of the back wound would place it at about the location shown in the picture on the next page. This was the same position shown on the autopsy "face sheet."

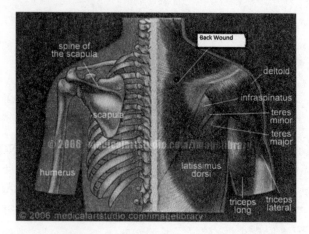

The back wound, right posterior thorax, was located at the level of the top of the scapula, approximately at the level of T2- T3, between the scapula and the spinal column not in the cervical area, C5-C7, where it is shown in the Rydberg drawings. The location at C5-C7 is where it would have to be located in order to support the entry from the back wound and exit through the neck wound i.e. single bullet theory. The measurement of this wound from the right mastoid process and the tip of the right acromion process seems to be unusual because both of these points of reference are movable and as the body moves these points of reference will different from any fixed point on the body. If the head is bent backward, or forward or if its turned to one side the distance from the mastoid process will change. The same is true of the movement of the shoulder (acromion process).

Situated in the lower anterior neck at approximately the level of the third and fourth tracheal rings is a 6.5 cm long transverse wound with widely gaping irregular edges.

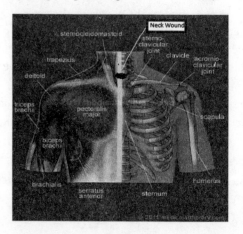

I have several comments and questions concerning the wound in the lower anterior neck, anterior thorax, as being at the level of the third and fourth tracheal rings. I never saw this wound examined during the autopsy at the Bethesda morgue. It seems that this location was derived from its anatomical position not from any actual physical examination of the wound itself. We were told during the autopsy that this was a tracheotomy performed in Dallas at Parkland Hospital and not to bother with it. We were not informed of Dr. Perry's statement that he performed this tracheotomy over a small entrance wound. While it is apparent that the tracheotomy was an emergency procedure, this tracheotomy seems to be highly unusual in that the incision is horizontal as opposed to vertical and the width and location could have possibly cause damage to the thyroid gland which lies below the Adam's apple. The only examination of this wound that I saw was a brief look under the chest flap during the autopsy examination of the body and its organs.

As you can see in the picture above, the neck wound is located above the clavicle at the level of the second or third tracheal ring, well above the back wound at the apex (top) of the scapula at the level of T2-T3 spinal vertebra.

Is it possible this description of the anterior neck wound location could be from a prior examination before the body was received in the morgue or was this an attempt to support the proposed "single bullet theory"?

In the "death stare" photo you can see what appears to be a lump on the right side of the neck just above the neck wound parallel to the Adam's apple. Could this be a bullet or fragment from the frontal entry as described by Dr. Perry at Parkland? This "death stare" was not seen at the Bethesda autopsy. As previously discussed there was no apparent damage to the face when the body was received at the Bethesda morgue and the eyes were closed with the exception of the right eye which was slightly open. This is noted in the official autopsy report.

Was this description of the anterior neck wound's location from a prior examination before the body was received in the morgue or was this an attempt to support the proposed "single bullet theory."

Unfortunately, I have no answer to this question, I like others can only speculate based on what I saw at the Bethesda autopsy and speculation is not within the purview of this book.

The second wound described above is presumably that of the right posterior thorax, the back, wound and is presumed to be connected with the wound in the lower anterior cervical region, the throat wound described by Dr. Perry as an entrance wound. The points Dr. Humes uses i.e. ecchymosis of the strap muscles of the right side of the neck and the fascia above the adjacent tracheostomy wound would have required a more thorough examination of those areas described. There was no examination of the areas described nor was there any examination of the tracheostomy wound. During the autopsy of the body Dr. Boswell gave a cursory look at the tracheotomy by lifting the chest flap and looking under it towards the tracheal wound.

Another point Dr. Humes uses to support the passageway of a projectile from the back wound to the throat wound is not consistent with the probing of the back wound by Dr. Humes and Dr. Fink as previously described nor is it consistent with the slight purplish- reddish area that I saw located on the bottom of the right upper lobe just above the apex of the middle lobe of the right lung. This reddish area was consistent with the termination of the back wound as probed by Dr. Humes and Dr. Fink.

The description of above parietal fascia, visceral fascia could have been seen on close examination and at microscopic examination if sections were taken at the autopsy. I don't remember any sections taken for microscopic examination other than the area of the slightly purplish bruise just above the apex of the middle lobe at the junction of the upper lobe the middle lobe and the lower lobe of the right lung and those taken from the body organs. There was also no through examination of the area described either internally or externally.

I heard no discussion of this proposed pathway during the autopsy or observed any probing of the pathway described above. As previously stated the back wound was probed by Dr. Humes and Dr. Fink and its trajectory was in a downward direction of approximately 45 to 60° which could be readily observed from inside the pleural cavity after the removal of the body organs.

To justify the description and supportive evidence given in the second wound section of the Bethesda autopsy report, the back wound would have to have moved upward from the upper back to the back of the neck in order to give a downward trajectory for exit at the throat wound. This is exactly what the Warren Commission did to justify the "single bullet theory." The placement of the back wound on the face sheet prior to beginning of the autopsy was at approximately second or third thoracic vertebra. This would have required an upward trajectory of approximately 15 to 30° for exit at the neck wound.

I saw no obvious bruising of the right side of the neck, but it is possible that the sudden left-backward movement of the head as depicted in the Zapruder film could have torn the fascia of the strap muscles and caused seepage of capillary blood.

Situated on the anterior chest wall at the nipple line are bilateral 2 cm long recent transverse surgical incisions into the subcutaneous tissue. The one on the left is situated 11 cm cephalad to the nipple and the one on the right 8 cm cephalad to the nipple. There is no hemorrhage or ecchymosis associated with these wounds. A similar clean wound measuring 2 cm in length is situated on the anterior lateral aspect of the left mid arm. Situated on the anterior lateral aspect of each ankle is a recent 2 cm transverse incision into the subcutaneous tissue. There is an old well-heeled 8 cm make Bernie abdominal incision. Over the lumbar spine in the midline is an old well-heeled 15 cm scar.

Missile wounds:

1. There is a large irregular defect of the scalp and skull on the right involving chiefly the parietal bone but extending somewhat into the temporal and occipital regions. In this region, there is an actual absence of scalp and bone producing a defect which measures approximately 13 cm at its greatest diameter.

From the irregular margins of the above scalp defect tears extend stellate fashion into the more less intact scalp as follows.

A. From the right inferior temporal parietal margin anterior to the right ear to the point slightly above the tragus.

B. From the anterior parietal margin anteriorly on the forehead to approximately 4 cm above the right orbital ridge.

C. From the left margin of the main defect across the midline and antero-laterally for a distance of approximately 8 cm.

Note:

My first view of the head wound was when Dr. Humes removed the wrappings from the head. The wound on first site appeared to be a large gaping wound in the posterior portion of the right side of the skull. As Dr. Humes was unwrapping the head, the wound gaped open along the fracture lines and appeared to be much larger than it actually was. After further examination and the reflection of the scalp from the skull, the actual area of the wound where the bone and scalp were missing could be better defined. The missing area was located in the posterior occipital parietal area extended slightly into the temporal area. This area of missing bone was approximately 3 to 3.5 x 2 to2.5 inches with an irregular triangular/rectangular shape with a larger curved upper portion located primarily in the posterior occipital/parietal and extending downward with the narrow portion extending downward just touching the posterior temporal area. This wound appeared to be slightly more cephalic than that described by Dr. McClelland but correlated more closely with the wound described by Dr. McClelland than the wound described in the autopsy report. The wound described in the autopsy report seems to be the appearance of the wound after fracture lines were extended and a coronal incision was made to remove the brain. During this later procedure some bone that was being held together by adhesion to scalp separated and fell into the cavity making the wound appear larger.

> Situated in the posterior scalp approximately 2.5 cm laterally to the right and slightly above the external occipital protuberance is a lacerated wound measuring 15 x 6 mm. In the underlying bone is a corresponding wound through the skull which exhibits beveling of the margins of the bone when reviewed from the inner aspects of the skull.

Note:

I never saw this wound during the autopsy even though, I had multiple opportunities during the positioning of the film cassettes for the head and body x-rays. I assisted Gerald Custer, the navy x-ray technician, during the taking of the first set of x-rays and I never saw this wound. This wound has been described in later testimonies by Dr. Humes and Dr. Boswell as being below the external occipital protuberance. There was never a discussion of this wound after viewing the x-rays. I believe the description of this wound given in the autopsy report above would have placed the wound within the area of missing bone that I saw after the scalp was reflected.

The statement, [In the underlying bone is a corresponding wound through the skull which exhibits beveling of the margins of the bone when reviewed from the inner aspects of the skull], is ambiguous and does not state whether the beveling of the margins of the bone were inward or outward toward the surface of the skull only that the margins exhibited beveling when viewed from the inside of the skull. One must ask, is this an inadvertent omission of a critical detail or is the wound itself a wound of convenience to support a preconceived conclusion that the shot was from the rear?

Though, it is possible that I could have missed seeing this wound. I feel that probability is very remote. Therefore, with the inconsistencies of the description of this wound in later testimonies by Drs. Boswell and Humes before the House Select Committee and the Assassination Records Review Board, it is difficult for me to believe that this wound exists as described.

The head wounds will be further discussed later.

Clearly visible in the above described large skull defect and extruding from it is lacerated brain tissue which on close inspection proves to represent the major portion of the right cerebral hemisphere. At this point it is noted that the falx- cerebri is extensively lacerated with disruption of the superior sagittal sinus.

In Dr. Humes' testimony before the Records Review Board, he said that the brain was visible through the defect but was not extruding.

The description of the brain above is more consistent with the Ida Dox drawings of the brain than with the brain removed from the head at the Bethesda autopsy. If the brain removed at autopsy, had been that extensively damaged there would've been no need to try and infuse it. The damage to the falx- cerebri and the disruption of the superior sagittal sinus would have caused massive damage to the vascular system of the brain. It would have also exposed a large amount of the underlying tissue in the brain and the fixation of the brain could have been accomplished by merely immersing the brain in the bucket of formalin without infusing it first. There would have been no advantage to the infusion of the brain.

The brain Dr. Humes removed from the cranium was infused. The appearance of the brain removed from the cranium at the Bethesda autopsy will be described in more detail in comments on the supplemental autopsy report.

Upon reflecting the scalp, multiple complete fracture lines are seen to radiate from both the large defect at the vertex and the smaller wound at the occiput. These vary greatly in length and direction. The longest measuring approximately 19 cm. These result in the production of numerous fragments which vary in size from a few millimeters to cm in greatest diameter.

The complexity of these fractures and the fragments thus produced, tax satisfactory verbal description and are better appreciated in photographs and roentgenograms which are prepared.

Received as separate specimens from Dallas, Texas are three fragments of skull bone which in the aggregate roughly approximate the dimensions of the large defect described above at one angle of the largest of these fragments is a portion of the perimeter of a roughly circular one presumably of exit which exhibits beveling of the outer aspects of the bone and is estimated to measure approximately 2.5 to 3.0 cm in diameter. Roentgenograms of this fragment reveal minute particles of metal in the bone at this margin. X-rays of the skull reveal multiple minute metal fragments along a line corresponding with a line joining the   above described small occipital wound and the right supraorbital ridge. From the surface of the disrupted right cerebral cortex two small irregular shaped fragments of metal are recovered. These measures 7 x 2 mm and 3 x 1 mm. These are placed in the custody of agents Francis X O'Neill Junior and James W. Sibert of the Federal Bureau of Investigation, who executed a receipt there for (attached).

Note:

These fragments were brought into the morgue late into the Bethesda autopsy, by an individual in a dark suit. These fragments were very small no more than a few millimeters and would not have been sufficient to cover the missing bone in the above described wound. The small twist tie bag which contained several small bone fragments and several small metal fragments, was placed on the table by the right ear. There was an attempt to fit these fragments into various fracture niches but by no means covered the area of missing bone. The bone received in the small twist tie bag was much less than the deficit of missing bone. I never saw the three bones described by Dr. Humes above nor did I ever observe any attempt to fit them in the area where the bone was missing. It should be noted that the autopsy report states that these three bone fragments were received from Dallas, but no time was given for the arrival at the morgue, in the autopsy report. It should be further noted that Dr. Humes stated that the three fragments approximated missing bone in the deficit. He, Dr. Humes, also gives the dimensions of one of these bone fragments as being 2.5 cm x 3 cm which is about 1" x 1.25." If this is the maximum size of the largest bone fragment and there were three bone fragments, then one can assume that the aggregate area of all three bone fragments was approximately 7.5 cm x 9 cm or about 3" x 3.6." The size of the missing area of bone described by me, Dr. McClelland and others at Parkland Hospital in Dallas, seems to be validated by Dr. Humes' own statement in the official autopsy report.

2. The second wound presumably of entry is that described above in the upper right posterior thorax. Beneath the skin there is ecchymosis of subcutaneous tissue and musculature. The missile path through the fascia and musculature cannot be easily probed. The wound presumably of exit was that described by Dr. Malcolm Perry of Dallas in the low anterior cervical region. When observed by Dr. Perry the wound measured "a few millimeters in diameter," however it was extended as a tracheotomy Incision and thus its characters distorted at the time of autopsy. However, there is considerable ecchymosis of the strap muscles of the right side of the neck and of the fascia above the trachea adjacent to the line of the

tracheostomy wound. The third point of reference in connecting these two wounds is in the apex (supra clavicular portion) of the right pleural cavity. In this region, there is contusion of the parietal flora and of the extreme apical portion of the right upper lobe of the lung in both instances the diameter of contusion and ecchymosis at the point of maximum involvement measures 5 cm. Both the visceral and parietal flora are intact overlying these areas of trauma.

These wounds are discussed above.

INCISIONS: scalp wounds are extended in the coronal plane to examine the cranial contents the customary (Y) shaped incision is used to examine the body cavities.

These coronal incisions could account for the flap seen on one of the autopsy photographs. The coronal extension of scalp lends support that the brain was removed by only extending scalp wounds.

THORACIC CAVITY:The body cage is unremarkable. Thoracic organs are in their normal position and relationship and there is no increase in free pleural fluid. The above description area of contusion in the apical portion of the right pleural cavity is noted.

LUNGS:The lungs are essentially similar appearance the right weighing 320 g, the left 290 g. The lungs are well aerated was smooth glistening pleural surfaces and gray pink color. A 5 cm diameter area of purplish red discoloration and increase firmness to palpitation is situated in the apical portion of the right upper lobe. This corresponds to the similar area described in the over allowing parietal pleural. Incision in this region reveals recent hemorrhage into pulmonary parenchyma.

The purplish red discoloration's location is discussed above.

HEART:The pericardial cavity is smooth walled and contains approximately 10 mL of straw colored fluid. The heart is of essentially normal external contour and weighs 350 g. The pulmonary artery is open in situ and no abnormalities are noted. The cardiac chambers contain moderate amounts of postmortem clotted blood. There are no gross abnormalities of the leaflets of any of the cardiac valves. The following are circumferences of the cardiac valves: aortic 7.5 cm full monic 7 cm tricuspid 12 cm mitral 11 cm. The myocardium is firm and reddish-brown. The left ventricular myocardium averages 1.2 cm in thickness, the right ventricular myocardium 0.4 cm. The coronary arteries are dissected and are of normal distribution and smooth wall and elastic throughout.

ABDOMINAL CAVITY: the abdominal organs are in their normal positions and relationships and there is no increase in free peritoneal fluid. The vermiform appendix is surgically absent and there are a few adhesions joining the region of the cecum to the ventral abdominal wall at the above described old abdominal incisional scar.

Note:

There is no mention of the atrophy and wasting of the adrenals as observed on the removed kidneys.

SKELETAL SYSTEM: Aside from the above described skull wounds there are no significant growth skeletal abnormalities.

ROENTGENOGRAMS: Roentgenograms are made of the entire body and of the separately submitted three fragments of skull bone, these are developed and were placed in the custody of agents Roy H Kellerman of the US Secret Service, who executed receipt therefor (attached).

SUMMARY: Based on the above observations it is our opinion that the deceased died as a result of two perforating gunshot wounds inflicted by high velocity projectiles fired by a person or persons unknown. The projectiles were fired from a point behind and somewhat above the level of the deceased. The observations and available information do not permit a satisfactory estimate as to the sequence of the two wounds.

The fatal missile entered skull above and to the right of the external occipital protuberance. A portion of the projectile transverse the cranial cavity and a posterior anterior direction (see lateral skull roentgenograms) deposited minute particles longest path. A portion of the projectile made its exit through the parietal bone on the right carrying with it portions of cerebrum, skull and scalp. The two wounds of the skull combined with the force of the missile produced extensive fragmentation of the skull, lacerations of this superior sagittal sinus and of the right cerebral hemisphere.

The other missile entered the right superior posterior thorax above the scapular and transverse the soft tissue of the supra scapula and the supraclavicular portions of the base of the right side of the neck. This missile produced contusions of the right apical parietal flora and of the apical portion of the right upper lobe of the lung. The missile contuses the strap muscles of the right side of the neck, damaging the trach and made it exit through the anterior surface of the neck. As far as can be ascertained this missile struck no bony structures in its path through the body.

In addition, it is our opinion that the wound of the skull produce such extensive damage to the brain as to preclude the possibility of the deceased surviving this injury.

Supplementary report will be submitted following more detail examination of the brain and of microscopic sections however, it is not anticipated that these examinations will materially alter the findings.

The above point discussions are based on what I observed and participated in during the autopsy. I was present at the right shoulder of the president's body during the entire autopsy with the exception when I left with Dr. Boswell to infuse the brain and examine the intestinal tract, and for a few minutes when Dr. Stover told me to grab a sandwich which accounted for no more than 15-20 minutes total. During this period, I was never out of sight of the autopsy proceedings. This is not to say that I saw everything that went on, but the extensive examinations needed to make some of the conclusions listed above would not have escaped my attention and probably would have required my assistance.

The following is included to give the reader a better understanding of the body wounds and their locations. Even though some of the materials discussed here have previously been presented in the discussion of the autopsy report, it is my hope that this section will bring more clarity to the reader.

HEAD WOUNDS

I guess the most controversial part of the presidents' autopsy is the head wound. The Dallas doctors' description of the large head wound supposedly the exit wound was different from what we saw at the Bethesda autopsy, or is it. The wound that Dr. McClelland described to me at a conference in Dallas appeared to be different from the initial appearance of the wound that I saw as it was being unwrapped during the President's autopsy, both in size and shape, until the scalp was reflected back from the wound. The location of the wound Dr. McClelland described would have been within the larger defect described by the Bethesda autopsy doctors in their autopsy report.

The head wounds seem to create the most controversy when being discussed. This is probably due to the differences between the Parkland doctor's descriptions of the wounds and the description of the wounds by the Bethesda autopsy doctors. It is also driven by the inconsistency of the autopsy doctors in later testimonies before various government investigative committees.

I first saw the head wound when Dr. Humes unwrapped the sheet and towel from the head. The wound was adhered to the towel-like material by dried blood and fluids and gaped open along a laceration that ran forward toward the anterior portion of the head, which immediately closed after the wrappings were separated from the head-wound gore. The scalp was torn and macerated with fractured bone fragments still clinging to the scalp. The entire area was covered with matted hair and dried blood. This made it difficult to determine the true extent of the wound. This made it appeared to be a massive "blowout" of the back of the head, but after the scalp was reflected back from the skull, the wound that had missing scalp and bone appeared to be more consistent with the shape and dimensions previously described by Dr. McClelland.

The wound, missing bone and scalp, was a large gaping wound in the occipital-parietal area of the right posterior side of the head. It looked to be about 2.5 to 3 inches (5 to 7 cm) by 1.5 to 2 inches (3 to 5 cm) in size with a rounded border at the top traveling downward in an elongated, rectangular/triangular shape with irregular margins. This irregular shape made it difficult to approximate the true diminutions of the missing bone area. This area was better defined when the scalp was reflected back from the skull. There was also a laceration of the scalp extending anteriorly from the upper frontal area of the wound (missing bone and scalp area) parallel to the sagittal suture, midline of the skull, and ending slightly past the coronal suture almost into the frontal bone. This scalp laceration closely followed underlying fracture lines of the skull. The scalp laceration resembled the other tears in the scalp created by the bullet, with one exception, there seemed to be neat, clean connections between several tears as if the tears had been surgically connected. This was the area that prompted Dr. Humes to ask someone in the gallery if there had been any surgery performed at Parkland Hospital in Dallas. Dr. Humes was told there had been no surgery at Parkland.

The 2.5 to 3 inches (5 to 7 cm) by 1.5 to 2 inches (3 to 5 cm) is not consistent with the description of 13cms (5+inches) which appears in the official autopsy report or the 17/19 cms (6.7/7.6 inches) described by Dr. Boswell in later testimony. The wound described in the autopsy report is more consistent with the appearance of the wound after the fracture lines and tears of the scalp and skull had been surgically extended and a coronal incision had been made to remove the brain by Dr. Humes as described to Dr. Fink by Dr. Humes. This is supported by Dr. Finks' report to Gen. Blumberg, when he, Dr. Fink, says that Dr. Humes told him that he, Dr. Humes, only had to extend some of the tears in the scalp, which were holding the fractured skull together, in order to remove the brain. I believe that Dr. Fink was present in the morgue when the head was unwrapped, which makes the Blumberg report questionable. I am sure he was present in the morgue before the brain was removed because the brain was still in the cranium when he, Dr. Fink and Dr Humes found the right temple wound. This supports Dr. Humes' statement that he only had to extend scalp tears to remove the brain.

I think it is only fair to say that my given measurements 2.5 to 3 inches (5 to 7 cm) by 1.5 to 2 inches (3 to 5 cm) of the wound, missing bone and scalp area, are approximations and not measured ones, even though the difference between 3 inches and 5 inches is obvious to most people. My given measurements also approximated more closely the diminutions given by Dr. McClelland at Parkland as he observed the wound in the emergency room than those listed in the official autopsy report.

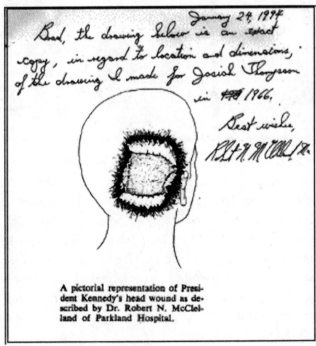

A pictorial representation of President Kennedy's head wound as described by Dr. Robert N. McClelland of Parkland Hospital.

This is the wound drawing that Dr. McClelland made to illustrate the wound he saw at Parkland in 1963. This closely matches the wound that I saw after the scalp was retracted from the skull. The area shown was the area where both bone and scalp were missing. While some bone was separated from the scalp as it was being refracted, you could still readily see the true area where there was an absence of bone and scalp. My original thought when I first saw this drawing was that the wound appeared to be a little more caudal, toward the neck, and lateral than the wound seen at autopsy. This may be perception on my part due to the slightly turned head in the drawing. The position of the wound in the drawing correlates well with the wound that I saw at autopsy after the scalp was retracted.

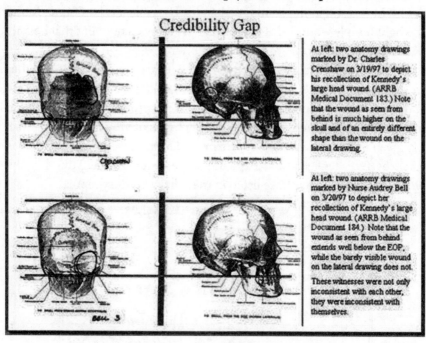

Credibility Gap

At left: two anatomy drawings marked by Dr. Charles Crenshaw on 3/19/97 to depict his recollection of Kennedy's large head wound. (ARRB Medical Document 183.) Note that the wound as seen from behind is much higher on the skull and of an entirely different shape than the wound on the lateral drawing.

At left: two anatomy drawings marked by Nurse Audrey Bell on 3/20/97 to depict her recollection of Kennedy's large head wound. (ARRB Medical Document 184.) Note that the wound as seen from behind extends well below the EOP, while the barely visible wound on the lateral drawing does not.

These witnesses were not only inconsistent with each other, they were inconsistent with themselves.

The above placement of wounds by Dr. Crenshaw and Ms. Audrey Bell for the record review board demonstrates a variance that one can see as individuals review and remember specific events. The top two placements of the head wound by Dr. Crenshaw more closely correlate with the location of the wound seen at autopsy after the scalp was reflected. Though there seems to be a conflict between the placement at the rear of the skull and the attempt to place the wound on the lateral or side of the skull. I believe this conflict is due to the difficulty of observing an irregular wound on the posterior portion of the skull and trying to relate that to its appearance from the lateral view.

The bottom drawings are those in which Ms. Audrey Bell attempted to place the head wounds. While the drawing on the left that depicts the head, wound appears to be more caudal, toward the bottom of the head, than that seen at autopsy. I believe the conflict described above is relative to the same difficulty that accounted for the conflict by Dr. Crenshaw. While Ms. Bell's placement of the wound at the back of the head appears to be lower than that seen in autopsy it is difficult to place a wound that is primarily in the posterior of the skull from the lateral view. The difficulty arises due to the skull being rounded and that the wound would probably have a different appearance from the lateral (side) view.

I would like again to remind the reader that the three individuals above had no opportunity to actually measure the defect of the wound and are only describing what they saw in very tense and dramatic circumstances.

There's been much discussion about the head wound by Douglas Horne in his interview with William Law. In this interview he (Horne) is adamant about the surgery to the head and believes that the surgery was done in the morgue by Dr. Humes and Dr. Boswell. The only problem with this theory is that I was present in the morgue all of the time from approximately 3:30PM Friday until 9:00AM Saturday, the following morning. If Dr. Humes and Dr. Boswell did Mr. Horne's "illicit" surgery then it would have had to have been done outside the morgue at another facility prior to 6:35PM, which is the time the body arrived at the morgue as given by Dennis David and collaborated by Sgt. Boyajian's action report which was later supported by William Law's conversation with Dr. Jay Cox, the Officer of the Day for the Bethesda Hospital. I have no direct knowledge of whether Dr. Humes or Dr. Boswell performed Mr. Horne's "illicit" surgery. The only thing that I know for sure is that it was not done in the Bethesda morgue between 3:30 PM and 9:00 AM the following morning, though I agree with Mr. Horne that the wounds were examined somewhere between Parkland and Bethesda.

Supplemental Autopsy:

Following Formalin Fixation, The Brain Weighs 1500 G.

The weight of 1500 g is approximately normal weight for an average human brain. This causes conflict with several witnesses who stated that there was up to 1/3 of the brain missing and some that say there was no brain at all.

131

The Right Cerebral Hemisphere Is Found to Be Markedly Disrupted. There Is A Longitudinal Laceration of The Right Hemisphere Which Is Pari-Sagittal and Positioned Approximately 2.5 Cm to The Right of the Midline Which Extends from The Tip of The Occipital Lobe Posteriorly to The Tip of The Frontal Lobe Anteriorly. The Base of The Laceration Situated Approximately 4.5 Cm Below the Vertex in The White Matter. There Is Considerable Loss of Cortical Substance Above the Base of The Laceration, Particularly in The Parietal Lobe. The Margins of This Laceration Are Association All Points Jagged and Irregular, With Additional Lacerations Extended in Varying Directions and For Varying Distances from The Main Laceration. In addition, There Is A Laceration of The Corpus Callosum Extending from The Genu to The Tail. Exposing This Latter Laceration Are the Interiors of The Right Lateral and Third Ventricles.

When Viewed from The Vertex Left Cerebral Hemisphere Is Intact. There Is Markedly Engorgement of Meningeal Blood Vessels of The Left Temporal and Frontal Regions with Considerable Associated Sub-Arachnoid Hemorrhage. The Gyri and Sulci Over the Left Hemisphere Are Essentially Normal Size and Distribution Those on The Right Are Too Fragmented and Distorted for Satisfactory Description.

When Viewed from The Basilar Aspect the Disruption of The Right Cortex Is Again Obvious. There Is A Longitudinal Laceration of The Mid-Brain Through the Floor of The Third Ventricle Just Behind the Optic Chiasm and The Mammillary Bodies. This Laceration Partially Communicates with An Oblique 1.5 Cm Tear Through the Left Cerebral Peduncle There Are Regulars Superficial Lacerations Over the Basilar Aspects of The Left Temporal and Frontal Lobes.

The above description of the damage to the brain would be readily discernible on first observation. The above states that the right cerebral hemisphere is severely damaged and that there is a longitudinal laceration that is parallel to the top of the brain. This laceration is located approximately 2.5 cm (1in) to the right side of the midline extending approximately 4.5 cm (1.8 in) through the gray matter into the underlying white matter. The description additionally states there is a considerable loss of cortical substance above the base (bottom) of the laceration. This statement would lead you to assume that a large portion of the right side of the brain was missing, which would support the descriptions of the Dallas Doctors and possibility support Paul O'Connor's and Jim Sibert's statement that there was no brain. This was not the description of the brain that was removed at the Bethesda autopsy.

The report further describes damage to the interior structures, a laceration of the Corpus Callosum from the genu to the tail (front to back) which exposes through the interiors of the right lateral and third ventricles. These structures are deep internal structures of the brain and would be exposed only by extensive damage of the brain.

I have serious questions about this description. First, the weight given for the brain is slightly above the 1200 grams to 1300 grams of the average adult brain. How could there be a considerable loss of cortical substance above the base of the described longitudinal laceration and still maintain a brain weight of greater than average. Some may argue that the weigh could be the result of an inadequate fixation with not enough time to equilibrate. This could well account for the weight given if the President's brain had suffered the extensive damage described above and had then been placed in formalin without infusion and autopsied two or three days later without adequate time to equilibrate. We usually infused the brains that we took at autopsy before they were placed in formalin. This procedure produced a faster and more through fixation and equilibration than the usual submersion in a container of buffered formalin for 7-10 days.

The above discussion of the left side of the brain tells us that the massive damage seen on the right was not seen on the left side of the brain. There was only engorgement of blood vessels and considerable subarachnoid bleeding. It also tells us that the gyri and sulci, the convolutions of the brain surface, on the left side are essentially of normal size and distribution and those on the right side were too damaged to describe.

The last description we are given is the appearance from the basilar (bottom) of the brain. The damage seen in the right lateral and third ventricles can also be seen through a laceration in the floor of the third ventricle. There is also a description of a small tear in the left cerebral peduncle.

You may be wondering why I have gone over this already published information. I have done this to prepare you for the information that I am about to discuss. This is not a description of the brain that was removed from the President's body by Dr. Humes, given to Dr. Boswell and which I attempted to insert the infusion needles to fix the brain. A brain in this condition would not have benefited from the infusion technique due to the massive disruption of the vascular system of the brain. The infiltration of the brain tissue would have been just as effective by immersing it in a container of formalin due to the vast area of cellular tissue that would have been exposed by the massive trauma as described in the above supplemental autopsy report. The massive disruption

133

as described in this report would not have allowed the retention in the brains vasculature long enough to have been effective.

In the Interest of Preserving This Specimen Coronal Sections Are Not Made. The following sections are taken for Microscopic Examination:

A. From the Margin of The Laceration in The Right Parietal Lobe.

B. From the Margin of The Laceration in The Corpus Callosum.

C. From the Anterior Portion of The Laceration in The Right Frontal Lobe

D. From the Contusion Left Fronto-Parietal Cortex.

E. From the Line of Transection of The Spinal Cord

F. From the Right Cerebellar Cortex.

G. From the Superficial Laceration of The Basilar Aspect of The Left Temporal Lobe.

During the Course of This Examination Seven (7) Black-And-White and Six (6) Color 4 X 5" Negatives Are Exposed but Not Developed (The Cassettes Containing These Negatives Have Been Delivered by Hand to Rear Adm. George W Burkley MC, USN White House Physician)

MICROSCOPIC EXAMINATION:

BRAIN:
Multiple Sections from Representative Areas as Noted Above Are Examined. All Sections Are Essentially Similar and Show Extensive Disruption of Brain Tissue Was Associated Hemorrhage. And None of The Sections Examined Are There Significant Abnormalities Other Than Those Directly Related to The Recent Trauma.

LUNGS:
Sections Through the Grossly Described Area of Contusion in The Right Upper Lobe Exhibits Disruption of Alveolar Walls and Recent Hemorrhage into The Alveoli. Sections Are Otherwise Essentially Unremarkable.

LIVER:
Section Show the Normal Hepatic Architecture to Be Well Preserved. The Parenchymal cells Exhibit Markedly Granular Cytoplasm Indicating High Glycogen Content Which Is Characteristic of the "Liver Biopsy Pattern" of Sudden Death.

SPLEEN:
Sections show no significant abnormalities.

KIDNEYS:
Sections show no significant abnormalities aside from dilation and engorgement of blood vessels of all calibers.

The adrenals are not mentioned.

SKIN WOUNDS:
Sections through the wounds in the occipital and upper right posterior thoracic regions are essentially similar. In each there is loss of continuity of the epidermis with coagulation necrosis of the tissues at the wound margins. The scalp wound exhibits several small fragments of bone at its margins in the subcutaneous tissue.

FINAL SUMMARY:
This supplementary report covers in more detail the extensive degree of cerebral trauma in this case. However, neither this portion of the examination nor the microscopic examination alter the previously submitted report or add significant details to the cause of death.

Autopsy photos:

I've been asked many times about the Fox photographs that are seen today in the public domain. It's difficult for me to comment on these photographs because none of them seem to be consistent with my memories of the body in the Bethesda morgue that night. There seems to be inconsistencies in all of the photographs which make me believe that theys may not have been taken during the Bethesda autopsy.

During the discussions, I will attempt to point out the inconsistencies which conflict with my memories of the morgue.

001 (picture on next page)

It appears that the scalp has been pulled up and stretched in an attempt to cover the wound. I remember an attempt to see if the scalp could be stretched to cover the wound. The stretched scalp covered the wound with the exception of an area a little larger than that of an old-style silver dollar.

The neck and ear seem to still be covered with the gore from the head wound while the hair is devoid of the bloody matting, that was seen when the head was first unwrapped.

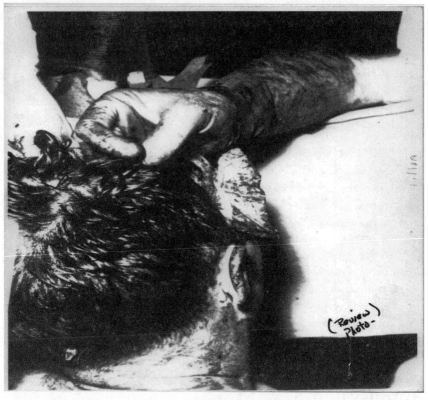

My third comment concerns the whitish tag-like spot located in the lower part of the head in the hair line. Many have identified this as an entry wound in the head as described in the official autopsy report. It appears to me that the protruding tissue could possibly be from the fatty tissue layer beneath the scalp. The protrusion of this tissue could indicate that it was pushed from the inside to the outside by the exit of a fragment rather than the entry of a bullet. I enter this possibility only as a thought, because I never saw the back-entry head wound described in the official autopsy report though I had ample opportunity when we were moving the head for placement of the x-rays plates.

As in most of the fox photographs, the anatomical reference points are masked. While I cannot say definitely that this is a photograph taken at the Bethesda autopsy, the horns of an autopsy head chock are seen just above the gloved hand holding the scalp up. This was the type of head chock used at our routine autopsies.

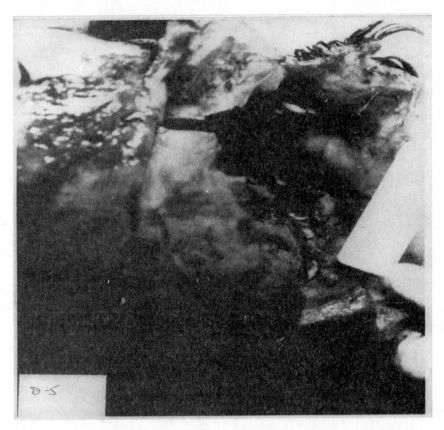

D-5

002

This photograph has been termed the "mystery photo" because of the difficulty in orientation due to the lack of visible anatomical points. While I believe this is a photo of the posterior head wound after the brain was removed and the scalp was reflected from the wound I cannot be sure. The wound seems to be larger than when I first saw it when the head was unwrapped. I believe that the original wound with the missing bone and scalp could still be defined within this larger deficit. It also seems that the rear-entry head wound would also fall within this area. I feel that the larger appearance was caused by bone fragments separated from the scalp as the scalp was reflected. Another contribution to the larger deficit would be the incisions connecting scalp laceration when the brain was removed.

I have talked with Dr. Chesser about this photo and the lack of my ability to orient it. Dr. Chesser has tried to help with my orientation but I am still not comfortable with my ability to do so. Dr. Chesser has been allowed to view the photos in the National Archives which I have been refused. Dr. Chesser has been able to orient the photograph from discernable anatomical points seen on the original photographs.

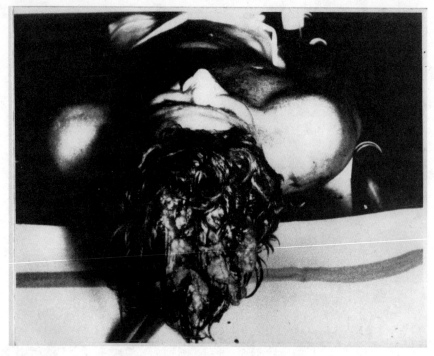

003

This photograph shows a wound that appears to cross the sagittal suture, midline, into the left side of the head. The wound proper did not cross the midline with the exception of maybe a few spider like radiating hairline fracture line.

The brain tissue seen in the above photograph appears to have normal convolutions with no maceration. In the area of the head wound the brain had some damage but not to the extent you would expect judging from the damage seen with the head wound.

There also appears to be some kind of structure over the body if that is a dissection table or a mayo instrument stand this is not a photograph taken in the Bethesda morgue during the autopsy. In this photograph there is no sign that the autopsy of the body has started. I only placed the dissection board over the table after the body cavity had been opened and we were ready to remove the body organs.

The above leads me to believe that this photograph may have been taken some other place and the object over the table was an instrument tray.

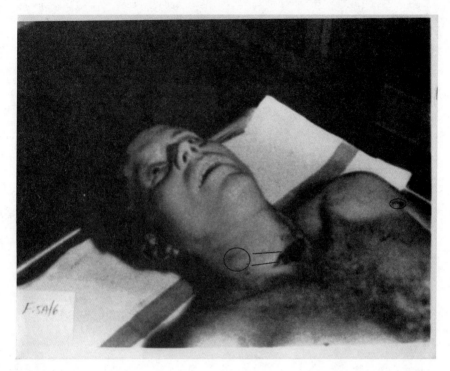

004

This photograph like the others presents questions for me. I watched Dr. Humes unwrap the head and I never saw this death stare on the face of the President's face. As previously discussed the left eye was closed and the right eyes was slightly open which the mortician closed with a small suture under the lid. The lips were slightly open.

As I viewed this photograph, I noticed a raised area on the throat parallel to the Adam's apple (circled area on side of neck). Upon closer scrutiny, this appears to be possibly something inside the tissue of the neck, a bullet or fragment from the throat wound which was described by Dr. Malcolm Oliver Perry in Dallas as an entry wound. If one looks closely, it appears that there could be the imprint of a tunneling from the right side of the throat wound, where Dr. Perry described the entry wound over which he did the tracheotomy, to the raised area on the neck.

The second notable mark seen in this photograph is on the left shoulder. I am unsure as to what this mark is and I use it only to make the case that if any of these marks had been found during the initial examination of the body in the Bethesda morgue, they would have been listed on the face sheet Dr. Boswell and I completed.

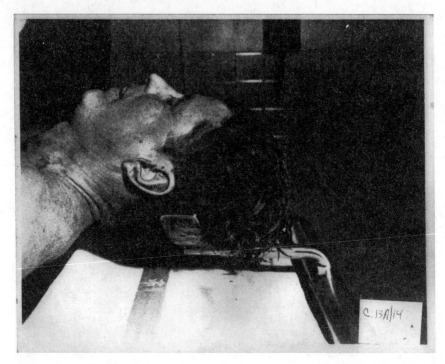

005

In the above photograph, you see the head being held in a metal cradle that is attached to the head of presumably the Bethesda autopsy table. This cradle not only seems to elevate the head but also the shoulders above the table. There also appears to be a wrinkling of the neck in the back as if the head had been pulled backwards from the body and it appears in this photograph that the body is so rigid, due to rigor mortis, that the elevation of the head also elevates the shoulder and upper chest. I remember that Dr. Fink and Dr. Humes were able to elevate the upper body to a partially sitting position as they were probing the back wound. During the initial face sheet examination, Dr. Boswell and I also had no difficulties related to an extreme rigor mortis as depicted in this photograph.

There are other things about this photograph that make me question if it was taken in the Bethesda morgue during the autopsy. I have no memories of such a metal cradle being used to support the head during any of the autopsies that I assisted with. I am not sure if the autopsy table had a place to attach such a head rest and I do not remember a telephone on that side wall. The telephone I remember was located by the deep sink just inside the passageway leading to the tissue room, linen room and the locker room in the back of the morgue. I specifically remember the location of the telephone because it had an extremely long curly cord to allow it to reach anywhere in the morgue proper. The tele-

phone on the wall does not appear to have the same definition as the wall tiles. It somewhat looks as if it was superimposed on the wall.

The discussion of the differences in the areas of the hair and other photographic anomalies seen in these photographs, I will leave to others which are more qualified in photography than I am.

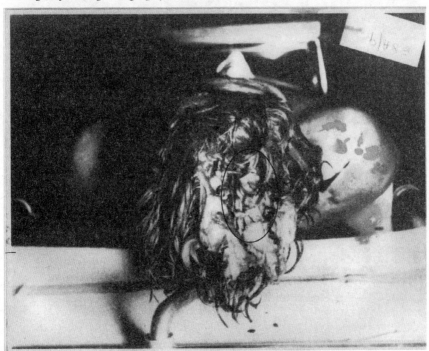

006

This photograph seems to be a close-up of the head wound seen in photograph 003. The area of brain tissue discussed is better defined in the circle shown in this time. The chest and body are not shown as in the number 003 photograph but the object over the table is better defined. My previous conclusion that this photograph was not taken during the Bethesda autopsy is further strengthened by this photograph.

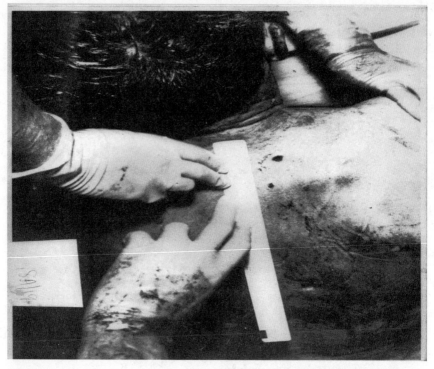

007

This photograph is of the back wound that was located at the apex of the scapular midway between the scapular and spinal column. In this photo the true location is difficult to see because the apex, top, of the scapula seems to be obscured by a bright light. The top wound seems to be higher in the back than it really was because the neck seems to be pushed backwards. The wound appears to be in the approximate location seen at autopsy and placed on the face sheet.

CHAPTER FOURTEEN

THE THREE CASKETS

The next entry is to answer questions that I am often asked concerning the caskets, to which I have to answer, "I had no hands-on and therefore have vague fragmented memories of the caskets."

The discussion of the caskets that came into the morgue the night of the autopsy presents some difficulty for me. I have distinct, but sometimes incomplete memories of three different caskets being in the morgue that night.

The first was the casket that the president's body arrived in. This memory was striking in that this casket appeared to be a common transport casket, not one that you would expect a president's body to arrive in. I remember this casket being brought just inside the morgue from the anteroom, where the cold boxes were located, and placed on the floor. My memory is that the body was removed from the casket, placed on a gurney and brought to the front table. This is a tentative memory because I didn't directly participate in the removal of the body from the casket or transporting it to the front table. Paul O'Connor, my counterpart, was directly involved in this process. Paul says that the casket was brought into the morgue and placed on the floor and the body was moved directly to the table from the casket. In our normal movement of bodies from the anteroom to the autopsy table, we would place the body on a gurney and move the gurney to the autopsy table, this may account for the possibility that my memory is merging the normal event with the event in the morgue that night.

The second casket that I remember from that night was a burial casket that was pushed up against the cold boxes in the anteroom. This casket was a highly polished high-end burial casket reddish in color. The colors in these descriptions may be biased due to my red-green color blindness that gives me problems with different hues of reds which often appear as shades of brown and greens that often appear as shades of gray. When I first noticed this casket, I asked the First- Class Hospital Corpsman, who

I believe was the duty Chief of the Day for the laboratory, about the casket and was told that the casket contained an Air Force major who was to be buried in Arlington the next day and had arrived too late to be received there. He said we were going to hold the casket for burial the next day. As I learned later, there are no military burials at Arlington on the weekends and the next day was Saturday.

This second casket is the one that holds the most uncertainty for me. In 2015 I attended a meeting in Chicago organized by Phil Singer and William Law. Phil had been able to find several of the Honor Guard members and had invited them along with me, Dennis David, Jim Metzler and several others to meet and discuss the arrival of the casket at the Bethesda morgue. After talking with the honor guard members and hearing their account of the casket arrival, I had come to accept that this was probably the casket that the honor guard removed from the Navy ambulance and brought to the anteroom door as described by several members of the honor guard at the conference. I have a vague memory of the head of a casket entering through the morgue doors from the hall into the ante-room with two members of the honor guard. I don't remember if the casket was brought into the ante-room or if it was just pushed through the doors. At the time, I was busy working with the doctors at the autopsy table. I could see the double doors that entered the ante-room from the hallway through the door that connected the ante-room to the morgue. It was just a cursory glance. During a later discussion with Hugh Clark, one of the Honor Guard members, I was able to identify the Honor Guard members that I saw with the casket entering the morgue door as James Felder(Army) and Tim Cheek (Marine).

While I now believe that the unclear memory described above is related to the casket that the honor guard removed from the Navy ambulance and brought to the morgue, I cannot be positive that the casket I saw pushed up against the cold boxes in the ante-room is the same casket that the honor guard delivered to the morgue. Never-the-less, I can say that the casket delivered to the morgue did not contain the President's body. The autopsy had begun some time before that delivery.

While reviewing some tape sessions of the Dallas conference organized by Harry Livingstone and a session in New York organized by Rick Russo I stated that my memory of the arrival of the casket that I saw against the cold boxes was prior to the arrival of the casket with the President's body. If this is the case, then the casket that Paul and I saw in the ante-room against the cold boxes cannot possibly have been the casket that was removed from the Navy ambulance by the honor guard. This may also give some credence to some researchers' "musical chairs" scenario of caskets, necessary to cover the multiple reported entrances of caskets into the morgue.

While I cannot say that my original memory of the arrival of the casket that was in the ante-room against the cold boxes was in error or that recent conversations with Dennis David and the honor guard member have influenced my current thoughts. I can say that the President's body was brought into the morgue in a shipping/transport type of casket and the body never left the morgue after it was placed on the autopsy table. The caskets could have been removed and replaced while I was busy with the body in the morgue proper, but if that was the case there would have been a lot of witnesses.

The last casket is one that I have a very explicit memory of, this was the casket that the President's body was placed in and removed from the morgue by the honor guard after the autopsy had ended and the mortician had finished preparing the body for burial. This casket was a large ornate mahogany burial casket appropriate to contain the body of the President of the United States. It was brought into the morgue sometime around midnight by Gawler's Funeral Home personnel and after the mortician had finished preparing the body, Paul and I helped the mortician dress the body and with the help of several others present, we placed the President's body in the casket. The casket was closed, and the Honor Guard removed it from the morgue.

The reader can get a better description of the transport casket that the body arrived in by reading Paul O'Connor's description given to and published by several research authors. Paul would have gotten a better view of the casket because he was directly involved in the removal of the body from that casket. I only saw the casket from a distance and was struck by the fact that it seemed to be an ordinary shipping casket.

CHAPTER FIFTEEN

Research of Michael Chesser, M.D. – After the Neurology-Radiology conference in Little Rock, I was intrigued with the information that Dr. Chesser gained from his viewings at the National Archives. I feel that it is critically important and this information should be presented to the general public. I hesitated to ask Dr. Chesser to share this information and was pleasantly surprised when he enthusiastically agreed to write this chapter, for which I am very grateful.

THE CRANIAL AUTOPSY X-RAYS AND PHOTOGRAPHS
MICHAEL CHESSER, M.D.

I would like to thank James Jenkins for asking me to contribute to this book. I met James at the JFK Lancer meeting in Dallas in 2015, and I enjoyed visiting with him, as we have much in common, growing up in the South, and serving in Navy medicine. I was initially awed by his experience at the autopsy of the President, and since getting to know him, I've found him to be a very humble, intelligent, and thoughtful man. He is clear headed, and not prone to exaggeration or embellishment. I know that he loves his country, as I do, and I believe that his story is incredibly important for our nation's history, and for future generations to be able to understand the events of November 22nd, 1963.

I'm always curious about the various reasons that people have for their interest in the assassination, so I'll briefly tell about my reasons. In James Jenkins' case, he had no choice in the matter, as he was under orders in the Navy. In my case, I volunteered for this, which might cause some to question my sanity. My interest goes back to childhood, when President Kennedy was one of my heroes, knowing about his courage in rescuing his shipmate after PT 109 was sunk. Later in life I realized how his policies, both domestic and international, were transformational, and it took an unbelievable amount of courage for him to propose many of these policies in the early 60's. After reading *JFK and the Unspeakable*, by James

Douglass, I was so curious that I attended the conference on the 50th anniversary of the Warren Commission conference in Bethesda, Maryland, in 2013. Many of the attendees there encouraged me to try and view the autopsy materials, after they found out that I'm a neurologist. I was eventually approved, and I made three visits to the National Archives II in College Park, Maryland, where the autopsy materials are stored.

This review will focus only on the head wounds, primarily focusing on the autopsy x-rays, and a brief review of the photographs. I would like to approach these images for what they tell us, separately from the eyewitness accounts from Parkland and Bethesda.

If there is *only one thing* that you know about the medical evidence, it should be this – two government sponsored medical panels overruled the military pathologists who performed the autopsy at Bethesda, and they moved the location of the skull entry wound from the lower occipital area over 4 inches up to the posterior parietal area (figure 1). Let that sink in – the military pathologists who saw the skull and brain, and explored the wounds during the autopsy, were told that they were wrong. They were told that they could not possibly have recorded the correct entry location in the back of the skull, and the entry location was moved up four and a half inches, to the top of the back of the skull. The two government-sponsored medical panels were the Clark Panel, in 1967, and the medical panel for the House Select Committee on Assassinations, which followed suit a decade later. There is no way that the importance of this can be overstated. How can a group of physicians overrule the pathologists who examined the body? What this tells us is that there was something seriously wrong with the medical evidence. I will try to describe this in more detail, and I will try to explain why I think the pathologists were overruled, and why they were told that they could not believe what their eyes told them. I will show why a standard forensic analysis of these skull x-rays shows that a minimum of 2 bullets struck the skull of the President, with the first striking the right lower occiput, and the second striking high in the right frontal region, in an area which was covered by hair and would have been easily missed by the Parkland ER team.

I reviewed the purported original cranial autopsy x-rays of President Kennedy, and the computer enhanced x-rays produced for the House Select Committee on Assassinations in 1978, at the National Archives II on April 22, 2015. I reviewed the original 1960 skull x-ray at the Presidential Library near Boston, where it is labeled as a sinus x-ray. Permission to view the autopsy films was granted by former Senator Paul Kirk, the attorney representing the Kennedy family, pursuant to the Deed of Gift of the autopsy materials.[1] Three skull x-rays (AP, right lateral, left lateral) have been stored in a temperature and humidity-controlled environment and are in fairly good condition. The x-ray images included with this review (Images 2,3,5-7) were published in the report of the House Select Committee on Assassinations in 1978[2]. My review of the x-ray films revealed details which are not visible on these public images. This review will document the differences between the actual films and the attached images, and lastly will include my conclusions.

The autopsy of President Kennedy was performed in the morgue of the Bethesda Naval Hospital during the evening of November 22nd, 1963. Commander James J. Humes, the lead pathologist for the autopsy, testified to the Warren Commission that the skull x-rays were made before the autopsy examination began. He stated that "before the postmortem examination was begun, anterior, posterior and lateral x-rays of the head, and of the torso were made"[3].

Dr. James H. Ebersole was the radiologist on duty during the autopsy, and the radiologic technicians were hospital corpsmen Jerrol F. Custer and Edward F. Reed[4]. There was no professional interpretation of the skull x-rays published with the Warren Report. The autopsy report notes only that the x-rays were placed into the custody of the U.S. Secret Service following the autopsy[5]. They were later given to the President's brother, Robert Kennedy, in 1965.

Edward Reed, the junior ranking of the x-ray techs, testified that he alone took the skull x-rays, and that he took a lateral and then an AP (anterior to posterior) x-ray of the skull[6], and that only two skull x-rays were taken during the autopsy. Jerrol F. Custer testified that he took a total of 5 skull x-rays (AP, two laterals, and two oblique films)[7]. Dr. Ebersole stated that there were 5 or 6 skull x-rays taken during the autopsy[8]. The reason

---

1. Archives HSCA Record No. 180-10001-10103; Letter from Burke Marshall to General Services Administration 29 Oct 1966.
2. Investigation of the Assassination of President John F. Kennedy; Hearings before the Select Committee on Assassinations of the U.S. House of Representatives; 95th Congress; Second session. 6 Sept 1978; Volume I; pages 239-244.
3. Report of The President's Commission on The Assassination Of President Kennedy; United States Government Printing Office; Warren Report, Volume II, page 349. 1964.
4. Warren Report, Volume II, page 8. 1964.
5. Warren Report, Appendix IX – Autopsy Report and Supplemental Report, page 5. 1964.
6. Assassinations Records Review Board, Testimony of Edward F. Reed, 21 Oct 1997, page 40.
7. Assassinations Records Review Board, Testimony of Jerrol Francis Custer, 28 Oct 1997, page 88.
8. Inside the Assassination Records Review Board; Horne, Douglas; Vol. II, page 418.

for the discrepancy between the number of skull x-rays taken versus the number transferred with the collection is not known.

The conclusion of the Warren Report was that a single bullet struck the skull, with entrance over the right lower occipital region, adjacent to the external occipital protuberance, and it exited in the region of the stephanion on the right side[9]. The first professional interpretation of the skull x-rays was provided by Russell H. Morgan, M.D., for the Clark Panel[10], which was appointed by Attorney General Ramsey Clark in response to criticism of the autopsy report. The Clark Panel inventory lists one AP skull x-ray and two left lateral skull x-rays. Dr. Morgan interpreted the x-rays as showing an entrance wound approximately 100 mm above the external occipital protuberance, and 25 mm to the right of midline. He identified a 6.5 mm metallic object visible on the AP x-ray, and he thought that this same object was visible on the right lateral x-ray, embedded in the outer table of the skull, adjacent to the entry. He postulated that the bullet fragmented and produced a large bony defect of the right frontal and parietal skull, with the defect extending approximately 25 mm across the midline to involve the left parietal skull.

The House Select Committee on Assassinations (HSCA) performed computer enhancement of the skull x-rays at the Aerospace Corporation in California in 1978, with the assistance of Gerald M. McDonnel, M.D., radiologist[11]. Dr. McDonnel concurred with the Clark Panel report that there was evidence of a single entry wound which he placed 96 mm above the external occipital protuberance. He agreed with Dr. Morgan regarding the 6.5 mm metallic object visible on the AP film. David O. Davis, M.D. reviewed the films for the HSCA and he also described the entry as located in the parietal bone, 90 to 100 mm above the external occipital protuberance. He was not able to positively identify the 6.5 mm metallic object on the lateral films[12]. He disagreed that this same 6.5 mm object, proposed to be a cross-section of the bullet that struck the skull, could be seen on the lateral x-rays.

To obtain approval to view the original autopsy x-rays and photographs, one must request permission from the attorney who represents

---

9. Stephanion: the point on the skull where the temporal line crosses the coronal suture.
10. 1968 Panel Review of Photographs, X-Ray Films, Documents and other Evidence Pertaining to the Fatal Wounding of President John F. Kennedy on November 22, 1963, in Dallas, Texas.
11. House Select Committee on Assassinations Report, Volume 1, pp 204-207. Dr. McDonnel was in private practice of radiology at the time of the HSCA, and teaching Defense Medicine at UCLA. He had been an Army radiologist in the 50's and early 60's and was the physician in charge of animal testing associated with nuclear weapons testing.
12. HSCA Report, Volume 1, pp 200-203.

the Kennedy family for the materials covered by the Deed of Gift. When I first heard of the Deed of Gift, I assumed that these materials were in fact a gift to the Archives. My assumption could not have been further from the truth. In 1965 the Justice Department, under Attorney General Nicholas Katzenbach, drafted House Resolution 9545, which required the transfer of the autopsy material and other assassination related materials to the National Archives. This bill was approved by Congress and became public bill 89-318. Robert Kennedy was "not sympathetic" to requests to turn the autopsy materials over to the Archives[13]. He was not allowed to keep this material privately, and he eventually had to turn over all of the autopsy materials in his possession.

I am not privy to the relationship between the Deed of Gift attorney and the Kennedy family, or between same attorney and the Archives personnel. I certainly don't blame the Kennedy family for these restrictions. But I do know that when these x-rays and photographs were placed into the Archives, and then access was restricted according to the Deed of Gift, the net effect was to severely restrict access. In addition, by placing them under the Deed of Gift, they are deemed private materials, and are not subject to Freedom of Information laws. To view this material one must first have the professional qualifications outlined in the Deed of Gift, and then demonstrate a specific reason for viewing the material. Very few people are even aware that the x-rays and photographs might be viewed, and then, the topic of the assassination remains so politically charged that very few physicians want to get involved. As a result, I was told by Archives personnel that there are many years in which the original films are not taken out of cold storage.

I requested to view the original skull x-rays and was approved, based upon my qualifications as a neurologist with an interest in the assassination. Actually, my first request was to view all of the x-rays and photographs, and the request was denied. I then narrowed my request to view only the skull x-rays, and Senator Kirk stated that I must have a specific reason for viewing them. I listed the primary goals of the viewing as repeating the optical density measurements of the x-rays, which had previously been done by Dr. David Mantik, and to measure the sella turcica, the bony "cave" which houses the pituitary gland. The sella turcica appeared to be enlarged on the images which were placed in the HSCA report. I was then approved to view the original skull x-rays only.

I spent one morning in April of 2015 viewing the x-rays and working with the Archives staff to take measurements of the film with an optical

---

13. HSCA Report, Appendix, Volume VII, page 28.

densitometer, to compare with the previous measurements made by Dr. Mantik. The optical densitometer has been used for quality control of x-ray film, and Dr. Mantik, with his background in physics and radiation oncology, came up with the idea to use the densitometer to compare the relative density of different areas of the autopsy x-rays.

The person viewing the x-rays at the Archives is never allowed to touch the actual film, and the x-rays are enclosed in a thin, perfectly clear mylar covering. The Archives personnel handle the film at all times, and there was a minimum of two people, and usually three, looking over my shoulder while viewing the films. In addition to dictating my findings, I was allowed to take notes and draw with pencil and paper supplied by the Archives. No photographs may be taken of these x-rays or of the autopsy photographs.

This may be redundant, but in this review, I will be reviewing the appearance of the x-ray film at the Archives, referred to as the original x-rays, and then the images of these x-rays which were placed into the HSCA report. And I will also review the HSCA computer-enhanced x-ray film which is stored at the Archives, and the images of these x-rays which were placed into the HSCA report. Anyone may order copies of the images placed into the HSCA report. These images however are of poor quality and there are some very important differences between these images and the x-rays stored at the Archives.

Something unusual happened during my first visit to the Archives, which in retrospect was fortuitous, as it allowed me to compare the original x-rays and the HSCA enhanced x-rays.

After spending the morning taking measurements of the films, we took a brief lunch break. After the break I began to view the x-rays again, and this time I dictated my findings into a microcassette recorder, since my handwriting is slow, and I must admit, very sloppy. After several minutes of dictating, one of the three Archives employees who were standing nearby and supervising my visit left the room and returned with the director of the Special Access section at the Archives, Martha Murphy. I had the impression that Ms. Murphy was upset, and she informed me that I had not been viewing the original x-rays, but had instead been viewing the computer-enhanced films which had been produced for the HSCA in 1977. I then asked if I could see the original x-rays, since I was approved to view them, and these were brought out for viewing. To this day I don't know exactly why this happened, but it allowed me to compare the HSCA films with the images of these same films which were placed into the HSCA report, and they are not the same.

I don't believe it was an accident that I was initially shown the HSCA films. Some of the Archives personnel have been working with these x-rays for decades. I had the impression that Ms. Murphy was brought into the room in response to something that I dictated, but I am not sure exactly what prompted them to notify her. As it turned out, I am glad that this happened, since I would have never thought to ask for permission to view the HSCA x-rays, in addition to viewing the original x-rays.

Figure 2 is the skull x-ray from 1960 which is stored at the Presidential Library near Boston. I initially thought that this was stored at the Archives, however they told me that it had been returned to the Library after it was viewed for the HSCA in 1977. When I contacted the Library, they stated that it must not have been returned, because they didn't have the film. After many conversations they looked again and it was found at the Library, where it was labeled as a sinus x-ray. I was allowed to view this x-ray and take optical density measurements, to compare with the autopsy x-rays.

Figure 3 is the image of the original right lateral film, and figure 5 is the image of the original AP film. These images which were published with the HSCA report are of very poor quality, and very blurred, compared to the x-ray films. The right lateral image especially appears different and much more difficult to review, compared to the original. Figure 4 is my replication of the left lateral skull x-ray, which was made by flipping the right lateral image, and then cropping the posterior third of the image out of view. It is interesting to note that the Clark Panel recorded that there were two left lateral skull x-rays, rather than a left and a right lateral film.

Figures 6 and 7 are the images of the HSCA films which were placed into the HSCA report. The computer enhancement resulted in brightening of the dark areas of the skull, and darkening some of the bright areas, so that there is a more uniform brightness. This wasn't strictly a matter of brightening or darkening certain areas of the film, however. Some important details were left out of the enhanced images, and this was not inadvertent, as will be explained.

BONE LOSS:

The anterior portion of the skull appears very dark on the lateral images, and the posterior half appears too bright. Because of this, it is very difficult to determine the areas of bone loss, especially over the anterior half. In any skull x-ray, the area of the temporal and sphenoid bones is the thinnest part of the skull, and therefore this area will appear darker than other areas of the skull, however this area of darkness on the autopsy lateral x-rays extends into the frontal and parietal bones. If the films were overexposed (too much radiation) or overdeveloped (developing solution too concentrated, developing time too long, or developer temperature too high), then the entire skull would have appeared darker than expected. The actual skull x-rays at the Archives do not show as much contrast between the front and back as you see on these images, however the contrast is still very unusual, and this has been noted by all the professionals who have viewed these films over the years. This could have been accomplished during the copying process, and it would not have been difficult. I agree with Mantik that the most likely way in which these x-rays were altered was through the copying process, by controlling the amount of light passing through certain areas of the film.

On the AP x-rays, and on the attached AP images from the HSCA report, there is an obvious loss of bone over the frontal and parietal regions. The right side of the frontal bone is heavily fractured, and the frontal sinus can be seen inside a large fragment which has separated from surrounding bone on the right side.

What is not usually appreciated on the AP x-ray is the loss of occipital bone, first described by Mantik. I agree with him that the AP image shows an area of bone loss extending into the left occipital region, demonstrated by figure 8. This appearance on the AP x-ray can only be caused by loss of occipital bone. The right lateral film also reveals a subtle change to the occipital bone, but there is a significant drop in the optical density measurements on the right lateral film over the occipital bone, and the outline of the bone in this region is disrupted, compared with the President's skull x-ray from 1960.

Figure 8 also demonstrates an area on the AP x-ray which corresponds to the posterior temporal and parietal skull covered by the "white patch" on the lateral x-rays. This area, enclosed by a circle, includes several fragments, which are most likely bone fragments, but there could be metallic fragments as well. I am convinced that the white patch was added to the lateral images to cover an area of bone loss and fragmentation.

Another area of bone loss is visible on the lateral x-ray, a small area over the right temporal bone, shown in figure 9. This loss of bone is consistent with an entry or exit wound. It is located at the same location as a wound which James Jenkins saw during the autopsy, just above the right ear. I viewed the autopsy photos stored at the archives, and there was a round blood-filled hole visible in this same area, on the photograph showing the right side of the head. This same photograph was not included in the digital images produced by the ARRB, which I viewed in June 2017.

RIGHT FRONTAL ENTRY:

My most important new finding is noted on figure 10, which is a replication of a portion of the right lateral film as viewed at the Archives. The gap noted in the frontal bone (a) on the original film revealed a cluster of tiny metallic-appearing objects within the gap, extending into the skull. This cluster of small objects, consistent with tiny metallic fragments, lies at the apex of the fragment trail located in the superior portion of the skull. The fragment trail widens from front to back, and the largest fragments were located toward the back of the skull. In general, larger fragments travel farther than smaller fragments, since the energy of a moving object is related to both mass and speed. Multiple researchers have proposed an entry in this area of the forehead, which was covered by thick hair.

Figure 11 demonstrates how the images were "enhanced" in this area, and the image which was placed in the HSCA report was altered to obscure both the gap between bone fragments and also the metallic fragments adjacent to the gap. If the image was only altered to increase the brightness of this area of the film, it would not have resulted in filling in of the gap in the bone, or the covering up of the fragments. This tells me that someone associated either with the enhancement process, or with the publication of these images, understood the importance of this finding, and did not want it to be widely known.

I was especially interested in this area before I visited the Archives, because the cone of the fragment trail points toward this area of the skull. I scanned the films with a 2X magnifier, and then, was able to use a 10X loupe magnifier to focus on areas of interest. The tiny metallic fragments were visible without the loupe magnifier, and they were faintly visible without the 2X magnifier. I viewed the perimeter of the skull thoroughly and did not see any other area with a similar appearance. The location of the fragments on the inner edge of the skull, at the apex of the fragment trail at the top of the skull, indicates that this was an entry wound.

When I saw these tiny fragments in this gap in the frontal bone, my first thought was – *why hasn't this been reported before?* I don't know the answer to this question. It might have been because I was very curious about this area on the x-rays before the visit, and it was one of the first areas that I viewed on the original films.

FRAGMENT TRAIL:

Figures 12 and 13 demonstrate the fragment trail and the silhouette of the skull. I did not include the full 6.5 mm object which appears within the right orbit on the AP x-ray (since I think that this was added to the film), but it is represented by an outline. I did include metallic densities which are present within the larger burn mark, in the right temporal region on the AP image.

The majority of the metallic fragments lie within the superior half of the skull, and most of these are situated within a cone which expands from front to back, with the apex of the cone directed toward a large fragment of the right frontal skull, which had collapsed backward and slightly downward into the skull. The original and the HSCA x-ray films revealed innumerable tiny metallic fragments in the anterior half of the skull. The images of both the original and the HSCA enhanced films placed into the HSCA report do not show most of these tiny fragments – they have been effectively removed from these images. The lateral films reveal that many of the tiniest fragments appear along a line extending from the right frontal skull toward the back of the skull. In one area these tiny fragments are layered along a thin, straight line, and it is possible that these tiny fragments were layered along the dura (leathery membrane surrounding the brain), which would have been sagging into the skull, due to skull fractures and absent bone. The most posterior fragment is located at the parietal-occipital junction on the right lateral image (figure 12, horizontal arrow). I agree with Mantik that this fragment was visible within the large 6.5 mm bright object which is the bright object on the AP film. McDonnel described this small fragment at the parietal-occipital as lying between the galea (thick fibrous layer of the scalp) and the outer table of the skull. Most of the fragments which are seen in the lower half of the skull on the AP image cannot be seen on the lateral image. The most likely explanation for this is that they are hidden by the white patch, an area which will be discussed later.

There appears to be a fragment embedded in the bone above the right eye, and above the orbit. I believe that this fragment came from the bullet which struck the right lower occipital skull.

If the Warren commission had been correct, and a single bullet struck the lower occipital skull, and caused a large exit wound in the right frontoparietal skull, why is there no fragment trail extending along this line?

If the HSCA medical panel had been correct, and a single bullet struck the skull in the posterior parietal region, why does the fragment trail expand from front to back? The smallest fragments on the x-ray are located at the opposite side of the skull from the HSCA entrance, which would defy the laws of physics. Another feature noted on the lateral x-ray, mentioned above, and first described by Dr. McDonnel, is the fragment which is embedded in the scalp in this location, and this would be difficult to explain. This fragment would have had to bounce backwards from the bone and lodge in the scalp which it had passed through, highly unlikely with a high velocity projectile. It would be impossible to explain the location of this fragment from a single entry wound at the Warren commission entry site – this would require the fragment to tunnel under the scalp at an angle greater than 90 degrees from its trajectory into the skull.

Intersecting fractures:

When fractures intersect, the fracture which formed last will terminate when it encounters the open space of an existing fracture (figure 14). This was first described by Georg Puppe, a German physician, in 1903, and this rule is very helpful when interpreting x-rays showing multiple fractures. Figure 15 shows a fracture terminating when it encounters a long radial fracture. The long radial fracture is fully consistent with an entry radial fracture from the lower occipital region. The shorter fracture is consistent with a short radial fracture from an exit wound at the posterior parietal region (the HSCA entry site). Fractures associated with entry wounds are typically much longer than fractures associated with exit wounds. This image also shows another radial fracture ending when it encounters the white patch.

This intersection of fractures argues against a single entry at the HSCA entry site, since the radial fracture which is associated with this area terminates when it intersects the long radial fracture. If there were a single entry wound at the HSCA site, this radial fracture would have occurred first, and it would not have ended when it encountered the second fracture. This was previously described by Dr. Randy Robertson, radiologist.

The manner in which the lower fracture terminates at the white patch is very unusual, and it adds further evidence that the white patch is artificial. Rather than tapering off, the wide fracture abruptly terminates at the white patch.

The HSCA enhanced x-ray films, not the images placed in the HSCA report, but the actual film at the Archives, reveals yet another set of intersecting fractures, as shown in a replication in figure 16. The fractures are drawn in white to delineate them from the dark surrounding area. The configuration of these fractures suggests that the arc-shaped fracture is a concentric fracture, and the relatively straight fracture is a radial fracture, likely emanating from the right frontal entry.

6.5 MM OBJECT:

The large white object visible in the upper aspect of the right orbit on the AP x-ray has a diameter of 6.5 mm, the diameter of the bullets supposedly fired by Lee Harvey Oswald, from a Mannlicher-Carcano rifle. I agree with Mantik that the appearance of this object on the original AP x-ray indicates that this is artificial. Attached is a drawing made by Mantik during one of his visits to the archives (figure 17) (my drawing is worse than my writing). There are densities within the outline of this fragment which appear to be fragments, and the largest of these fragments lines up on the lateral film with the fragment embedded in the scalp, the same object described as embedded in the scalp by McDonnel. The only thing that I can add to Dr. Mantik's description is that I thought there was a gradual increase in the density of the lower portion of this object, from its lower margin toward the midportion of the object.

There are too many problems with this object to mention them all. The Warren Commission noted that the nose and the tail of this bullet were found in the limousine, so that would leave this object coming from the mid portion of the bullet, and this defies explanation. There were no large fragments even approaching this size which were removed at the time of the autopsy. There is no corresponding fragment seen on the lateral x-rays. When I presented these images to a Neuroradiology conference at my local medical school, the first comment was that there was no corresponding fragment on the lateral image, and none of the neuroradiologists believed that it could be seen on the lateral. A fragment of this brightness on the AP x-ray should have stood out like a sore thumb on the lateral image. Dr. Mantik took more optical density measurements of this object than I did, and he has described how impossibly dense this would have to be, if it were real. When Dr. Mantik interviewed Dr. Ebersole by phone, the conversation abruptly ended when he asked Ebersole about this 6.5 mm object. The most likely way in which this was added to the film was through copying, and it would have been easy for this to have been done.

Dr. Ebersole, the radiologist attending the autopsy, made some comments in his HSCA testimony which may be relevant here[14]. He noted that the x-rays "showed no evidence of a slug, a bullet," and that this was "disconcerting." He told a strange story about communicating within the next few days with Dr. James Young at the White House by phone, to give measurements to help prepare a bust of the late President. He told of communicating with him cryptically, "something to the effect that Aunt Margaret's skirts need the following change." It must be asked why these measurements would be obtained from the fractured and deformed skull as shown on the x-rays, and why would there be a need to talk in such cryptic terms? Could this have had something to do with copying (and alteration) of the x-rays? Dr. Ebersole was certainly uncomfortable with the subject of the 6.5 mm object.

For me, the bottom line in discussing the 6.5 mm object is the appearance of the object on the original AP film. I have no doubt that this object is artificial, and that it was added to the film to implicate the Mannlicher-Carcano rifle.

WHITE PATCH:

The white patch, as described by Mantik, is demonstrated on the negative image of the HSCA lateral in Figure 15, and labeled "A." This could have been easily added to a copy of the film, by covering these areas and reducing exposure to light, during the copying process. The white patch is actually two areas, separated by a fracture line. Another fracture abruptly ends when it encounters the lower part of the white patch, adding weight to the argument that this area is artificial.

The optical density measurements of this area on the right lateral film placed the density of the skull in this area as almost the same density as the petrous ridge, at the base of the skull. The petrous ridge is almost solid bone across the base of the skull when viewed on the lateral projection. The optical density of the left lateral film placed the density of the white patch as more dense than the petrous ridge. Naked eye observation tells you that this area appears very strange, but the optical densitometer proves beyond doubt that this must be artificial.

BURN MARKS:

There are two burn marks on the AP film, and figure 18 is a replication of the larger burn mark. The larger burn mark is located in an area

14. HSCA Testimony of James Ebersole, March 11th, 1978, pages 6-8.

158

of the AP film which corresponds on the anterior to posterior axis with a line which extends from the right temporal bone back through the white patch to the posterior parietal skull. (This is not apparent until you take into account the angle of the AP film – it was taken at an angle of 15 degrees below the normal angle of the AP x-ray. This angle is easily calculated by measuring the distance between the lower rim of the orbit and the top of the petrous ridge on the AP x-ray, and then applying this distance to the lateral film.)

Burn marks on an x-ray could occur if the film was held over the "hot lamp" too long. The hot lamp is the term for a bright light which is housed in a metal frame, and it can be used for viewing areas which are too dark when viewed on the standard view box. In the days of viewing x-ray film, rather than digital images on a monitor, burn marks were rarely produced if the film were held over the bright light for too long. I've talked with multiple radiologists and neurologists who spent their careers viewing film, before digital images became available, and they all agreed that they were rare, and many had never seen a burn mark. They all agreed with me that a perfectly round burn mark would be extremely unusual. In addition, it would not be expected to create the metallic-appearing densities which are visible within the burn mark on the AP film.

The burn marks are raised and crinkled. Since I believe that these "original" films are actually copy films, this implies that the marks had to be recreated on the copy film, to cause the crinkled appearance, and to strongly imply that they were the true originals.

Dr. Ebersole testified to the HSCA that he "may have" made the burn marks, by holding the film too close to the hot lamp[15]. It is difficult to believe that he could not definitely remember making such burn marks, on the most important x-rays that he had ever viewed. Jerrol Custer stated in his ARRB testimony[16] that "this is where Dr. Ebersole got it too close to the heat lamp." He added "Isn't it funny how where it starts to burn is the area that I suggested was an entry wound?"

I would not expect a burn mark made by a hot lamp to be perfectly circular, but rather it would be expected to have irregular margins. The old hot lamps had a metal frame, with a large hole a few inches in diameter in the frame covering the bright bulb, and the film was placed over this hole to illuminate the area of concern. I speculate that the burn marks added to the copy film were caused by something other than a hot lamp, possibly

15. HSCA Testimony of James Ebersole, March 11th, 1978, page 20.
16. ARRB deposition of Jerrol Custer, October 28th, 1997, page 115.

with a cigarette lighter. In my opinion this area deserves further study. I'm very skeptical of the official story surrounding these burn marks.

DIGITIZATION OF THE AUTOPSY X-RAYS:

After viewing the x-rays in 2015, I requested permission to view them again, and the request was denied. I was approved, however, to return to the Archives and view the autopsy photographs of the head wounds, and these were viewed in September of 2015. Following that visit, I corresponded with Senator Kirk, and with Martha Murphy at the Archives, and several other researchers were corresponding with them as well, encouraging them to make high quality digital images of the x-rays. This would preserve these images and would also allow for better analysis of the images. In late 2016 I thought that some progress was being made, and Senator Kirk appeared to be in favor of digitizing the x-rays. Subsequently Martha Murphy called and relayed that this could not be done, however she said that they would try to retrieve digital images which were made by the ARRB, at the Kodak facility in Rochester in 1997. It turned out that the x-rays were not included in the digital images made at Rochester, but the digital images of the photographs were converted from their Jaz drive format to a usable format by the Archives personnel. I was then able to view these digital images of the photographs at the archives in early June of 2017. I again corresponded with Senator Kirk and with Ms. Murphy, recommending digitization of the x-rays, and our group of researchers offered to cover the cost of making these digital copies. As of this writing, after six months there has not yet been a response to this request.

AUTOPSY PHOTOGRAPHS:

As noted, I've viewed the autopsy photographic prints in 2015, and also the digital images of the photographs in 2017. The digital images are of very high quality and they should be viewed with the prints, because the viewer can magnify the images on the monitor and see much more detail. The prints may be viewed with a stereoscopic viewer and this gives the viewer a 3D image, which is especially helpful when viewing the photograph labeled the scalp retraction photo.

Some of the autopsy photographs were not turned over to Robert Kennedy by the Secret Service, and copies were subsequently sold by James Fox, a Secret Service photographer, in the 1970's. These "Fox" images are now widely seen on the internet. There were apparently no repercussions from the sale of these photographs, and this makes a mockery of the Deed of Gift and the sequestration of the original photographs. The Fox photographic images on the internet are of poor quality, and because of this the evidence of alteration of some of these photos is hidden. In the case of the scalp-retraction photographs, the Fox version is cropped and this causes difficulty in interpreting the image.

There are three versions of the scalp-retraction photograph (also referred to as the mystery photo) at the Archives, numbered 1,2,44,45, 17JB, and 18JB, according to the Clark Panel report. I did not record the numbers of the prints when I viewed them at the archives, which I should have done in retrospect. There are two black and white versions, and onecolor version. One of the black and white versions appears to show the glare of a light shining across the image from the right side. The light casts shadows across the image, which appeared to be caused by small particles on the surface of the photograph. This photograph appeared to be a photograph of a photograph (figure 19). Why would there be a photograph of a photograph in this collection? The most likely explanation is that it would have served to replace one of the existing photographs, although if that were the case, it was performed sloppily and in haste. Obviously, I don't know where or when this would have been done. I have not been able to obtain a copy of this image, and this image (figure 19) was made from a screenshot of a GIF, described with the text below the figure. I think that this photograph in the Archives was made from the other black and white photo in the collection. The image in the GIF is not exactly the same as the photo that I observed – in that part of the image the GIF appears as if it is covered by a glass cover and it appears to be partially magnified.

The color version of the scalp-retraction photo was the most helpful to me when viewing at the Archives. In the left upper portion of the photo there is plainly seen a layer of retracted fat from the abdominal wall. The nipple on the right chest wall is barely visible. The V incision is seen on the right forehead, and the right eyebrow and lashes are visible. There is a wide fracture pointing toward the frontal region, and the curve of the right side of the skull and the posterior fossa is visible.

One of the most telling things about the back of head photographs in the collection, is that you never see the full back of the head in any of them. The left occipital region is never fully seen on the same photo showing the right occipital region. Also, the whorl of hair is seen just to the right of the midline on these autopsy photos, however there are multiple photographs of President Kennedy during life which show that this whorl of hair was on the far left side of his scalp. The autopsy images of the back of the head show that someone is holding the scalp, and I believe, as do many researchers, that the scalp was mobilized and stretched to cover the back of the head for some of these photos.

The lower area of the back of the head on these photographs appeared very strange, and it almost defies description. This was even more apparent on the digital images, but it was also seen on the prints. The hair in this area appeared to be much too fine to be real, and in the background, there appeared to be a phantom image which was darker, suggesting that this part of the photograph was added as a layer over this region.

The print of the photograph which was taken from the right side of the autopsy table shows the right side of the head, with the bone flap visible above and slightly behind the right ear. A small blood-filled hole is visible on the print, just anterior to the bone flap. James Jenkins saw what he thought was a bullet wound in this location during the autopsy. To my disappointment, this particular photograph was not included in the set of digital photos which I was allowed to view at the Archives. James Jenkins has not been allowed to view the autopsy photographs at the Archives, and I and others have written to support his request.

Included in the collection of digital photographs prepared for the ARRB were three photographs which were recovered from a roll of film taken by Floyd Riebe, Navy photographer, on the night of the autopsy[17]. This roll of film was taken from Riebe and exposed to light by Roy Kellerman of the Secret Service. Two of these three images show the right side of the head, from slightly different angles. Although the images are somewhat dark, the only area of these images which appeared to be blurred was over the back of the right side of the head, and the left side of the head was not seen. The area behind the ear appeared to be smudged. The facial features were clearly seen, and the gallery rails were visible in the background, on the left side of the autopsy table. These photos were labeled A1-01, A1-02, B4-01 and B4-02.

This set of photos included two photos with barely any image at all, appearing as a bright flash with a faint oval outline in the center, and no information could be gleaned from these identical photos, labeled A2-01 and A2-02.

The photographs of the brain were viewed only on the prints, as they were not included in the digital images. I have no doubt that these photos could not be photos of President Kennedy's brain. Figure 20 is a draw-

17. ARRB deposition of Floyd Riebe, May 7th, 1997.

ing of the dorsum of the brain from the HSCA report, figure F-302. The photograph of the dorsum of the brain at the Archives showed swelling of the left hemisphere, and subarachnoid blood was present. The left hemisphere shows no evidence of laceration on this dorsal view. The brain was somewhat deformed or twisted, and the Ida Dox drawing of this photograph doesn't portray this. There was no hemorrhage visible in the wide-open wound of the right hemisphere.

The ventral (undersurface) of the brain showed that the cerebellum was completely intact, except for a small sliver of folia hanging loose on the left side, which can occur with handling of this delicate tissue. There was a faint linear laceration extending along the lateral surface of the temporal lobe and the frontal lobe on the left side, barely extending into the brain substance. This appeared to be a saw-cut laceration, which I have seen on many occasions, during my time as a morgue assistant in medical school, and later during brain cutting sessions when I was a resident and then when I was a faculty member for several years.

I believe that one of the reasons that the Clark Panel and the HSCA medical panel moved the entry location was because they knew that an entry in the right lower occipital region would have caused a massive amount of damage to the cerebellum. There was no way to reconcile the brain photographs with the Warren Commission entry location. Not only that, but there are no fragments extending from the Warren Commission entry site and the proposed exit site at the top of the skull. They moved the entry site to a location 100 mm above the WC entry, however this site is disproved as an entry site by the x-ray evidence of intersecting fractures. They saw an area on the back of head photographs which they determined must be an entry wound, however this area appeared to me to be a superficial scrape or abrasion. The fragment trail cone expands from front to back, while it should have expanded from back to front, if the HSCA entry location were correct.

Another reason that the HSCA medical panel moved the entry location must be because of its own trajectory analysis. If a shot fired from the TSBD 6th floor entered at the right lower occiput, it would have blown out the front of the face, rather than exiting at the top of the skull. This trajectory analysis was subsequently buried in the HSCA data.

Dr. J. Thornton Boswell, one of the Navy pathologists at the autopsy, drew a diagram showing the width of the large defect of the skull, and he also noted that the falx was torn from the "coronal suture back"[18]. The falx

18.   https://www.historymatters.com/essays/jfkmed/How5Investigations/How5Investigations-

is a tough fibrous membrane which separates the upper portion of the hemispheres of the brain. It would be impossible for there to be such a loss of bone and also a laceration of the falx over this large area, without having a speck of injury to the left hemisphere of the brain.

By the time of the President's autopsy, James Jenkins had considerable experience in assisting the pathologists with removal of the brain at autopsy, and his remarks should carry weight. He described Dr. Humes as saying that the brain literally fell out of the skull into his hands, and he did not see Dr. Humes make the usual cuts of the dura and vessels needed to remove the brain from the skull. This brings up multiple issues which I won't go into here, but are better explored by reading David Lifton, Doug Horne, William Law, and others. This involves the shell game involving the two separate teams who thought they were bringing the casket bearing the President into the morgue at Bethesda, the two separate brain examinations, and other issues. There was deception involved in the autopsy, and I don't pretend to be an expert on all of the evidence of deception, but I agree that it was done to hide the true nature of the wounds.

Conclusions:

There is x-ray evidence of at least two shots striking the skull, based upon the pattern of intersecting fractures, loss of bone, and the fragment trail. If there were only two shots impacting the skull, then the right lower occipital entry occurred first, followed by the right frontal entry. The bullet which struck the right forehead fragmented into innumerable tiny fragments, while the bullet which struck the right lower occiput was likely jacketed and there was little fragmentation.

There is x-ray evidence of a small bony defect in the right temporal bone, in an area in which James Jenkins saw a round wound with gray margins. I saw this on the autopsy photograph of the right side of the head. If this were an entry wound, then that implies 3 shots striking the skull. David Mantik and Doug Horne have described their 3-shot scenario and I haven't seen any evidence to refute their ideas. I'm not ready to totally agree yet, since I think it is still possible that the right temporal wound could have been an exit wound from the right lower occipital entry. Such a shot would have more likely come from a lower floor of the DalTex building, with a direct line of sight. When considering a multiple shooter scenario, I recommend reading Carol Hewett's essay, and her discussion of the use of silencers and sound suppressors[19]. I will be the first to admit that David Mantik and Doug Horne understand the totality of the evidence much better than I do, and I strongly recommend reading their 3-shot scenario[20].

Why did the military pathologists report only one bullet entry to the skull? I don't think that they were incompetent, although the two Navy pathologists were not experienced in forensic autopsies. In my opinion, it is much more likely that they were coerced in some way to follow the official story coming out of Dallas, that there was a single shooter, from the rear. They could have been told that they must support this theory, in the interest of national security. In his depositions, Dr. Humes seems to be talking around many subjects, and he was less than forthcoming in his testimonies.

In the case of the enhancement of the x-rays for the HSCA, I am more skeptical. The changes made to the enhanced x-rays were done in a way which obscured important information. And then, the images of the original and enhanced films were altered when they were placed into the HSCA report, and I strongly believe that this was a deliberate attempt to hide evidence. I requested any records pertaining to the enhancement of the x-rays, and I was informed that the Archives has no records pertaining to this process.

I still have many questions about the medical evidence, but there is already overwhelming evidence that the Warren Commission and the HSCA conclusions were far from the truth.

Personally, this has been a humbling experience. Before going to the Archives, I didn't really grasp the importance of the medical evidence, and I didn't know what I was getting into. It is humbling to look at the x-rays and the photographs, and to see the massive amount of injury inflicted upon President Kennedy. It looked bad enough on the HSCA films, and when I was told that I had not been looking at the originals, I found myself breathing a sigh of relief, even hoping that the evidence wouldn't look so bad on the original films. But then they brought out the original films, and it just looked worse. I cannot imagine how it felt to be part of what James Jenkins experienced. It makes me appreciate his honesty and his courage even more.

---

19. https://kennedysandking.com/john-f-kennedy-articles/silencers-sniper-rifles-the-cia. When considering multiple shooters it should be remembered that some of the weapons could have been equipped with silencers or sound suppressors, if the shooter was located in a more vulnerable position. Thanks to Milicent Cranor for pointing out this review by Carol Hewett

20. *Inside the Assassination Records Review Board*; Horne, Douglas. *John F. Kennedy's Head Wounds: A Final Synthesis*; Mantik, David.

I must admit to a certain ambivalence about telling of my findings from reviewing the autopsy photographs and x-rays at the Archives. There are times when I wonder if I'm doing the right thing, by describing the evidence, and how it was manipulated and deceptively presented by the Warren Commission report and by the House Select Committee report. I still love my country, and in this day of turmoil in Washington, I don't want to weaken our institutions further. During my medical career, I've seen many patients who were working or retired from agencies such as the CIA, FBI, Secret Service, and military intelligence. I was always impressed with their honesty and integrity – how a person faces personal illness says a lot about them. I don't think that we can hold the current employees of agencies of the government responsible for what happened over 50 years ago, even though we know that some of these agencies are still working to hide the evidence. In my opinion, these agencies have changed, compared to the early 60's when they were treated like a personal fiefdom by men such as Allen Dulles, James Angleton, and J. Edgar Hoover. Some changes were made as a result of the Church Committee; however, the country has never really faced up to the extent of the abuses of the 60's. So, I believe that it is not incongruent to support their work today, while strongly supporting a search for the truth surrounding the assassination. Eventually I decided that anyone who has seen the primary evidence has a responsibility to speak the truth, and that we need to learn why this tragic event happened, and only then can we safeguard the country from having something like it happening again.

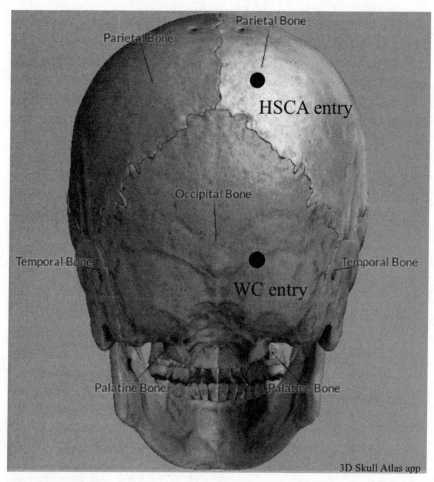

Figure 1. The House Select Committee on Assassinations and the Clark Panel moved the entry site up 10 cm from the Warren Commission entry site.

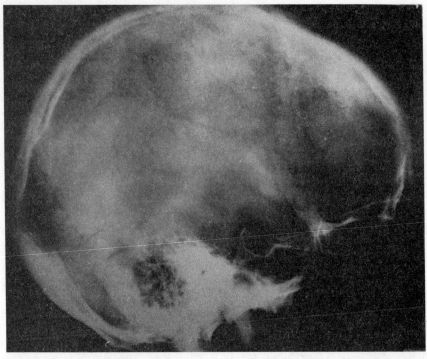

Figure 2: Right lateral skull x-ray dated 1960. The original film is stored at the Presidential Library in Boston, and this image was published in the HSCA report, 1978. The facial bones were obscured for the HSCA report.

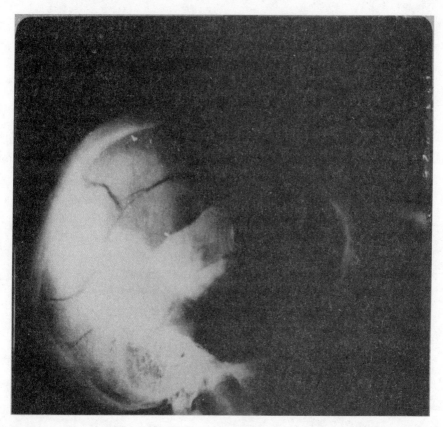

Figure 3: Image of the "original" right lateral x-ray published in the HSCA report.

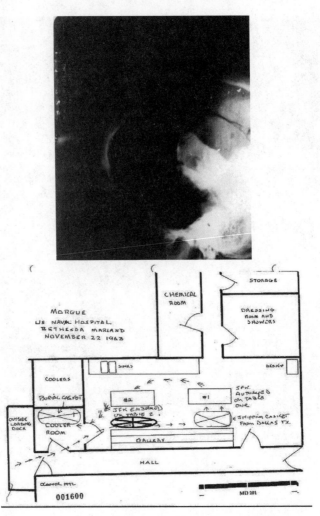

Figure 4: Approximate *replication* of the left lateral x-ray, demonstrating how the posterior aspect of the skull was not seen on this film. The right lateral skull image was flipped and cropped to prepare this replication. Jerrol Custer stated that the cutoff left lateral film was caused by his inability to position the GE 250 portable x-ray unit between the autopsy table and the gallery[21]. The adjacent diagram is a drawing of the morgue which was made by Paul O'Connor, Navy corpsman. There is an obvious problem with Custer's explanation – for a left lateral x-ray, the film is placed on the left side of the body, and the portable x-ray unit is placed on the right side of the body. There should have been no problem taking the left lateral skull x-ray. If the limited space had caused a problem, it would have been with the right lateral skull x-ray.

21. ARRB deposition of Jerrol Custer, October 28th, 1997, page 68.

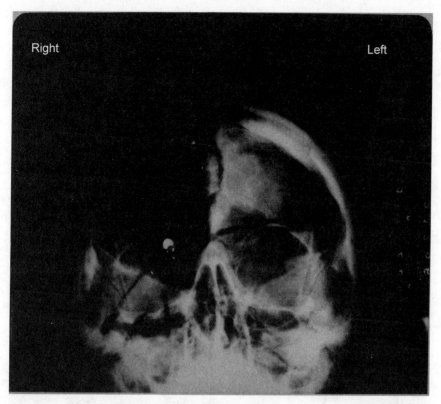

Figure 5: Image of the "original" AP film, published in the HSCA report. (please note that right and left are reversed for the viewer). The bright object to the right of the nasal bones is termed the 6.5 mm object.

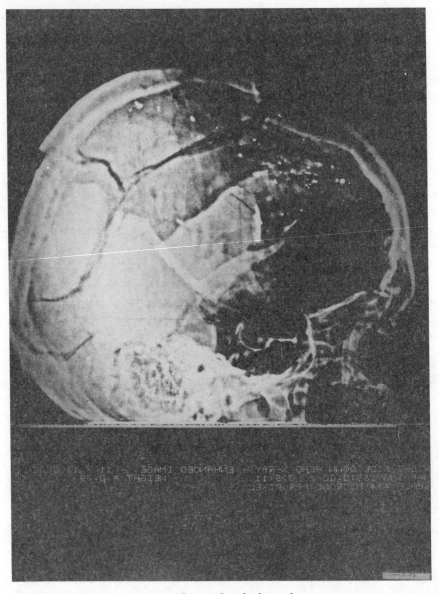

Figure 6: HSCA computer enhanced right lateral x-ray image.

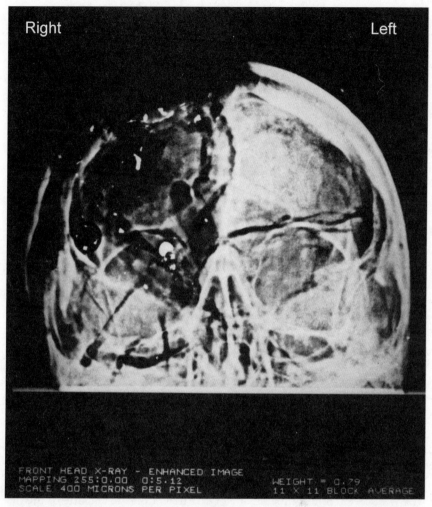

Figure 7: HSCA computer enhanced AP image (from the HSCA report)

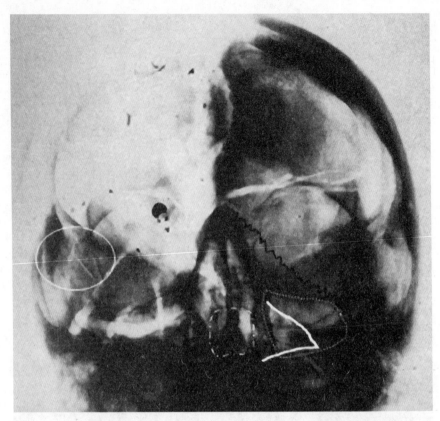

Figure 8: Negative of the AP image. The black squiggly line extending from near the midline diagonally down toward the left side is the lambdoid suture. The dash and dot line outlines the sphenoid sinus. The dotted line below the lambdoid suture is the outline of the maxillary sinus. The white solid line is the edge of a bone defect on the left side of the occipital bone. The white oval on the right side encircles several dark objects which appear to be fragments of bone or metal in the posterior temporal area. This area corresponds with part of the "white patch" region seen on the lateral images.

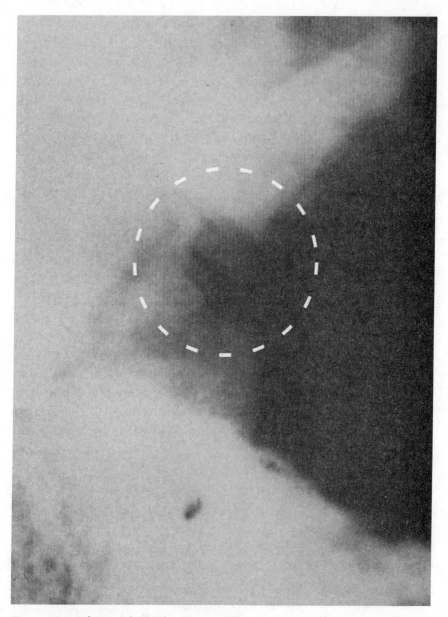

Figure 9: Defect in the right temporal bone, inside the circle above, just above the petrous ridge and the auditory canal. This is not seen on the premortem lateral x-ray. It is consistent with an entry or exit wound. The bone flap visible on some of the autopsy photographs extends over the upper margin of this bone defect.

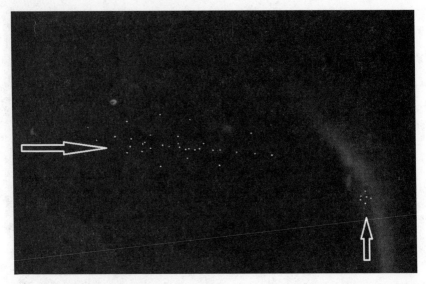

Figure 10: The horizontal arrow points toward the trail of fine dust-like fragments in the frontal region, which lead back to a small gap between frontal bone fragments which appears to be an area of entry. The vertical arrow points toward tiny fragments which were visible on the original x-rays, but are not seen on the HSCA film or on the images placed in the HSCA report. The brightest object on the image, above the trail of dust-like fragments, is actually an area of damage to the film. The frontal bone fragments on the right side had collapsed slightly into the cranial vault.

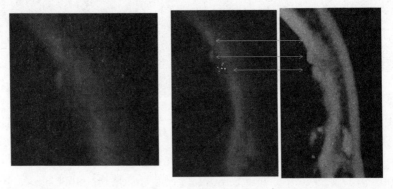

Figure 11: On the left is the frontal entry site as seen on the image of the original lateral x-ray placed in the HSCA report. The middle image is a rough replication of the original x-ray as viewed at the Archives, and the image to the far right is the image of the HSCA film which was placed in the official report. The "enhancement" effectively covers the tiny fragments and the gap in the bone.

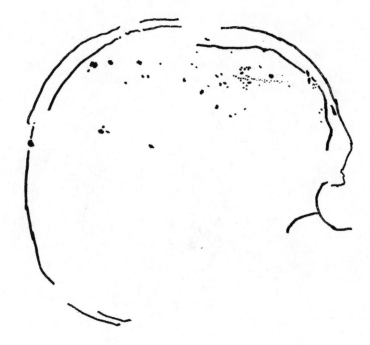

Figure 12: The fragment trail as seen on the original right lateral x-ray, with the outline of the skull.

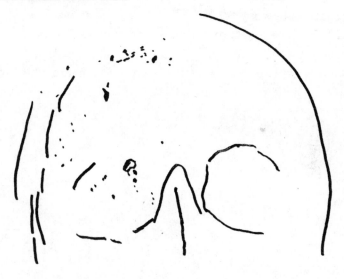

Figure 13: The fragment trail as seen on the AP X-ray, against the outline of the skull. The large 6.5 mm fragment which appears on the right is outlined. The cluster of fragments at the top of the skull corresponds to the fragment trail on the lateral film.

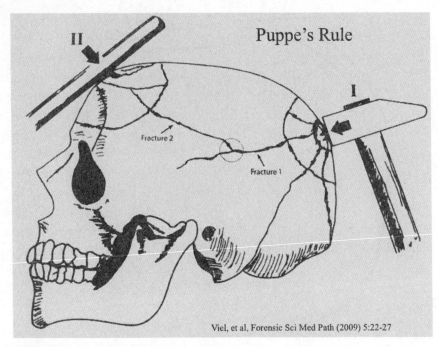

Puppe's Rule

II

Fracture 2

Fracture 1

I

Viel, et al, Forensic Sci Med Path (2009) 5:22-27

Figure 14: Fracture 2 terminates when it encounters fracture 1. According to Puppe's rule, fracture 1 occurred first (a fracture cannot propagate over an open space). These intersecting fractures are radial fractures, which radiate out from the entry or exit wound. Radial fractures associated with entry wounds are typically much longer than those associated with exit wounds. Concentric fractures are also seen in this figure, often appearing in a circular pattern, interrupted by the radial fractures which develop first.

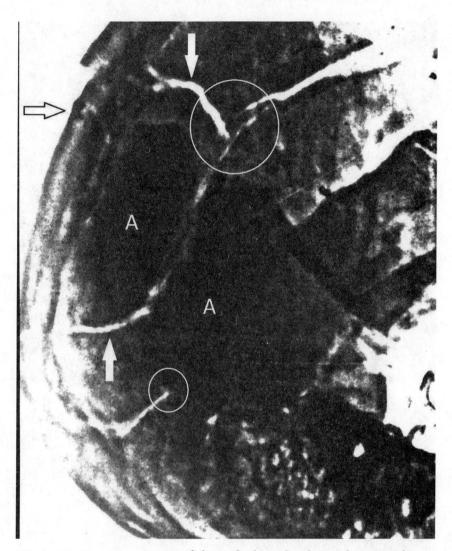

Figure 15: Posterior aspect of the right lateral enhanced image, shown here as a negative. The horizontal arrow points toward a fragment embedded in the scalp, and this fragment is visible on the original AP x-ray, situated within the diameter of the large 6.5 mm object. The upward arrow points toward a long radial fracture, and the downward arrow points toward a short radial fracture, which terminates when it encounters the long fracture (top circle). This indicates that the long fracture occurred first. The white patch (A) is shown in this negative image as darker than the surrounding area. The lower circle shows where a fracture terminates at the white patch. The occipital area of the skull on this lateral image appears heavily fractured.

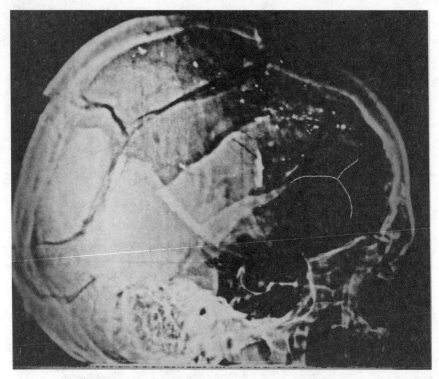

Figure 16: The HSCA enhanced lateral skull x-ray films at the Archives revealed these faint intersecting fractures, *replicated* here in white. This area of the x-rays is so dark that it is almost impossible to know if there was loss of bone over the entire area, however the presence of these fracture lines confirms the presence of bone.

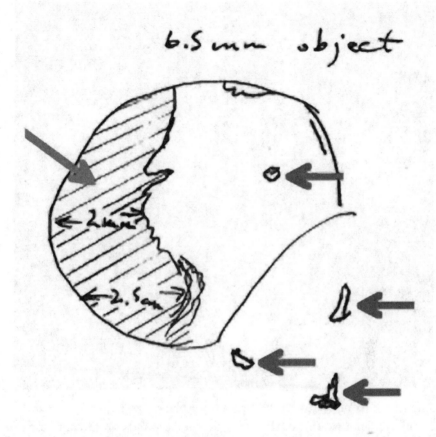

Figure 17: from John F. Kennedy's Head Wounds: A Final Synthesis — and a New Analysis of the Harper Fragment; Mantik, David, 2015. The blue arrow points to the fragment which appears to correspond with the fragment which is embedded in the scalp adjacent to the HSCA entry site. I believe that this was an exit site.

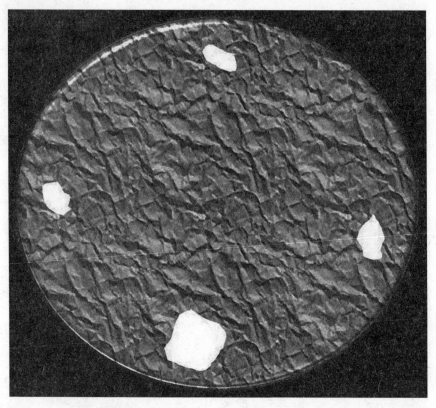

Figure 18: **Replication** of the larger burn mark. The larger burn mark is located in an area of the AP film which corresponds on the anterior to posterior axis with a line which extends from the right temporal bone defect, back through the white patch to the posterior parietal skull.

Figure 19: This image is a close-up of a part of a "GIF" image of a scalp retraction photograph from the Pat Speer website. In the center of the image is a shadow which appears to be a shadow across a flat surface. The shadows appeared to be created by small particles on the surface of the photograph. Most of these looked like dust particles, however one over the border of the photograph looked like a tiny piece of fabric.

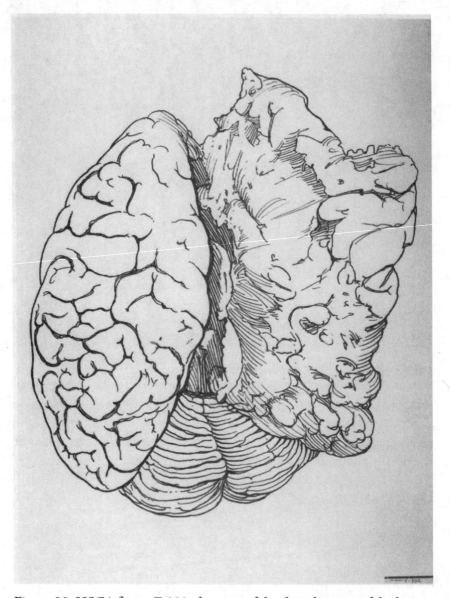

Figure 20: HSCA figure F-302, drawing of the dorsal aspect of the brain.

Sources:

Archives HSCA Record No. 180-10001-10103; Letter from Burke Marshall to General Services Administration 29 Oct 1966.

Investigation of the Assassination of President John F. Kennedy; Hearings before the Select Committee on Assassinations of the U.S. House of Representatives; 95th Congress; Second session. 6 Sept 1978; Volume I; pages 239-244.

Report of The President's Commission on The Assassination of President Kennedy; United States Government Printing Office; Warren Report, Volume II, page 349. 1964.

Warren Report, Volume II, page 8. 1964.

Warren Report, Appendix IX – Autopsy Report and Supplemental Report, page 5. 1964.

Assassinations Records Review Board, Testimony of Edward F. Reed, 21 Oct 1997, page 40.

Assassinations Records Review Board, Testimony of Jerrol Francis Custer, 28 Oct 1997, page 88.

Inside the Assassination Records Review Board; Horne, Douglas; Vol. II, page 418.

Stephanion: the point on the skull where the temporal line crosses the coronal suture.

1968 Panel Review of Photographs, X-Ray Films, Documents and other Evidence Pertaining to the Fatal Wounding of President John F. Kennedy on November 22, 1963, in Dallas, Texas.

House Select Committee on Assassinations Report, Volume 1, pp 204-207. Dr. McDonnel was in private practice of radiology at the time of the HSCA, and teaching Defense Medicine at UCLA. He had been an Army radiologist in the 50's and early 60's and was the physician in charge of animal testing associated with nuclear weapons testing.

HSCA Report, Volume 1, pp 200-203.

HSCA Report, Appendix, Volume VII, page 28.

HSCA Testimony of James Ebersole, March 11th, 1978, pages 6-8.

HSCA Testimony of James Ebersole, March 11th, 1978, page 20.

ARRB deposition of Jerrol Custer, October 28th, 1997, page 115.

ARRB deposition of Floyd Riebe, May 7th, 1997.

https://www.historymatters.com/essays/jfkmed/How5Investigations/How5InvestigationsGotItWrong_tabfig.htm

https://kennedysandking.com/john-f-kennedy-articles/silencers-sniper-rifles-the-cia. When considering multiple shooters, it should be remembered that some of the weapons could have been equipped with silencers or sound suppressors, if the shooter was located in a more vulnerable position. Thanks to Milicent Cranor for pointing out this review by Carol Hewett.

Inside the Assassination Records Review Board; Horne, Douglas. John F. Kennedy's Head Wounds: A Final Synthesis; Mantik, David.

ARRB deposition of Jerrol Custer, October 28th, 1997, page 68.

James Jenkins at JFK's gravesite

EPILOGUE

I hope this text will answer many of the questions that I've been asked over the 50+ years since the autopsy occurred. As I have previously stated, it not is my intent to refute or judge the materials that have been published prior to this book. I will leave that to the reader. The material discussed in this text is related only to the medical evidence collected during the autopsy. I have tried to relate this information as I remember it. I'm aware that I could not have possibly remembered everything that transpired that night. It is not my intent to claim that what I remember is all-inclusive of the transactions or procedures that occurred during the autopsy that night in the Bethesda morgue.

There've been many theories put forth about what transpired in the morgue and the results of the conclusions of the medical evidence gathered that night. I can only say that these are only theories, because there were only five people at the autopsy table examining the body and doing the autopsy procedural work. Those individuals were Dr. James Humes, Dr. Pierre Fink, Dr. J. Boswell, Paul O'Connor, and myself (James Jenkins). There has been much maligning of the three pathologist who performed the autopsy and the reporting of their findings. I believe these were good, honorable men caught up in an untenable situation. Being career military officers, they were ordered to a predetermined conclusion by their superiors. If you have been in the military you will understand this and to those who so stridently say that they should have told someone what was going on, we asked, "Who was there to tell, the President or the head of the FBI, the two government officials who benefited the most. I think not?

Over the last 54 years I've been asked many questions about how I felt during the autopsy of the President of United States, John Fitzgerald Kennedy.

I really had no personal feelings about the President either emotional or political. I was just a young Navy hospital corpsman whose duty assignment happened to be assisting with autopsies in the Bethesda Naval Hospital morgue. Though I have to admit this particular autopsy was a little bit more trying than the others that I had been involved in.

At the time, I knew very little about President Kennedy. I had no political agendas and my only goals were to finish my Navy enlistment and continue my medical education. Even though, I must admit that I began this autopsy with a little more trepidation than others – after all, this was the president of the United States of America. I knew that I must be more attentive to what I was doing and to the needs of the pathologist performing the autopsy. Because Paul and I were the lowest people on the totem pole present in the room, our satisfactory performance sometimes seemed to present a daunting task. This pressure did not come from the pathologist that we were working with, but from the subtle hostile atmosphere generated by frustration and sometimes outright anger from the gallery.

Emotionally, I approached this autopsy as I have always approached autopsies. I have always had a solemn, sad, respect for those autopsied. After all, it always represents a loss of life and tragedy for family and loved ones and in this case, the tragic loss for a nation. While I believe that an autopsy is an opportunity to learn invaluable information, I also believe that it should be accomplished in a reverent manner, respecting the life of the individual and family that it represents.

As I think back through what I have written in this book and how it has affected my life, it seems that the real tragedy was not the assassination of a president or the taking of a life but the assassination of a nation and the degradation of its citizens. While the assassination of a president or any man is tragic and devastating for those that are close to him as family, friends and acquaintances, the use of this devastating and cruel act to gain personal political power and wealth by entrenched evil political entities is the real tragedy for the nation.

The insistence of long-serving powerful political figures, that the citizen people would not be able to handle or deal with the truth, therefore the truth must be hidden from them for their own sake, is simply a self-serving gratification of their own imposed superior egos. This is a prime example of people in power who begin to believe that they know what is best for all of those that they govern, which they considered to be inferior.

It is always said that we should learn from history but we too often forget that history is written by those that win. In the case of the assassination of John Fitzgerald Kennedy, President of the United States of America, we the people and citizens of this great country are the losers. We have been treated like small children being put to bed early so the adults can talk.

We the people, citizens of our country, were unknowingly a part of an experiment conducted by powerful political entities within our own government to test just how much they could get away with subverting and controlling our lives. I believe that the assassination was not only a tragedy for the moment, but a slow clandestine, controlled change from a country governed by its people to a country governed by a select, powerful and wealthy few.

Today, in this country, we are beginning to see the fruition of the events that were put in place by the assassination of this great People's President. This must be stopped.

It is time that We the People take back those inalienable rights, given to us by God, as stated in our Constitution and Bill of Rights, as written by our founding fathers. We must stand up and tell our governing entities that they must adhere only to the limitations and duties given to them by our Constitution and the will of the people.

Index

Dr. Mary's Monkey
How the Unsolved Murder of a Doctor, a Secret Laboratory in New Orleans and Cancer-Causing Monkey Viruses are Linked to Lee Harvey Oswald, the JFK Assassination and Emerging Global Epidemics

BY EDWARD T. HASLAM, FOREWORD BY JIM MARRS

Evidence of top-secret medical experiments and cover-ups of clinical blunders The 1964 murder of a nationally known cancer researcher sets the stage for this gripping exposé of medical professionals enmeshed in covert government operations over the course of three decades. Following a trail of police records, FBI files, cancer statistics, and medical journals, thisscontaminated polio vaccine, the genesis of the AIDS virus, and biological weapon research using infected monkeys.

Softcover: **$19.95** (ISBN: 9781634240307) • 432 pages • Size: 5 1/2 x 8 1/2
Hardcover: **$24.95** (ISBN: 9781937584597)

Me & Lee
How I Came to Know, Love and Lose Lee Harvey Oswald

BY JUDYTH VARY BAKER
FOREWORD BY EDWARD T. HASLAM

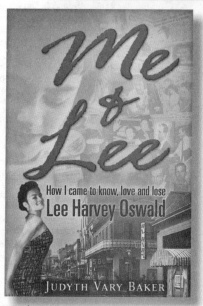

JUDYTH VARY WAS ONCE A PROMISING science student who dreamed of finding a cure for cancer; this exposé is her account of how she strayed from a path of mainstream scholarship at the University of Florida to a life of espionage in New Orleans with Lee Harvey Oswald. In her narrative she offers extensive documentation on how she came to be a cancer expert at such a young age, the personalities who urged her to relocate to New Orleans, and what lead to her involvement in the development of a biological weapon that Oswald was to smuggle into Cuba to eliminate Fidel Castro. Details on what she knew of Kennedy's impending assassination, her conversations with Oswald as late as two days before the killing, and her belief that Oswald was a deep-cover intelligence agent who was framed for an assassination he was actually trying to prevent, are also revealed.

JUDYTH VARY BAKER is a teacher, and artist. Edward T. Haslam is the author of *Dr. Mary's Monkey*.

Hardcover • $24.95 • Softrcover • $21.95 ISBN 9780979988677 / 978-1936296378 • 608 Pages

A Secret Order
Investigating the High Strangeness and Synchronicity in the JFK Assassination
by H. P. Albarelli, Jr.

Provocative new theories that uncover coincidences, connections, and unexplained details of the JFK assassination

Reporting new and never-before-published information about the assassination of John F. Kennedy, this investigation dives straight into the deep end, and seeks to prove the CIA's involvement in one of the most controversial topics in American history. Featuring intelligence gathered from CIA agents who reported their involvement in the assassination, the case is broken wide open while covering unexplored ground. Gritty details about the assassination are interlaced throughout, while primary and secondary players to the murder are revealed in the in-depth analysis. Although a tremendous amount has been written in the nearly five decades since the assassination, there has never been, until now, a publication to explore the aspects of the case that seemed to defy explanation or logic.

H. P. ALBARELLI JR. is an author and reporter whose previous works can be found in the Huffington Post, Pravda, and Counterpunch. His 10-year investigation into the death of biochemist Dr. Frank Olson was featured on A&E's Investigative Reports, and is the subject of his book, A Terrible Mistake. He lives in Indian Beach, Florida.

Softcover • **$24.95** • ISBN 9781936296552 • 469 Pages

Survivor's Guilt
The Secret Service and the Failure to Protect President Kennedy
by Vincent Michael Palamara

The actions and inactions of the Secret Service before, during, and after the Kennedy assassination

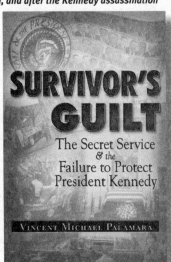

Painstakingly researched by an authority on the history of the Secret Service and based on primary, firsthand accounts from more than 80 former agents, White House aides, and family members, this is the definitive account of what went wrong with John F. Kennedy's security detail on the day he was assassinated.

The work provides a detailed look at how JFK could and should have been protected and debunks numerous fraudulent notions that persist about the day in question, including that JFK ordered agents off the rear of his limousine; demanded the removal of the bubble top that covered the vehicle; and was difficult to protect and somehow, directly or indirectly, made his own tragic death easier for an assassin or assassins. This book also thoroughly investigates the threats on the president's life before traveling to Texas; the presence of unauthorized Secret Service agents in Dealey Plaza, the site of the assassination; the failure of the Secret Service in monitoring and securing the surrounding buildings, overhangs, and rooftops; and the surprising conspiratorial beliefs of several former agents.

An important addition to the canon of works on JFK and his assassination, this study sheds light on the gross negligence and, in some cases, seeming culpability, of those sworn to protect the president.

Vincent Michael Palamara is an expert on the history of the Secret Service. He has appeared on the History Channel, C-SPAN, and numerous newspapers and journals, and his original research materials are stored in the National Archives. He lives in Pittsburgh, Pennsylvania.

Softcover • **$24.95** • ISBN 9781937584603 • 492 Pages

In the Eye of History
Disclosures in the JFK Assassination Medical Evidence
SECOND EDITION
BY WILLIAM MATSON LAW

An oral history of the JFK autopsy

Anyone interested in the greatest mystery of the 20th century will benefit from the historic perspective of the attendees of President Kennedy's autopsy. For the first time in their own words these witnesses to history give firsthand accounts of what took place in the autopsy morgue at Bethesda, Maryland, on the night on November 22, 1963. Author William Matson Law set out on a personal quest to reach an understanding of the circumstances underpinning the assassination of John F. Kennedy. His investigation led him to the autopsy on the president's body at the National Naval Medical Center. In the Eye of History comprises conversations with eight individuals who agreed to talk: Dennis David, Paul O'Connor, James Jenkins, Jerrol Custer, Harold Rydberg, Saundra Spencer, and ex-FBI Special Agents James Sibert and Frances O'Neill. These eyewitnesses relate their stories comprehensively, and Law allows them to tell it as they remember it without attempting to fit any pro- or anticonspiracy agenda. The book also features a DVD featuring these firsthand interviews. Comes with DVD.

Softcover: **$29.95** (ISBN: 9781634240468) • 514 pages • Size: 6 x 9

JFK from Parkland to Bethesda
The Ultimate Kennedy Assassination Compendium
BY VINCENT PALAMARA

An all-in-one resource containing more than 15 years of research on the JFK assassination

A map through the jungle of statements, testimony, allegations, and theories relating to the assassination of John F. Kennedy, this compendium gives readers an all-in-one resource for facts from this intriguing slice of history. The book, which took more than 15 years to research and write, includes details on all of the most important aspects of the case, including old and new medical evidence from primary and secondary sources. JFK: From Parkland to Bethesda tackles the hard evidence of conspiracy and cover-up and presents a mass of sources and materials, making it an invaluable reference for anyone with interest in the President Kennedy and his assassination in 1963.

Softcover: **$19.95** (ISBN: 9781634240277) • 242 pages • Size: 6 x 9

The Polka Dot File on the Robert F. Kennedy Killing
Paris Peace Talks connection
BY FERNANDO FAURA

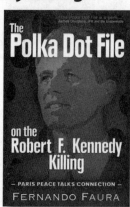

"THE POLKA DOT FILE IS A GEM IN THE FIELD OF RFK ASSASSINATION RESEARCH. READ IT AND LEARN."
—JIM DOUGLASS, AUTHOR, JFK AND THE UNSPEAKABLE

The Polka Dot File on the Robert F. Kennedy Killing describes the day-to-day chase for the mystery woman in the polka-dot dress. The book comments on but does not dwell on the police investigation, and reads like a detective thriller instead of an academic analysis of the investigation. It incorporates actual tapes made by an important witness, and introduces the testimony of witnesses not covered in other books and it is a new take on the assassination and the motives for it introduces a new theory for the reasons behind the assassination. Original and highly personal, it reaches a startling and different conclusion not exposed by other books.

FERNANDO FAURA graduated cum laude with a degree in journalism from the California State University. In 1967 he joined The Hollywood Citizens News. Fernando has won awards from the Press Club, the National Newspaper Publishers Association, and was nominated for a Pulitzer Prize.

Softcover: **$24.95** (ISBN: 9781634240598) • 248 pages • Size: 6 x 9

From an Office Building with a High-Powered Rifle
A report to the public from an FBI agent involved in the official JFK assassination investigation

by Don Adams

An insider's look at the mysteries behind the death of President Kennedy

The personal and professional story of a former FBI agent, this is the journey Don Adams has taken over the past 50 years that has connected him to the assassination of the 35th president of the United States. On November 13, 1963, Adams was given a priority assignment to investigate Joseph Milteer, a man who had made threats to assassinate the president. Two weeks later John F. Kennedy was dead, and Agent Adams was instructed to locate and question Milteer. Adams, however, was only allowed to ask the suspect five specific questions before being told to release him. He was puzzled by the bizarre orders but thought nothing more of it until years later when he read a report that stated that not only had Joseph Milteer made threats against the president, but also that he claimed Kennedy would be killed from an office building with a high-powered rifle. Since that time, Adams has compiled evidence and research from every avenue available to him, including his experiences in Georgia and Dallas FBI offices, to produce this compelling investigation that may just raise more questions than answers.

DON ADAMS is a former FBI agent who participated in the investigation of the assassination of John F. Kennedy. He is the author of numerous articles on the subject and is considered a respected authority on the topic. He lives in Akron, Ohio.

Softcover • **$24.95** • ISBN 9781936296866 • 236 Pages

Betrayal
A JFK Honor Guard Speaks

by Hugh Clark

with William Matson Law

The amazing story that William Law has documented with his historical interviews helps us to understanding our true history. This compelling information shreds the official narrative.In 2015, Law and fellow researcher Phil Singer got together the medical corpsman, who had been present at Bethesda Naval Hospital for President Kennedy's autopsy with some of the official honor guard, who had delivered the president's coffin. What happened next was extraordinary. The medical corpsmen told the honor guards that they had actually received the president's body almost a half-hour before the honor guard got there. The honor guard couldn't believe this. They had met the president's plane at Andrews, taken possession of his casket and shadowed it all the way to Bethesda. The two sides almost broke into fisticuffs, accusing the other of untruths. Once it was sifted out, and both sides came to the understanding that each was telling their own truths of their experience that fateful day, the feelings of betrayal experienced by the honor guards was deep and profound.

HUGH CLARK was a member of the honor guard that took President Kennedy's body to Arlington Cemetery for burial. He was an investigator for the United Nations. After Hugh left the service he became a New York City detective and held that position for 22 years.

WILLIAM MATSON LAW has been researching the Kennedy assassination for over 25 years. Results of that research have appeared in more than 30 books, including Douglas Horne's magnum opus Inside the Assassination Records Review Board. Law is the author of In the Eye of History and is working on a book about the murder of Robert F. Kennedy with the working title: Shadows and Light. He lives with his family in Central Oregon.

Softcover • **$19.95** • ISBN 9781634240932 • 144 Pages

Silent Coup
The Removal of a President
by Len Colodny & Robert Gettlin
25th Anniversay Edition – Includes Updates
Foreword by Roger Morris

This is the true story of betrayal at the nation's highest level. Unfolding with the suspenseful pace of a le Carre spy thriller, it reveals the personal motives and secret political goals that combined to cause the Watergate break-in and destroy Richard Nixon. Investigator Len Colodny and journalist Robert Gettlin relentlessly pursued the people who brought down the president. Their revelations shocked the world and forever changed our understanding of politics, of journalism, and of Washington behind closed doors. Dismantling decades of lies, *Silent Coup* tells the truth.

LEN COLODNY is a journalist. In 1992 he co-wrote with Robert Gettlin: *Silent Coup: The Removal Of Richard Nixon*. In the book the authors claim that John Dean ordered the Watergate break-in because he knew that a call-girl ring was operating out of the Democratic headquarters. The authors also argued that Alexander Haig was not Deep Throat but was a key source for Bob Woodward, who had briefed Haig at theWhite House in 1969 and 1970.

Softcover • **$24.95** • ISBN 9781634240536 • 520 Pages

Bond of Secrecy
My Life with CIA Spy and Watergate Conspirator E. Howard Hunt
by St. John Hunt
Foreword by Jesse Ventura

A father's last confession to his son about the CIA, Watergate, and the plot to assassinate President John F. Kennedy, this is the remarkable true story of St. John Hunt and his father E. Howard Hunt, the infamous Watergate burglar and CIA spymaster. In Howard Hunt's near-death confession to his son St. John, he revealed that key figures in the CIA were responsible for the plot to assassinate JFK in Dallas, and that Hunt himself was approached by the plotters, among whom included the CIA's David Atlee Phillips, Cord Meyer, Jr., and William Harvey, as well as future Watergate burglar Frank Sturgis. An incredible true story told from an inside, authoritative source, this is also a personal account of a uniquely dysfunctional American family caught up in two of the biggest political scandals of the 20th century.

Softcover • **$24.95** • ISBN 978-1936296835 • 192 Pages

Dorothy
The Murder of E. Howard Hunt's Wife – watergate's Darkest Secret
by St. John Hunt
Foreword by Roger Stone

Dorothy Hunt, "An Amoral and Dangerous Woman" tells the life story of ex-CIA agent Dorothy Hunt, who married Watergate mastermind and confessed contributor to the assassination of JFK. The book chronicles her rise in the intelligence field after World War II, as well as her experiences in Shanghai, Calcutta, Mexico, and Washington, DC. It reveals her war with President Nixon and asserts that she was killed by the CIA in the crash of Flight 553. Written by the only person who was privy to the behind-the-scenes details of the Hunt family during Watergate, this book sheds light on a dark secret of the scandal.

Softcover • **$24.95** • ISBN 978-1634240376 • 192 Pages

Saint John Hunt is an author, a musician, and the son of the infamous and legendary CIA covert operative and author, E. Howard Hunt. Saint John spent more than ten years searching for the truth about his father's involvement in JFK's death, resulting in his first book Bond of Secrecy. In his second book, Dorothy, he explored his mother's life as a CIA spy and her war with Nixon, which resulted in her murder. He lives in south Florida.

David Ferrie
Mafia Pilot, Participant in Anti-Castro Bioweapon Plot, Friend of Lee Harvey Oswald and Key to the JFK Assassination

by Judyth Vary Baker

One of the more eccentric characters linked to the JFK assassination

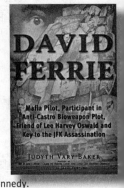

Of the all the people surrounding the assassination of President Kennedy, few are more mysterious and enigmatic than David William Ferrie of New Orleans. Author Judyth Vary Baker knew David Ferrie personally and worked with him in a covert project in New Orleans during the summer of 1963, and this book examines his strange and puzzling behavior both before and after the assassination. At the time of the assassination, Ferrie was a 45-year-old New Orleans resident who was acquainted with some of the most notorious names linked to the assassination: Lee Oswald, Clay Shaw, Guy Banister, Jack Ruby, and Carlos Marcello. He possessed assorted talents and eccentricities: he was at one time a senior pilot with Eastern Airlines until he was fired for homosexual activity on the job; he was also a hypnotist; a serious researcher of the origins of cancer; an amateur psychologist; and a victim of a strange disease, alopecia, which made all of his body void of hair. His odd lifestyle was embellished with an equally bizarre appearance featuring a red toupee and false eyebrows. This is the first book focused solely on David Ferrie and his alleged involvement in the conspiracy to assassinate President John F. Kennedy.

JUDYTH VARY BAKER is an artist, writer, and poet who first became known as a young prodigy in cancer research, then, later, for her assertion that while conducting cancer research in New Orleans in the summer of 1963, she had a love affair with Lee Harvey Oswald. She is the author of *Me & Lee: How I Came to Know, Love and Lose Lee Harvey Oswald*. She lives in Europe.

Softcover • **$24.95** • ISBN 9781937584542 • 528 Pages

LBJ and the Kennedy Killing
By Eyewitness

James T. Tague

This is unlike any other book about the assassination of President John F. Kennedy. The author, James Tague, was there and he was wounded by the debris from a missed shot on that fateful day. He stood up to our Government when the Warren Commission was about to ignore what really happened and spoke to the true facts. James Tague's testimony changed history and the "magic bullet" was born in an effort by the Warren Commission to wrongly explain all the wounds to President Kennedy and Governor Connally, and to try and convince the public that Lee Harvey Oswald was the "lone nut assassin." Tague, a long time Dallas area resident, initially believed the Warren Report, but time, diligent research and amazing revelations told to him by prominent Texans has given James Tague an inside look at what really happened. Be prepared to learn new facts, never before published, about one of our nation's darkest moments.

JAMES T. TAGUE spent 5 years in the Air Force, had a career in the automobile business rising to top management and is today recognized as a top researcher on the Kennedy assassination. It was an accident of timing that he was in Dealey Plaza that November day in 1963, receiving a minor injury.

Softcover • **$29.95** • ISBN 9781937584740 • 433 Pages

Kennedy & Oswald   *–The Big Picture–*
by Judyth Vary Baker and Edward Schwartz

Unraveling the many strands of hidden history behind the assassination of President Kennedy is not an easy task. Co-authors Baker and Schwartz guide us toward the conclusion that ultimately, the motivation was total governmental control, a coup d'état, changing us from a democratic republic to a oligopoly – a corporatocracy. With help from new witnesses regarding the "Crime of the Century," we are led to the realization that the "War of Terror" and the Patriot Act were predesigned to undermine our US Constitution and our Bill of Rights. The very moment Kennedy died our own government turned against "We the People." Baker and Schwartz provide a compelling narrative showing Oswald's innocence and a condemnation of the conspirators who planned and carried out the assassination of our 35th president and our Republic.

Softcover • **$24.95** • ISBN 9781634240963 • 408 Pages

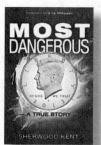

Most Dangerous   *–A True Story–*
by Sherwood Kent

OUT OF THE BOWELS of the sleepy southern town of Tupelo, Mississippi, the birthplace of Elvis Presley, emerges a darkly-humorous true story of staged terror, occult ritual and mind control. The book reads like a Faulkneresque tall tale but is, unfortunately for the main character and those around him, all-too-true. Author S.K. Bain finds himself caught up in the middle of something bigger and uglier than he can at first fathom. Yet, much to his dismay, he catches on rather quickly to what's taking place around him—and near-simultaneously elsewhere across the county in places such as Boston, MA and West, TX—because he's seen this sort of thing before. He wrote the book on it, literally, and he soon realizes just how much danger he and his family are in.
The year is 2013, the 50th anniversary of the JFK assassination, and Bain discovers that he is enmeshed in a year-long series of scripted events meticulously planned and brilliantly executed by some of the most ruthless, diabolically-creative, powerful psychopaths on the planet. As the story unfolds, it turns out that Bain has an idea who, specifically, might be behind his woes, and if he's correct, it's even less likely that he's going to get out alive.

Softcover • **$24.95** • ISBN 9781634240406 • 408 Pages

Sinister Forces
A Grimoire of American Political Witchcraft
Book One: The Nine
BY PETER LEVENDA, FOREWORD BY JIM HOUGAN

A shocking alternative to the conventional views of American history.
The roots of coincidence and conspiracy in American politics, crime, and culture are examined in this book, exposing new connections between religion, political conspiracy, and occultism. From ancient American civilization and the mysterious mound builder culture to the Salem witch trials, the birth of Mormonism during a ritual of ceremonial magic by Joseph Smith, Jr., and Operations Paperclip and Bluebird. Fascinating details are revealed, including the bizarre world of "wandering bishops" who appear throughout the Kennedy assassinations; a CIA mind control program run amok in the United States and Canada; a famous American spiritual leader who had ties to Lee Harvey Oswald in the weeks and months leading up to the assassination of President Kennedy; and the "Manson secret.

Softcover: **$24.95** (ISBN 9780984185818) • 432 pages • Size: 6 x 9

Book Two: A Warm Gun
Readers are provided with strange parallels between supernatural forces such as shaminism, ritual magic, and cult practices, and contemporary interrogation techniques such as those used by the CIA under the general rubric of MK-ULTRA. Not a work of speculative history, this exposé is founded on primary source material and historical documents. Fascinating details on Nixon and the "Dark Tower," the Assassin cult and more recent Islamic terrorism, and the bizarre themes that run through American history from its discovery by Columbus to the political assassinations of the 1960s are revealed.

Softcover: **$24.95** (ISBN 9780984185825) • 392 pages • Size: 6 x 9

Book Three: The Manson Secret
The Stanislavski Method as mind control and initiation. Filmmaker Kenneth Anger and Aleister Crowley, Marianne Faithfull, Anita Pallenberg, and the Rolling Stones. Filmmaker Donald Cammell (Performance) and his father, CJ Cammell (the first biographer of Aleister Crowley), and his suicide. Jane Fonda and Bluebird. The assassination of Marilyn Monroe. Fidel Castro's Hollywood career. Jim Morrison and witchcraft. David Lynch and spiritual transformation. The technology of sociopaths. How to create an assassin. The CIA, MK-ULTRA and programmed killers.

Softcover: **$24.95** (ISBN 9780984185832) • 508 pages • Size: 6 x 9